Working Text

Working Text

Teaching Deaf and Second-Language Students to Be Better Writers

Sue Livingston

Gallaudet University Press
Washington, DC

6/2/11
WW
FP45 —

Gallaudet University Press
Washington, DC 20002
http://gupress.gallaudet.edu

16 15 14 13 12 11 10   1 2 3 4 5 6

ISBN 1-56368-466-7, 978-1-56368-466-1

The excerpts on p. 109, 111, and 204 are from *A Letter to Mrs. Roosevelt* by C. Coco de Young,
copyright © 1999 by C. Coco de Young. Used by permission of Doubleday, an imprint
of Random House Children's Books, a division of Random House, Inc.

Contents

Acknowledgments   v

PART 1

Teaching Deaf and Second-Language Students to Be Better Writers

           Introduction: The Role of Oral/Aural Abilities in Writing   2

CHAPTER 1   The What and Why of Writing Instruction   12

CHAPTER 2   The How of Writing Instruction   25

CHAPTER 3   Reading and Writing to Link Lexis and Grammar—I   41

CHAPTER 4   Reading and Writing to Link Lexis and Grammar—II   51

CHAPTER 5   How Will Students Know When They Are Becoming Better Writers?   77

CHAPTER 6   Best Practices: Not Just for Hearing Students   88

           References   96

PART 2

Teacher's Guide and Supplement to *Working Text: X-Word Grammar and Writing Activities for Students*

           To the Teacher   101

SECTION 1

Discovering X-Words and Subjects, How X-Words Show Time, How X-Words Match with Subjects, Editing Practice

ACTIVITY 1   Using X-Words: 20 Yes/No Questions   104

ACTIVITY 2   Make an X-Word Chart   105

ACTIVITY 3   X-Words and Subjects: Statements   106

ACTIVITY 4   X-Words and *Not* and *n't*: Negative Statements   107

ACTIVITY 5   Finding X-Words and Subjects #1   *Wayside School Is Falling Down*   108

ACTIVITY 6   Finding X-Words and Subjects #2   *A Letter to Mrs. Roosevelt*   109

ACTIVITY 7   X-Words and Time #1   *Wayside School Is Falling Down*   110

ACTIVITY 8   X-Words and Time #2   *A Letter to Mrs. Roosevelt*   111

ACTIVITY 9   X-Words and Time #3   "My Parents"   112

ACTIVITY 10   Subject and X-Word Match-Ups #1   113

ACTIVITY 11   Subject and X-Word Match-Ups #2   114

ACTIVITY 12   X-Words and Time #4   "On the Evening of September 11th, 2001"   **115**

ACTIVITY 13   Subject and X-Word Match-Ups #3   **116**

ACTIVITY 14   Subject and X-Word Match-Ups #4   **117**

ACTIVITY 15   Subject and X-Word Match-Ups #5   **118**

ACTIVITY 16   A Brief Word about Most *WH-* (information) Questions   **119**

ACTIVITY 17   Practice Editing I   "The Necklace"   **120**

ACTIVITY 18   Practice Editing II   *Charlotte's Web*   **121**

ACTIVITY 19   Practice Editing III   *Charlotte's Web*   **122**

Editing Quiz I: Editing for Missing X-Words, Time, and SX   **123**

Editing Quiz I: Answers   **124**

SECTION 2
X-Words and Main Verbs, Hidden X-Words, Editing Practice

ACTIVITY 20   X-Word and Main Verb Match-Ups #1   "The King and the Bees"   **126**

ACTIVITY 21   X-Word and Main Verb Match-Ups #2   "Saving the Birds"   **127**

ACTIVITY 22   X-Word and Main Verb Match-Ups #3   **129**

ACTIVITY 23   X-Word and Main Verb Match-Ups #4   *A Christmas Treasury*   **130**

ACTIVITY 24   X-Word and Main Verb Match-Ups #5   "The Glass Dog"   **131**

ACTIVITY 25   X-Word and Main Verb Match-Ups #6   *Red Scarf Girl*   **133**

ACTIVITY 26   Hidden X-Words in Main Verbs: The Powerful X-Word *Does* #1   **134**

ACTIVITY 27   Hidden X-Words in Main Verbs: The Powerful X-Word *Does* #2   **135**

ACTIVITY 28   Hidden X-Words in Main Verbs: The Powerful X-Word *Do* #1   **136**

ACTIVITY 29   Hidden X-Words in Main Verbs: The Powerful X-Word *Do* #2   **137**

ACTIVITY 30   Finding Hidden *Does* and *Do*   *Bob and Mary*   **138**

ACTIVITY 31   Hidden X-Words in Main Verbs: The Powerful X-Word *Did* #1   **139**

ACTIVITY 32   Hidden X-Words in Main Verbs: The Powerful X-Word *Did* #2   **140**

ACTIVITY 33   Finding Hidden *Did*   *Bob and Mary*   **141**

ACTIVITY 34   Finding X-Words, X-Word and Main Verb Match-Ups, and Hidden X-Words #1   "The Midnight Ride"   **142**

ACTIVITY 35   Finding X-Words, X-Word and Main Verb Match-Ups, and Hidden X-Words #2   "The Story of a Great Story"   **144**

ACTIVITY 36   Practice Editing I   **146**

ACTIVITY 37   Practice Editing II   *Charlotte's Web*   **147**

ACTIVITY 38   Practice Editing III   *Reading for Concepts*   **149**

ACTIVITY 39   Practice Editing IV   *New Practice Readers*   **151**

Editing Quiz II: Editing for X-Words, Verbs, and Infinitives   **153**

Editing Quiz II: Answers   **154**

Sentence Patterns and Editing Practice

ACTIVITY 40 Review of Changing Statements into Yes/No Questions   156

ACTIVITY 41 What Is a Trunk?   157

ACTIVITY 42 Changing Trunks into Yes/No Questions   158

ACTIVITY 43 Joining Trunks: T, + T with *and*   159

ACTIVITY 44 Joining Trunks: T, + T with *but*   160

ACTIVITY 45 Joining Trunks: T, + T with *so*   161

ACTIVITY 46 Joining Trunks: T, + T with *or*   162

ACTIVITY 47 Practice with Joiners   163

ACTIVITY 48 One Trunk with Two Predicates: T=   164

ACTIVITY 49 One Trunk with Three (or more) Predicates Joined by *and*   165

ACTIVITY 50 Practice with T, + T and T=   166

ACTIVITY 51 Sentence Combining with T, + T and T=   167

ACTIVITY 52 Linkers and Trunks (LT) "The Hotel Owner's Mistake"   168

ACTIVITY 53 Other Linkers and What They Mean   169

ACTIVITY 54 Practice with Linkers   170

ACTIVITY 55 Practice Editing for Sentence Patterns I   171

ACTIVITY 56 Practice Editing for Sentence Patterns II   172

ACTIVITY 57 Front and End Shifters (FT and TE)   174

ACTIVITY 58 Shifting Shifters *Harvey Slumfenburger's Christmas Present*   176

ACTIVITY 59 Shifting Shifters "Cinderella"   177

ACTIVITY 60 A Word about Fragments   179

ACTIVITY 61 Another Word about Fragments   180

ACTIVITY 62 Inserts (TI)   181

ACTIVITY 63 Inserting Inserts   182

ACTIVITY 64 Practice Identifying FT, TE, and TI *Drip! Drop!*   183
             How Water Gets to Your Tap, "The Paddle Wheel Boat"

ACTIVITY 65 Identifying All Sentence Patterns *Ant Cities*   184

ACTIVITY 66 Practice Editing for Sentence Patterns III   185

ACTIVITY 67 Practice Editing for Sentence Patterns IV   187

ACTIVITY 68 Practice Editing for Sentence Patterns V *Killing Mr. Griffin*   189

             Editing Quiz III: Editing for Sentence Patterns   191

             Editing Quiz III: Answers   193

SECTION 4

Boxes and Main Words, Countable and Uncountable Boxes, *THE* Boxes, Referents, Editing Practice

ACTIVITY 69   Boxes and Main Words   *The Magic School Bus Inside the Human Body*   196

ACTIVITY 70   Practice with Boxes   *New Practice Readers*   197

ACTIVITY 71   More Practice with Boxes   "The Year is 1902"   198

ACTIVITY 72   Focusing on Nouns   199

ACTIVITY 73   Countable and Uncountable Boxes   200

ACTIVITY 74   Practice with Countable and Uncountable Boxes   201

ACTIVITY 75   Practice Correcting Countable and Uncountable Errors   202

ACTIVITY 76   *THE* Boxes   203

ACTIVITY 77   Recognizing Reasons for *THE* Boxes   *A Letter to Mrs. Roosevelt*   204

ACTIVITY 78   Practice with *THE* Boxes #1   *Wayside School Is Falling Down*   205

ACTIVITY 79   Practice with *THE* Boxes #2   "Two Great Painters"   206

ACTIVITY 80   Practice with *THE* Boxes #3   *Reading Fluency*   207

ACTIVITY 81   Referents   *The Ways of Written English*   208

ACTIVITY 82   Understanding Different Forms of Referents   210

ACTIVITY 83   Choosing the Correct Referent   *Chicken Soup for the Teenage Soul*   211

ACTIVITY 84   More Practice with Referents   212

ACTIVITY 85   Practice Editing Inside Boxes and for Referents I   213

ACTIVITY 86   Practice Editing Inside Boxes and for Referents II   214

Editing Quiz IV: Editing Inside Boxes and for Referents   215

Editing Quiz IV: Answers   216

Appendices

APPENDIX A   X-Words: Before and Now   218

APPENDIX B   X-Words: 1 or 2 or Many   219

APPENDIX C   Some Main Verb Forms   220

APPENDIX D   Linkers   223

APPENDIX E   Common Shifter Words and Phrases   224

APPENDIX F   Countable and Uncountable Nouns and Boxes   225

APPENDIX G   X-Word Grammar Correction Symbols   226

APPENDIX H   Model Essays   228

APPENDIX I   Model Essays Grammatically Analyzed   235

References   244

Index   246

Acknowledgments

I have been teaching Deaf students for thirty-eight years, and for thirty of those years knowing how to successfully integrate the teaching of grammar with the teaching of good writing evaded me. I knew that my students needed to learn basic grammatical principles of written English as well as the craft of essay writing, but I was stymied by the questions of what grammatical principles to teach and how to teach them so that students could actually use them to make their essays clearer. But eight years ago, when I was introduced to Linda Ann Kunz, a colleague of mine at LaGuardia Community College, my questions started to find answers. Linda, a renowned linguist, published author, and teacher of English as a Second Language par excellence, introduced me to X-Word Grammar and to the body of work she created to teach it to hearing ESL students. X-Word Grammar, Linda explained, is a system that derives from the work of Robert Allen, who taught at Teachers College, Columbia University. Professor Allen's original system, *sector analysis*, was a way of syntactically analyzing written English sentences. In the 1970s, to fit their needs as teachers of English, Allen's graduate students adapted his system into X-Word Grammar.

It was Linda's approach to X-Word Grammar that drew me in: it was teacher-friendly, clear, and engaging. I begged her for all the texts and explanatory information she had, and after countless lunches, dinners, and visits to her home, I found myself falling in love with a way of teaching grammar—as odd as that may sound. Equally important, I started to understand that the relationship between teaching grammar and writing is more like a Y than an equal sign (=). Rather than teaching grammar alongside but very separate from real writing, as in an equal sign, I saw that X-Word Grammar could allow teachers to teach grammar both alongside, as the top V-part of the Y shows, but then, very quickly, right onto writing as seen in the stem part of the Y. Why? Because X-Word Grammar simplifies grammar by systematizing it. Its elements come together to make constructions bigger, relatable, and clearly visual. It doesn't burden students with trying to figure out how very discrete and disparate rules apply to writing; instead, it shows them how these bigger constructions are patterns in the language and how these patterns are very much dependent on one another. Linda, how I only wish there was time for innumerably more lunches and dinners, but your untimely passing has so very unfortunately precluded this.

I would also like to thank Jack Gantzer and Jane Selden, colleagues at LaGuardia, for sharing their very positive experiences with X-Word Grammar with me, and Jack for loaning me Robert Allen et al.'s *Working Sentences* (1975), which I have yet to return. (Sorry, Jack!) The concept behind that title intrigued me, and I piggybacked off of it to create my own title, *Working Text: Teaching Deaf and Second-Language Students to Be Better Writers.* In his "Foreword to the Instructor," Allen states, "The title of this book is intentionally ambiguous. It refers not only to sentences that work—that is, sentences that serve their purpose—but to the process of working sentences to improve their effectiveness. This second sense of *working* suggests the image of a potter or sculptor working his raw material into a desired form." Allen's concept of working raw material stayed with me, and I began to think more about the teaching of writing as working *text*—not just sentences—right from the beginning of a writing assignment. Couldn't all the bridge work between reading and writing that my students needed to do prior to and during a writing assignment be considered "working text"? And couldn't, then, all my students be considered potters and sculptors? As this book hopefully shows, yes, it could, and yes, they can.

And so, to all my potters and sculptors over all the years, a big thank you for the pleasure of watching you present your finished products and for the pleasure of seeing your sense of accomplishment. To John Mayher, Peter, Jenna, Grace, and Linda Ann Kunz: this piece of pottery is for you.

Part 1

Teaching Deaf and Second-Language Students to Be Better Writers

Introduction: The Role of Oral/Aural Abilities in Writing

Here are some examples of writing by Deaf and hard of hearing students, representing the kind of writing that has crossed my desk at one time or another during my twenty-four-year career as a teacher of developmental writing at LaGuardia Community College. These are conclusions to the first drafts of essays that my students wrote at the beginning of the term, in response to what they had been reading.

Speculating about the reasons for the unethical behavior of an interpreter named Comstock, one student concludes:

> I can't know why Comstock spoke so negatively to Abel and Janice because I don't know his background and also I don't know about between him and his deaf parents. How can I guess the reason that Comstock said negatively about them? Because there are many reasons that is hard to find the right answer. I don't know an interpreter like Comstock would probably not exist today in my country still exist, but I heard in USA not exist today, but I am wondering if a naïve deaf foreigner come to USA without knowing ASL does it exist an interpreter like Comstock would probably not exist today? Unfortunately, I don't have my conclusion.

Offering an opinion as to whether a certain deaf peddler in a fictional piece fit a description of a prototypical peddler, another student concludes:

> Deaf peddlers make me very abhorrent. Last several summers ago, I remembered that I went to subway station in Manhattan. I was stand up and waited for the train. I saw some of Deaf friends are peddlers in the subway. I noticed their communicates wasn't very well. Image if I am Deaf peddler myself on the street . . . . How do I do survive myself? I have to travel in the United States for peddler. If my friends saw me street sell to people. I could embarrassed myself because of my friends already notice me. I know that is not very easily. But I feel sorry for them. I believe that their family don't care about their life. I prefer an education school then get good job for my goal. I never give up in college.

I really want to earn my highest degree then get good job in the future. What if I have Deaf kids. I will tell my kids do not peddler on the street. I want them very smart than them.

Offering possible reasons as to why the author of *The Broken Cord*, Michael Dorris, decided to take his life, a final student writes:

I am really fascinated to read the catalogue about Michael's life. It made Me shock and inspire me to feel sad. I wished help to consuel with Michael. I hope Michael would be quiet in the heaven and watch on his ex-wife and children.

The authors of these excerpts are all adults in their twenties. One is a proficient American Sign Language (ASL) signer, deaf from birth, and two are fairly proficient hard of hearing signers with fairly clear articulation skills. While one sample might be easier to understand than another, none reflects writing abilities necessary to exempt its author from a basic skills writing course at the college level. As these examples show, and as over the years I have come to see, a student's oral ability (which includes sign language) or aural ability does not predict quality of writing. Stated differently, a command of sign or some speaking and hearing abilities are insufficient for writing well.

For parents and educators of hard of hearing students who might assume that speaking and hearing abilities are necessary precursors to writing competence, this point might not sit well. One would expect that having some hearing and some command of the spoken form of English could only make learning its written form easier; indeed, this is part of the rationale for cochlear implants and intensive auditory and speech training. Yet there are thousands, perhaps millions, of speaking and hearing college students whose first language is English who do not write well. Developmental writing courses at the college level across the nation are filled with American-born hearing students who cannot express their ideas clearly and coherently. Here is a conclusion to the first draft of an essay written by a hearing student in a developmental writing course at LaGuardia. In the essay, he argues that parents should not show more respect to male children than female children:

I think disrespecting our children is so embarrass because our children won't realize the way we are raising them. It's good to see in which kids give us an impression when they bring us gift, honors from school and especially when they ask us to tell them a storie before they go to sleep. That's why I argue all the parents to take care of their own children.

While we do not have to read through as many lexical or grammatical errors as we do in the excerpts by Deaf and hard of hearing students, we see similar issues of missing foci and off-the-point ways for ending essays. Why do hearing and speaking students, who have full access to spoken language, have difficulty writing clearly?

Differences Between Spoken and Written Discourse

Deborah Tannen (1982), citing the research of Chafe (1980), asserts that differences exist between spoken conversation and written prose. In general, written discourse is compact because it "is characterized by a high degree of integration made possible by the slowness of writing. . . . Spoken discourse, in contrast, is characterized by fragmentation, resulting from the spurt-like nature of speech which probably reflects the jerky nature of thought" (7). To achieve its compactness, written discourse recruits more complex syntactic structures such as embedded clauses beginning with *who*, *what*, or *which*; spoken discourse gets by with basic conjoiners such as *and*, *but*, and *so*. In addition, writers tend to show relevance by explicitly stating connections between and among ideas in their writing whereas speakers rely on listeners to infer meaning.

Tannen also maintains that there are other language features that differentiate genre types. That is, in addition to the differences between written and spoken modes, people produce language in expected ways that are appropriate to their communicative goals. Offering an opinion in speech or writing and telling a story in speech or writing are different communication contexts that each requires its own features of language use. Consider the example of Deanna, a proficient, middle-aged signer. Deanna was asked to first "tell" and then write about a memorable dream as part of an informal research project that compared how dreams were signed with how they were written. I wanted the students in the project to "talk" about something with which they were very familiar and then to subsequently write about it. Here is the signed version of Deanna's dream as transcribed from videotape by a certified ASL interpreter:

> My mother was really a domineering woman. One day . . . I remember very well, my mother always loved my brother. She showed favoritism towards him. Sonny-Lee this, Sonny-Lee that over and over. So, one day, I went to bed and then to sleep. My mother was very, very fussy. Everything was spic and span. I remember there was a table, yes, I remember a table my father was there, seated across the table from my mother and I was across the table from my brother. It was a round table with a beautiful white, linen tablecloth. I don't know why, but it was white, with a bottle of red, tall red. It could have been wine or borscht, my mother was expert at making borscht soup, you know, it's beets. It happened in the dream that my brother pushed the borscht or wine and it spilled all over and turned everything red. It was white no longer, everything was red.

To lessen the possibility that the written version would be a direct translation of the signed version, I waited approximately three months before I asked Deanna to do the written version of this same dream:

A Red Tablecloth

> My mother was a domineering woman and she kept her apartment spic and span. She loved my older brother much more than me. She always called him "Sonaly" instead of Daniel.
>
> One day during a dinner time, she set the table up with a beautiful, white linen tablecloth with her new dishes, silverware and a crystal bottle, which was

filled with red wine or red borscht. My mother cooked very tasty borscht and my father loved red wine.

We all sat down to dinner. I couldn't remember which one was spilled all over the white tablecloth and of course, it became red all over. She slapped my face hard and blamed me for ruining her white tablecloth, but it was not really my fault. The bottle was knocked down by my brother and he got away with murder.

The differences between the oral and written versions are clear. First, there are asides in the oral version ("I don't know why, but"; "you know it's beets") as well as repetition ("and turned everything red," "everything was red") that give it the jumpy feel of thinking on your feet. Second, there is location setting ("there was a table, yes, I remember a table my father was there, seated across the table from my mother and I was across the table from my brother"), which is characteristic of narrative in ASL as people and objects are first placed in space and then commented on or moved. Third, the description of how the table was set is composed with a sophisticated expanded prepositional phrase ("with her new dishes, silverware and a crystal bottle"), and a subordinate clause used to more specifically describe what was in the crystal bottle ("which was filled with red wine or red borscht"), instead of a separate sentence as in the oral version ("It could have been wine or borscht.") Rhetorically speaking, character traits of the mother are more tightly clustered in the written account ("fussy" and "keeping everything spic and span" are separated from "domineering" in the oral account but mentioned together in the written), and, perhaps most important, the point of the whole narrative—that the mother, true to her favoritism, blamed the ruined tablecloth on Deanna even though her brother was the culprit—is only implied in the oral version but explicitly stated in the written version. Finally, the explicitly stated interpretation that her brother "got away with murder" brings the short narrative around full circle; the significance of the dinnertime fiasco is that it is a case in point of the supposed stronger love that Deanna's mother had for her brother.

Undoubtedly, the second pass at thinking about her dream gave Deanna the advantage of starting with some initial language to further embellish; also, because writing afforded Deanna more time to think about her dream, her written version contained more relevant ideas that cohered better. With time for rereading, Deanna had more opportunities to extend and connect her thinking, a communicative benefit not afforded speakers. However, these advantages notwithstanding, knowing how to write about a certain event clearly entails more than just knowing how to sign about it clearly. Deanna knew how to recruit grammatical and rhetorical strategies for writing a short narrative.

The incoherent nature of the conclusions to student essays excerpted above—all written by fairly proficient oral-language users—might make us wonder what the differences are between these student-writers and Deanna. Deanna happens to be a bookworm with a propensity for short stories and memoir and an avid *Reader's Digest* fan—a proficient reader of narrative. She most likely internalized the look and feel of anecdote as well as the look of and feel of English through her many exposures to them in print. On the other hand, none of the three other students were proficient readers of the essay form. None understood how to end an essay most likely because they had not read enough essays to get a feel for how conclusions work. Without being able to read essays well, they were unable to write essays well. Extending this idea a bit further, we can hypothesize that reading experience in general wields powerful influence over writing abilities.

Reading Privileges Writing

My basic writing courses over the past twenty-four years have been a virtual United Nations of oral or through-the-air languages/communication systems in use. I have had students like Lucy, who only uses spoken English; like Juan, who only uses ASL; like Fred, who uses "total communication"(speaking and signing at the same time); and like Dan, who has cochlear implants and depends on oral and aural input during class time but signs with his Deaf friends outside of class. These students, like the ones whose essay conclusions are excerpted above, were all required to take a basic writing course based on the nature of their writing, so, as we have seen, there does not appear to be a through-the-air-communication type that privileges writing. However, if reading and writing abilities are linked, we would expect to see some predictive relationship between my students' abilities as readers and their abilities as writers, regardless of their communication preference. Were my better readers also my better writers?

Lucy, Juan, Fred, and Dan placed into my basic writing course as a result of the City University of New York (CUNY)/ACT writing test that all incoming students are required to take. The test asks students to write a letter to a school official or community board member in support of one of two proposed ways of spending grant money to improve the school or community. Students must explain why their choice is the better one in an organized and focused essay. I was struck by the fact that Lucy, Juan, Fred, and Dan had not shown up in my basic reading course. Where were they? Checking their transcripts, I noted the phrase "reading requirement fulfilled." This does not happen often. Most of my students require extended time in basic reading courses and then in special test-preparation courses for the CUNY/ACT reading test, a test similar to the reading component of the SAT where students read an extended passage and answer multiple-choice questions. Without this course these students were judged "reading proficient" by the CUNY/ACT reading test, and right from the outset, these students were indeed better writers. Being "reading proficient" they were fluent writers—they had lots to say and the words and phrases to say it with. They benefited from instruction in fine-tuning their essays, but their writing was not as needy as the three students whose work is excerpted above who, you may have correctly assumed, did not fulfill their reading requirement. Lucy needed help with establishing a point and sticking with it; Juan needed to liven up his writing with some voice; Fred needed help with ordering his ideas to make them flow logically; and Dan—who wrote "Stranger in the Nest" in chapter 2, and, as you will see, could have taught me a thing or two about good narrative writing—needed assistance with incorporating quoted material into his texts.

How did Lucy, Juan, Fred, and Dan learn the words and phrases that helped them to be fluent writers? We can assume that they did not hear them fully or even hear them at all, and we can assume that even if they lip-read the words and phrases in conversation, they would not necessarily know how to spell them. Instead, they learned the words and phrases they needed through *seeing* them again and again in print—through reading. Did they pass my basic writing course on the first attempt? Yes, they did. Did they pass the ACT writing test on the retest? Three on the retest, one on the next try. Once these students learned ways to bridge their reading and writing, the requirements of the essay form, and some light grammar, they were off and running.

Broached from a different vantage point, consider Whitney. Whitney, who does not sign, has told me again and again that she has a "speaking problem." She is mildly hard of hearing but actually speaks very well. Whitney hears only parts of words and phrases, and she makes best guesses as to how to say the words her hearing is distorting. She was not a reader before coming to my class. Because she depended on her ears to write as opposed to her eyes, her writing—as you probably have already predicted—was wrought with mis-spellings and contorted phrasings. After two semesters of intensive reading and writing, however, Whitney understood that it wasn't a speaking problem that she had, but a "seeing problem"—she, for all these years, never realized that text, being 100 percent accessible, could have been a "supplemental mother tongue" for her had someone, somewhere along her educational twelve-year path, taught her how to read and write by making connections for her between other writers' texts and her own.

Let's linger for a moment on the idea of print being a supplemental mother tongue for Deaf students. I first discovered this notion in a talk given by Michael Chorost at a conference at Lehman College in 1985. Michael wrote his presentation when he was a student at Brown University to explain how he learned to read as a hard of hearing child. Here he explains how his father reacted to the discovery that Michael could not hear in full (this was the mid-1960s when the use of sign language by hearing parents of Deaf children was not accepted as easily as it is today):

> My father, a psychologist, recognized the meaning-crisis when the diagnosis was made. He knew I was nearly at the end of the crucial language-development period, and desperately behind. He reasoned, if not language through the ears, why not the eyes? Since my eyes seemed to work fine, he began teaching me how to read, even before I got my hearing aids. . . . He started me on the Dolch word-picture cards, i.e., "hat" on one side, a picture of a hat on the other. He didn't waste time on the alphabet. He chose instead to teach me to recognize words by their total shape . . . instead of painlessly working them out by their meaningless letters. I think this was a brilliant move, because it exposed me to meaningful language instantly. Starved as I was, meaning was the greatest motivator of all. Thus print, rather than speech, was my first true language. . . . [and] reading led to writing for me as naturally as hearing leads to speech in hearing children. (Chorost 1985, 194–96)

Considering the fact that print is the only language modality that offers total and full access to English for Deaf students, the primacy of print in learning to write seems obvious. While I would not argue that print should be a surrogate mother tongue for Deaf students, I have seen that *leaning on* print while writing is a sure sign that students are recognizing its value in upgrading their phrasing and expanding their lexicons. Here is Jack leaning on phrases from the text *13 Days* by Robert Kennedy (1969), which was part of his basic reading course. He was given the following assignment: "You are President Kennedy. You are speaking to the American people tonight in a live broadcast about the decision to create a blockade around Cuba in response to finding out that Russia has placed nuclear missiles there. You must explain to the American people why a blockade is a better idea than a military strike." In Jack's response below, note the phrases that are italicized.

> Hello Americans! Today I going to give you short information. I, the Congressmen, the CIA been working really hard and time running out. What best we have our plan is the blockade in Cuba. We send the ships surround the Cuba for not want Russian carry a missiles. Reason because the blockade does

not attack. We want some information from Russian or Cuba or we can convince them. Because it is the chance we have to discuss and not to start a war. *We, the American* never treat (threatened) Cuba, because *we, the United States* are the big country than the Cuba. We are not bully. We are not allow *to rain bomb over Cuba* and will be *destruction of the human race*, we don't want that.

We see Jack's attempts at what I might call "proclamation speech" in "We, the American" and "We, the United States" where he "borrows" the language from several of the formal correspondences included in the book (between the Executive Committee working under the direction of Robert Kennedy and Nikita Khrushchev), as well as his use of sophisticated infinitive and noun phrases.

Here is Justine leaning on Joanne Greenberg's short story "And Sarah Laughed" to explain how Sarah, a hearing woman, desperately wanted to converse with her Deaf husband, Matthew, even though she did not sign:

> Sarah feel that she really wants to tell Matthew about she needs laughing from him or *a little meaningless talk* such as affection. But Sarah doesn't tell him because she feels like *bondage of silence* with him. . . . She prefers to keep her *habit of silence* for years.

Jack and Justine did not lip-read or hear the phrases italicized above in their through-the-air communication. They read them. Of course, without a doubt, they better understood their meaning through class discussion in Sign, but that through-the-air use could not have assisted them in writing the phrases correctly. The text, once they fully understood it, served as the scaffolding from which they recruited specific phrases for the formulation of their own ideas, to create text that came infinitely closer to college level.

Putting Down Our Swords

Among other reasons, I wanted to write this book because I felt that, for far too long, the profession of educating Deaf students has been obsessed with the oral/aural language development of Deaf students, and this obsession has overshadowed the real need of students to understand and interact with language in print. We have argued endlessly about the best ways to communicate through the air, but we have failed to understand that even skilled hearing English-language users are not necessarily competent writers or see the profound implication this has for students who are Deaf and hard of hearing. If hearing and speaking students struggle with writing well, we must look for solutions for improving writing above and beyond oral/aural language development.

But I fear that many of my colleagues hold strongly to the notion that there is a one-to-one relationship between language-through-the-air and writing. We think that if students speak or sign English, they will write better essays. They will not. We think that if students sign their essays first in ASL or view essays signed in "academic ASL" and then are assisted in translating the videotaped signs into print, they will eventually write better essays. They will not. We must distance ourselves from teaching based on these notions, on the incorrect belief that writing is a direct translation of the language we speak or sign. These teaching practices stem from outdated principles and practices from the fields of bilingual education and Teaching English to Speakers of Other Languages (TESOL), methods such as *contrastive analysis* and *grammar translation*. The former teaching methodology compares and contrasts grammatical structures between source and target languages; the latter creates written transcriptions of a source language that are translated into a target language so that differences in the two languages can be discussed. Thankfully, ESL instruction today, for the most part, has a new look and feel, and it gives high priority to the kinds of methodologies discussed in this book. However, there are additional language-teaching practices within TESOL that are still being rethought.

This past winter, I attended a conference sponsored by the ESL and English faculty at CUNY. The conference was called "Conference on Teaching, Language, and the CUNY Student," but its focus was on a group of students found nationwide who are now pegged as "Generation 1.5." I had no idea what that meant until I attended the conference and did some background reading. This is what I discovered:

> Generation 1.5 students are U.S.-educated English language learners. There is great diversity among them in terms of their prior educational experience, native and English language proficiency, language dominance, and academic literacy. Some of these students immigrated to the United States while they were in elementary school; others arrived during high school. Still others were born in this country but grew up speaking a language other than English at home. They may see themselves as bilingual, but English may be the only language in which they have academic preparation or in which they can read and write. At the same time, these students may not feel that they have a full command of English, having grown up speaking another language at home or in their community. Equipped with social skills in English, Generation 1.5 students often appear in conversation to be native English speakers. However, they are usually less skilled in the academic language associated with school achievement, especially in the area of writing. (Harklau, Losey, and Siegal 2003, 1)

I learned that Generation 1.5 students fall in between Generation 1 students, those whose native language is not English and where no English is spoken in the home (typically ESL students), and Generation 2 students, those whose native language is English and where English is spoken in the home (typically native English speakers; Crook 2007). Generation 1.5 students, despite having attended mainstream classes in high school, upon coming to college are placed in ESL classes based on writing placement exams such as the CUNY/ACT essay exam. This infuriates them because even though they are comfortable with spoken English, they are placed with students who have had limited exposure to spoken English.

They have the right to be infuriated, because they have indeed been wrongly placed. The faulty placement decisions are based on the faulty notion that writing problems stem from problems with oral language and that English for communication and correctness needs to be learned prior to the kinds of writing tasks that allow students to enter and add to conversations with the authors they read. It does not. Students can enter these conversations at all levels because they all can think. What needs to be adjusted is the difficulty level of the texts they interact with. Even in the hearing world, then, we see the inability to understand the intimate connections that students need to draw between reading and writing, as opposed to speaking and writing, if they are to become competent college-level writers.

My Deaf and hard of hearing students can be considered Generation 1.5 students. They have (except for my international students) studied in the United States for about a decade, some more, some less; for the hard of hearing students, English is not necessarily the language spoken at home, and for the Deaf students, because hearing parents do not typically sign well and parents and children must resort to lip-reading and gesture, communication in the home is highly restricted. English has been the language of academic preparation for all, and most of them do just fine communicating with one another through the air—including the hard of hearing students who learn ASL rather quickly to be part of our social group. The problem, as we have come to see, is when they are asked to write in an academic context, as it is with the hearing Generation 1.5 students. Like Generation 1.5 students, then, instead of linkages between speech and writing, they need opportunities to read and write about ideas that broaden their horizons. And, without a doubt, these new ideas need to be written clearly and correctly. But how?

When I was first hired to teach writing to LaGuardia's Deaf students, I came to the job armed with the latest research on teaching writing to hearing students. Culling from the work of teacher-writers such as Calkins, Atwell, Mayher, and Elbow, leaders in the field of writing education, my students made great strides with their writing as they learned to draft and redraft mostly personal responses to readings until what they said was clearer and more convincing. As curricular changes were instituted and students were required to use readings to argue a point of their own, my students followed suit. I noticed how they were beginning to push the boundaries of their thinking to allow new, more sophisticated thoughts in as they interacted with other authors' ideas and their own. I saw that the readings pushed their vocabulary to a new level and that our conversations during conferencing time became, well, actually interesting. But then the sky fell in and interrupted our progress: The administration mandated that in order for developmental students to move on to freshman composition, they would have to pass the CUNY/ACT writing test—and grammar counted. I had a big problem. Wasn't it enough that my students were really thinking now in their essays? How perfect did their English have to be? I soon learned that correctness mattered, big time.

Fortunately, at about the same time that the requirements changed, I discovered a teaching method called X-Word Grammar. As I learned the system and thought long and hard about it, I realized that X-Word Grammar was an approach that could help my students first to discover grammatical principles and then apply them to their own writing—and it seemed to be an approach they could really master. Most important, I found that I could integrate this system into the kinds of text-based writing assignments required of my students. Rather than create separate courses for writing and for grammar, grammar would be overlaid onto writing assignments; language and content would be combined. Students in my developmental writing course who learned X-Word Grammar were able to build bridges among their reading, their writing, and their grammar, and their writing vastly improved. X-Word Grammar gives students a way to engage with ideas that say something to them and a way to say something back—and to say it well.

I would like to ask educators of Deaf students to rethink the "language wars" that have torn and continue to tear our field apart, and to put down our swords. By language wars I mean the cycle of implementing, discarding, and re-implementing language mandates and policies that has continued for more than 100 years, in schools for Deaf students across the

United States that have touted one form of through-the-air language/communication system over another. We started with manualism (the exclusive use of ASL) and the Rochester Method (the exclusive use of fingerspelling), then moved on to oralism (the exclusive use of speech with support from aural abilities) and then on to Total Communication (the combined use of signs and speech) and to Cued Speech (where hand symbols placed close to the mouth disambiguate distinct phonemes) and Visual Phonics and on to various combinations of these "isms" and "tions" for different instructional purposes. We have screamed at each other, shaken fingers in one another's faces, and written diatribes about the virtues of one language/communication system over another, but the fact remains that when our students arrive in college, mostly all communicate through the air in fairly competent ways and some are good readers, but few are competent writers. This book, then, is a plea to end the language wars and devote our energies to what has been and continues to be missing in writing instruction for Deaf students: forging intensive links among reading, writing, and grammar, as early as possible. I invite you to read on to see how these links are forged in self-contained classes of Deaf students at LaGuardia Community College, and how all students can learn to work text to become better writers.

Chapter 1

The What and Why of Writing Instruction

Although the personal narrative essay is my favorite form of essay to teach, read, and respond to, my students can no longer pass their developmental skills writing course by writing a personal narrative. Because my students must now pass a rigorous proficiency test in order to graduate, the ante has been upped to exit from developmental writing. Developmental writing has taken on a more expository, academic look that requires students to engage with texts by using supporting examples to back up their points and offer personal analyses to extend the significance of the examples chosen. Reading has become the basis for writing, and although there are times when I long for some of the intriguing and engaging personal essays of the past, I have come to see how this new requirement better prepares students for the variety of writing assignments they will meet in college in the years to come.

This new way of writing does not come easily to my students. For too many years, they have not had opportunities to engage with interesting ideas to write about, for the simple reason that they have not had opportunities to read and discuss interesting ideas. Students have been asked to write about general topics that presume familiarity ("Should the government fund space exploration projects or research on human diseases?") or are contrived to afford students practice with a particular rhetorical form ("Explain the steps involved in preparing something you like to cook") or a particular grammatical structure ("Describe a favorite room in your house. Be sure to use locative prepositions."). More recently, in order to enroll in freshman composition, my students have to prove their worth as writers by doing something similar to this: "Write a letter to the dean of your college arguing for either upgrading the computer labs or improving the college bookstore." What students, honestly, would want to roll up their sleeves and get to work on these topics?

Writing assignments should ideally come from topics or questions students would like to think more deeply about after reading a required text or texts, slowly and carefully. Such texts should have themes that fire students up and introduce them to characters with whom they can easily identify because the characters' trials and tribulations tug at some similar emotional chord. Finding the right text is the key to successful writing experiences because I see how utterly motivating it is for students to read something they actually enjoy. Typically, I choose short stories or full-length novels in which intrigue builds over time and characters can be known up front and personally as their growth or decline is tracked through the text. "Because of their imaginative nature and narrative structure, [stories] invite their audiences into them. . . . Literature encourages us to empathize with or react against the characters who attract our attention, vicariously experience what they do as we identify with them, and speculate on those aspects of their lives that the authors have not described for us" (Hirvela 2001, 117). There are always ways into fictional texts for students because such texts are about the kinds of problems people have to deal with in real life—and students generally want to snoop a bit into the lives of others to see how their own problems match up, or hypothesize reasons for problems, or offer some advice. Students also tend to remember story episodes rather well, which means, at times, they can write longer essays that draw upon information gleaned from wider expanses of text—which will most likely be required in full-credit classes.

In *Engaging Ideas*, John C. Bean (1996) offers teachers a variety of ways to structure academic writing assignments. He makes the point that the best writing topics require students to become involved with controversy, to take a stand and roll up their sleeves and prove that their take on a particular issue is the right one. Such is the backbone of academic writing that my students must learn. And although I find there is more engagement with writing when students are afforded opportunities to theorize on their own about an issue in a text that calls to them in some way and to create their own writing topics, the majority of my students welcome ideas to write about and choose teacher-created writing topics. They need an issue to support or not support, a question to answer or a problem to solve.

Topics should assist students in addressing the issue, question, or problem being raised by way of a single thesis statement. Here are two sample topics, the first from our study of Laura Esquivel's (1989) *Like Water for Chocolate* and the second from two short stories on the theme of stereotyping. Notice that the assignments give students a key idea from the readings to support or not support, as well as specific questions that will extend their thinking about the idea so that their essays say something significant and have a finished feel to them.

> **At the end of the April chapter in *Like Water for Chocolate*, Mama Elena shouts to Father Ignacio, "Men aren't very important in this life, Father." Using examples from the first four chapters of the story, show how this quote either does or does not accurately describe the way Mama Elena leads her life. What reasons can you offer for the behaviors you describe?**
>
> **In "What my Mother Knows" by Carole Glickfeld and "Cathedral" by Raymond Carver, a Deaf person (Ruth's mother) and a blind person (Robert) are stereotyped by people who do not know them. Have you, like Ruth's mother or Robert, ever been stereotyped? Citing examples from each of the stories, show how your experience is either similar to or different from Ruth's mother's and Robert's experiences. Why do you think you have or have not been stereotyped?**

There is no more time for vapid writing topics about funding space exploration or writing letters to deans about more computer labs. Brenda Jo Brueggemann (1999) would say that writing topics such as these appeal to those who value literacy for communication rather than for its use as language. Brueggemann writes, "When literate acts are seen as being only about or for the purpose of communication, when literacy is only about or for the correct use of skills to convey a message clearly . . . then the beauty, of what language can do, as well as its power, is lost" (37). Brueggemann relates the story of Ellen, a Gallaudet University graduate, a gifted user and teacher of ASL, and a comedian, storyteller, and poet in the Deaf community:

> Despite the enormous troubles she has had, and continues to have, with English, Ellen professes a "love" for it. She has a history of "lousy grammar"—a picture of herself as a somewhat "screwed up" user of English that she's come to internalize after all these years: "I always had a problem with writing because [just as] with lipreading, I could catch certain things, but then I would miss so much. I put things together, but it was usually screwed up". . . . She has spent more than enough educational time trying to learn to just *communicate* in English: " . . . I was giving up my recess at the deaf schools so that I could have private speech lessons one on one. I benefited, yeah, because I can communicate with my family better and with some people. And sometimes I feel like I can talk and that is really nice. But really skilled sentences, no. Little phrases I can say, short and sweet.". . . [Ellen] is currently enrolled in a Ph.D. program in a state university, and it is through that program, she tells me, that she continues to use and attempt improving her "English reading and writing."And she does so for far more than purely functional, instrumental, communicational reasons: "I love English because it really broadens my horizon so much. . . . English helps me express more, writing jokes and stories—like that. . . . I find it a challenge to find a way to say things that will make people laugh in English too." (44–45)

For Ellen, then, writing is for learning, through reading, how to be a better comedian. The more she reads and writes, the more she broadens intellectually, and, I am sure, the funnier and more interesting her jokes and stories become. Ellen's reading and writing work is purposeful; she does it not to prove her competence in English in order to pass a test, but to write a piece that is a creation, something that is branded with her distinct thinking, something that sustains her interest over time, something that engages her. And this, according to Brueggemann, is exactly why Deaf students should write. This is how literacy becomes language: "Literacy is about 'broadening' oneself and one's community—about expression, laughter, challenge, and appreciation shared across, through, within that language" (45). If we, as teachers, can offer readings that students enjoy and that inspire them to think about and learn from, the hardest part of our job as teachers of writing has been done.

Writing into Reading

In order to produce a well-written essay, students must have a solid understanding of the stories they are being asked to analyze. For lower-level readers, this means we must create ways to pull students into the text and have them interact with it. They must read a text slowly and deeply. Most students, for a variety of reasons, do not spend enough time on their reading assignments. They rush through them hoping to come upon the gist of the author's purpose, missing details that could tie important connections together. This is not to say that their actions are always deliberate; many times, given the fact that most Deaf developmental writers are also developmental readers, certain texts are too difficult for students who are Deaf to digest on their own. I tell my students that to better understand what they read, they must sit down with their tools: something to write with, a good dictionary, their reading, and their writing-into-reading activity.

Guide or Comprehension Questions

Writing-into-reading activities such as answering guide or comprehension questions slow students down in their reading and provide opportunities for them to try to piece together text details on their own. Part of the appeal of guide questions is that inside many of these questions lies a true statement about the text. So, for the short story "Lifeline" by Gloria Anzaldúa (1991), inside the question "How does Suel reject la Prieta?" is the information that Suel rejects la Prieta, which helps students through their reading. These hints that students decipher by reading the questions slowly and carefully, as well as with diligent use of an accessible dictionary such as the *Newbury House Dictionary of American English* (2004), offer ways of digging deeper into text that cannot be read independently. The *Newbury House Dictionary*, a learner's dictionary, is particularly helpful because definitions are easy to understand and sample sentences show how words are used in everyday life. Students have told me that the practice of writing the page numbers where the answers to the questions can be found right next to each question also helps them navigate the text on their own.

Be careful to create questions that are not too big ("What is the significance of Suel's rejection?") or that cannot be answered until more details about the text are known. Start with small questions that assist students in understanding the flow of ideas in the reading (who, what, where, when, how), and, if you are asking a question that requires students to do some inferring—a question that calls for their opinion or some reading between the lines—tell them that you will signal that by adding the phrase "do you think" to the question, as in "Do you think la Prieta will continue to pursue Suel?" If you ask, "Will la Prieta continue to pursue Suel?" some students might think the answer lies in the text.

Marking Text

Another writing-into-reading activity that I encourage of my students is *marking text*: underlining key ideas, writing side responses or paraphrases about ideas, adding questions that come to mind, writing dictionary definitions of unknown words right onto the text, and using arrows to connect related ideas. As Mary Fjeldstad (2006) explains in *The Thoughtful Reader*, students need ways of actively engaging with text to help them remember what they've read. Marking text makes visible what good readers do to help them understand text. However, students require extended practice in marking text, so teachers must model the process many times. In classrooms with hearing students and teachers, students follow along in their books as the text is being read aloud or discussed. Deaf students cannot watch text and teacher simultaneously; they need their eyes to follow the teacher's signs. But a teacher signing about text is not enough. Students need to literally see how more able readers take text in and let it out, in ways that help them understand it better.

Therefore, to level the playing field, it is essential that classrooms for Deaf students be equipped so that text can be projected and teachers can write on and next to it. The text can be projected onto a whiteboard either through the use of transparencies and an over-head projector or a document camera connected to a projector. (Document cameras allow teachers to project any text—either single sheets of paper or open books—without having to make transparencies.) Of course, digital files of text can be viewed on a whiteboard by connecting the computer to a projector. Deaf students can thus focus their attention on both the projected text and the teacher, who stands and signs d irectly next to the projected text, working the text.

Here is an example of a marked-up excerpt from de Maupassant's (1907) story "The Necklace" that I go through with my students as they watch. I tell them that I first need to read this section without marking anything, to get a feel for what it is about. After reading it silently to myself, I mention that the excerpt is a dispute between a husband and a wife. With this initial understanding of the text, I can now read to find out more details about the conflict:

[But one evening her husband came in with a proud air, holding in his hand a   *seems happy*

large envelope.]

"There," said he, "there's something for you."

She quickly tore the paper and took out of it (a printed card) which bore these

words:—

"The Minister of Education and Mme. Georges Rampouneau beg M. and

Mme. Loisel to do them the honor to pass the evening with them at the palace

of the Ministry, on Monday, January 18."

[Instead of being delighted, as her husband hoped, she threw (the invitation) on

the table with annoyance, murmuring—   *odd response*
                                                        . . . why?

"What do you want me to do with that?"]

"But, my dear, I thought you would be pleased. You never go out, and here's a

chance, a fine one. I had the hardest work to get it. Everybody is after (them) (they)

are greatly sought for and not many are given to the clerks. You will see there

all the official world."

?

She looked at him with an irritated eye and she declared with impatience:—

"What do you want me to put on my back to go there?"

He had not thought of that; he hesitated:—

"But the dress in which you go to the theater. That looks very well to me—"

He shut up, astonished and distracted at seeing that [his wife was weeping.

Two big tears were descending slowly from the corners of the eyes to the

!! strong reaction

corners of the mouth.] He stuttered:—

What's the matter? What's the matter?"

But by a violent effort she had conquered her trouble, and she replied in a

calm voice as she wiped her damp cheeks:—

"Nothing. Only I have no clothes, and in consequence I cannot go to this

Oh...

party. Give your card to some (colleague) whose wife has a better outfit than I."

→ (N) someone husband works with

He was (disconsolate.) He began again:—

→ (ADJ) very unhappy

"See here, Mathilde, how much would this cost, a proper dress, which would

do on other occasions; something very simple?"

[She reflected a few seconds, going over her calculations, and thinking also *planning how to get what she wants*

of the sum which she might ask without meeting an immediate refusal and a

frightened exclamation from (the frugal clerk).] → *(ADJ) husband doesn't like to waste money*

At last, she answered hesitatingly:—

"I don't know exactly, but it seems to me that with [four hundred francs] I *A lot of money!!!*

might do it."

[He grew a little pale, for he was reserving just that sum to buy a gun and *doesn't tell Mathilde this*

treat himself to a little shooting, the next summer, on the plain of Nanterre,

with some friends who used to shoot larks there on Sundays.]

But he said:—

"All right. I will give you four hundred francs. But take care to have a

pretty dress."

Notice that my markings fall into several categories.

1. My interpretations (brackets): This is where I add my own ideas about what I am reading. I sense that Mathilde's husband is initially happy about the invitation but that Mathilde's response is odd; that Mathilde knows to be careful to not ask for too much money for a dress; that her husband does not speak up about his own desires. None of these ideas are actually stated in the text, but I am jumping off from the text to add my own two cents. My goal is to have these two cents grow into a provocative claim about the story through continued discussion written into notes on the whiteboard.

2. My questions (question marks): I wonder why Mathilde's reaction to the invitation is so strange and strong, what "all the official world" might mean.

3. Big points (underlines): I underline the reason why Mathilde says she cannot go to the party.

4. Unfamiliar words (circles) and phrases (wavy lines): I circle and look up words students might not know, including their parts of speech—students must understand how words function in a sentence before they can use them properly (for more about why this is so important, see chapter 3). I also try to massage

definitions to fit the story, situating them in an understandable context, as seen in the definitions for *colleague* and *frugal*. This will help students remember definitions; wavy lines call their attention to how meaning needs to be discerned from groups of words.

5. Referring back to what was already said (double-headed arrows): the word *card* is referred to as *invitation*, *them*, and *they* later on in the text. Students might not recognize this if it was not marked for them.

By copying several exact mark-ups that teachers model onto their own copies of the same text, students begin to learn how to approach or work new texts independently. Using brackets slows students down to reflect on text; question marks help them see where to keep reading to perhaps find answers, or to know where to begin a class discussion by asking their own questions; underlines shout out, "This is important!" Finding understandable definitions of unknown words moves students along in their reading and offers them new ways of lifting the level of their writing once they understand their meaning. Most important, the markings give students something to go back to when they are asked to think more deeply about a possible thesis and to subsequently write their essays. They will remember better the aspects of the story they have already made some notation about, and right before them are words and phrases to draw upon when they reference points in their essays. As I see it, this is one of the most authentic ways of learning English: learning it simultaneously with making a point about something of interest.

Focused Reading Notes

John Bean (1996) describes an approach to writing into reading called "focused reading notes" (144), in which teachers create four or five topic headings for students to fill in with notes from their texts. Each topic heading represents a key idea from the readings that teachers want students to walk away with. Topic headings for "The Necklace" might include "Mathilde's Wants and Desires," "Husband's Response to Mathilde's Needs," "The Cover-Up," and "The Debt." Under each heading, teacher and students jot down story information in note form. Marie Clay (1982) notes that many times students need only the slightest of clues to facilitate their understanding of a text—just a taste of what the text is about helps students orient their thinking. Having the students take focused notes serves this purpose well; the category headings provide frames of reference for story parts from which students can piece together the details of the specific part on their own. Teachers can also include the number of bullets that would satisfactorily fill out a frame, so students know to keep digging if they discover fewer than the requisite number. This requires students to do some rereading, which few students might do on their own.

Writing to See Our Deeper Thinking about Reading

Formulating Discussion Notes

In *Rewriting: How to do Things with Texts*, Joseph Harris (2006) claims that in order to offer a response to a text, students first have to come to terms with it by offering "an accurate account of [the] work" (5). Writing-into-reading activities lead students into a text's meaning and from there into more substantive class discussions. When students have put in the time necessary to understand the specifics of a particular piece, class discussion flies with more accurate gists, insightful comments as well as personal opinions, and thoughtful lingering questions. It is during this discussion that teachers can entice students to think about their reading from a different angle—to think of something different to say about it. As Janet Angelillo (2003) explains in *Writing About Reading*, we want students "to be changed by what they read, and to use some of that change as the basis for their writing" (107). After having read several chapters in Laura Esquivel's *Like Water for Chocolate*, Philip, a student studying to become a priest, was taken by the immoral behavior of Tita, the main character in the novel. In class, he said that he was convinced that Tita was not the victim the author was making her out to be, and that rather than being the unfortunate daughter condemned to take care of her mother for the rest of her life instead of marrying and having her own family, she was a temptress who took pleasure in flirting with her sister's husband. You can imagine the stir this discussion caused! Philip's deeper thinking spoke to his particular take on the text. As Laura Hennessey DeSena (2007) would say, he "talked back" to the text and took his own unique stance. There was a plethora of information in the chapters that we had read up until that point that he could use to back up his theory.

Ideally, teachers will propose more than one text to consider for an essay, so that parallels can be drawn between and among texts. Harris (2006) refers to taking concepts from one text and applying them to another as *forwarding*, or extending the range and power of ideas (62). The more students see an essential theme of a particular text appearing in another, the stronger the understanding of the ideas under discussion. One grouping of essays whose themes I have asked students to think about includes "An American Dream" by Rosemarie Santini (1990) and "The Struggle to Be an All-American Girl" by Elizabeth Wong (1990). Both essays relate the difficulties that immigrant parents face trying to preserve specific cultural traditions in their children once they move to America. The essays introduce us to children who would prefer to be more American than Italian or Chinese, respectively. Class discussion meanders. We talk about rigid and unrealistic parenting as opposed to flexibility in decision making, lack of respect as opposed to respectful independence, and creating new allegiances at the expense of losing family connections. Discussed from the perspective of the different characters in the essays, the theme of cultural conflict between the generations, broached over and over again, becomes easy to understand and subsequently to jump off from. My student Olga argued that because the immigrant parents made the decision to bring their children to America, they now had to accept the consequences of this decision—only a high level of engagement with the text could have evoked this response.

As discussion flies, I jot down notes on the whiteboard. The form of these notes is dictated by the meanings that are being formed through discussion of the text. Notes can be just phrases alone, or phrases structured into concept groupings, depending on how many similar ideas are generated. The more savvy of my students begin to see that the quality of their essays is directly tied to how well they understand their readings and the ensuing class discussion, and I notice them taking extreme care in jotting down these notes as we talk. Here, then, is perhaps the most important writing-into-reading activity that I think has been overlooked by teachers of Deaf students. Deaf students do not necessarily know how to take notes, how to choose from among the phrases that pop up in class discussions the ones they may need for their essays and should write down. Participating in a discussion and sharing ideas in ASL does not necessarily mean that students will know how to phrase those ideas in English, because ASL is not English. Most hearing students discussing that Mathilde in "The Necklace" "wished for a lifestyle that she could not afford," or that Monsieur Loisel "lived to please his wife" or that Madame Forrestier "was just as guilty of pretense as Mathilde" would have no trouble jotting this language down because they would know how to spell most words and how to order them. They lean on everyday words they have heard again and again and use their knowledge of sound patterns to help them attack words new to them.

While good Deaf readers might have no difficulty with translations from ASL to print, most Deaf students in developmental reading and writing courses need to see the discussed language in print. When the language of key ideas is made accessible, students walk away from class discussion with phrases they can integrate into their essays, and they produce more fluent first drafts. Typically, this is language that is idiomatic, uses advanced vocabulary, and is syntactically embedded —and is therefore important for college-level writing. As with writing-into-reading activities, there is no better motivation to learn a language than the need to create an important message with it.

Using Discussion-Board Software, Social Networking Tools, and Blogs

Today, writing to see our deeper thinking about texts is not limited to the classroom. Students can participate in discussions online via discussion-board software or social networking platforms such as Ning, or blogs. Asynchronous or synchronous, electronic discussions engage students and can play an important role in improving their writing, especially at the stage where ideas are being gathered. What holds true for the formulation of good writing topics holds true for the formulation of good online discussion prompts: They should be based on readings that offer students chances to take a stand one way or another, to jump off from and develop an idea in a different direction, to forward a concept from one reading to another, to personalize in some way, or to begin to formulate answers to questions they may have been puzzling over. While some teachers are very structured in their requirements ("at least three substantial responses for each online session; have your books open and be ready to support your ideas with quotes") and grade students on a highly specified rubric based on quality of response, others ask students to select an idea or quote that interests them and leave it at that. Some teachers participate in the discussion; others are spectators to it.

Having dabbled with blogs, discussion boards, and Ning over the years, I have found that these tools are most helpful when students are in groups and a selected group "summarizer" collects the thoughts of the group members to present in paragraph form. The quality of response in these summaries raises the discussion to a new level, as the summarizer has had the benefit of working with several ideas from several students and thinking becomes more complex. It is also productive to instruct students that their responses will be viewed in class the next day. Knowing that their work will be showcased, students step up and try harder to have a better product to show. I like to peruse posts the night before class and cut and paste those that will make for good continued discussion when the class comes together. Here is the opportunity for students to stretch their thinking about a particular point or points: As students view the selected posts (through the use of a document camera or computer and projector), I stand right next to the post and write alongside it on the whiteboard any additional thoughts that arise from class discussion.

Now the discussion points have been broached three times: once by the students individually, once in groups, and once as a class with me. This is sure to help students elaborate and enhance their thinking, something we ask of them all the time. Online discussions are particularly effective as students can revisit them at any time. One of my colleagues requires her students to go back into their electronic discussions to find quotes of interest from other classmates and incorporate these quotes into their more formal essays, crediting classmates through in-text citation—this is a brilliant way to begin to teach documentation.

As with face-to-face discussions, electronic discussions engender more productive thinking when students have already come to terms with what they have been reading through writing-into-reading activities, which should be considered first-step activities that remain primary regardless of the modality of instruction.

Thinking in Chunks

Before I started writing this book, I filled four or five 8 ½ × 11–inch yellow pads with reading notes. I headed each page with the name of the book the notes were from and then, gradually, on additional pages of additional notepads, I created my own headings based on what I had been reading; typically, these were the big ideas I wanted to think more about and probably write about. Here I was being creative, putting my own spin on what others had done before me. I would then scribble each new smaller, related thought under the appropriate heading, in no particular order. Once I felt I had enough to say, I smoothed out the order, again being creative but now trying to figure out the most logical way to present my ideas so that my readers would see the logic as well. I kept at this, creating the big ideas (chunks) from the little ideas of my reading and then smoothing out the ideas—for eight years! This is what composing is all about: thinking in chunks and then smoothing out the ideas within the chunks.

Our students are neither writing books nor keeping at their writing projects for eight years. Nevertheless, their writing processes should not be much different from mine. We have already seen the need for reading notes and discussion notes. Discussion notes are the equivalent of my own headings on the yellow notepads—they are the new thinking that evolved from the details of reading notes. The students now need to fill in their discussion notes with the details of their reading notes, in no particular order at this point.

I had my class read chapter 9 of *In This Sign* by Joanne Greenberg (1970). Margaret Ryder, the seven-year-old hearing daughter of Abel and Janice Ryder, who are Deaf, must negotiate the purchase of a coffin for her four-year-old brother who recently died. She is with her parents, but she alone must speak with the funeral director and for her parents. In our discussion of this chapter, students felt that Margaret, Janice, Abel, and the funeral director are all to be held accountable for the breakdown in communication that transpires at the funeral parlor. This became a big discussion idea that we wrote on our whiteboard. After the discussion, I sent the students back to their reading notes to fill in this big idea with smaller ideas that would serve as proof of their thinking. As I walked around the room, I saw that students were thinking in chunks fairly well. I saw things like this:

> Margaret's Fault
>
> > should have told the funeral director she didn't understand his big words like *coffin* and *deceased*
> >
> > had never heard those words before
> >
> > messed up the interpretation of *value* when the funeral director asked her if Bradley's life had any *value* to her parents. Thought he was asking if Bradley was *expensive* to raise
>
> Abel and Janice's Fault
>
> > should not have allowed a 7-year-old to interpret for them—too young
> >
> > could have written back and forth with the director themselves
> >
> > should have known that Margaret's vocabulary was limited because she didn't go to school
>
> The Funeral Director's Fault
>
> > knew Margaret wasn't understanding but kept on talking
> >
> > screamed at Margaret and insulted her parents which made Margaret silent

This was a fine beginning. Then I asked the students to think back to our discussion of an even bigger point. For a conclusion to this prospective essay, I wanted them to think about this question: "What was Joanne Greenberg trying to tell us by writing chapter 9?" They went back to their discussion notes and found the following ideas:

- Some Deaf parents might depend on their hearing children to interpret too much for them, stealing their childhood from them.

- Mistakes in interpretation can ruin communication between Deaf and hearing people.

I am not a proponent of very detailed outlines because I feel that rigid forms constrict composing; writing from outlines often results in the outlined ideas transposed into connected prose and nothing more, which I find disheartening. If I can see a certain logic to my students' thinking, I'm satisfied. I want my students to think on their feet, if you will, as they are composing, and see where this freedom takes them. I know they will come up with more ideas because they will be thinking more about their topics, and this sustained thought will trigger a new idea here and there.

Our discussion on the book chapter spawned good ideas, and those students who wanted to pursue this topic further were ready to grow an essay, which I assure you did not take eight years to write! But consider what went into this particular essay thus far: Students answered guide questions and kept focused reading notes. They marked up their copies of the chapter and kept discussion notes. They did a rudimentary chunking of their ideas. It was a lot of work, and it extended into several class sessions—before the students wrote one word of their essays. There was just too much writing into reading, thinking, and discussing to worry yet about drafting.

Chapter 2

The How of Writing Instruction

In the introduction to this book, I mentioned that one of the reasons why my developmental writers have difficulty writing conclusions to essays is because they have not had sufficient exposure to essays—they have not read and understood enough essays to be familiar with how conclusions to essays work. I must now further qualify this thought: My students have not learned to write essays because they have not had opportunities to *study* excellent, readable models of exactly what is expected of them. This is particularly unfortunate considering how real writers approach much of their own creative work—they cry out for models. Joan Didion, as a beginning writer, typed the stories of Ernest Hemingway to get a feel for how he crafted his sentences; Gay Talese did the same with F. Scott Fitzgerald (Thomason and York 2002). In other fields, too, we seek out models who are expert at what we aspire to: Competitive chess players study the moves of the masters; professional football players watch videotapes of their competitors' plays to frame their own; and ice dancers practicing for the Olympics study the moves of those pairs who have come before them and won gold.

Writers study how skilled writers craft their writing in particular works, how they organize their ideas and choose specific words and phrases—their "ways with words" or "writerly moves" (Ray 1999). Isoke Titilayo Nia (1999) calls these model texts *touchstone texts*. "For several days students will read and talk about the text, discussing anything they notice about the writing. The focus of the inquiry at this point is to try to figure out how the writer went about the writing" (5–6). Here are four of Nia's criteria for touchstone texts:

1. You (the teacher) have read the text and you love it.

   You and your students have talked about the text a lot as readers first. Our first response . . . should be as readers. Talk first and talk well before you begin to dissect any piece of writing for your study.

2. You find many things to teach in the text.

   The text feels full—teaching full. You see so much that you can teach using just this one piece.

3. Your students can read the text independently or with some support.

   Because you are going to invest so much time and talk in this one piece . . . you don't really need to worry about whether every [student] can read the text independently. This text is going to come with lots of support.

4. The text is a little more sophisticated than the writing of your best students.

   You want every [student] to have to work to write like this author. (6)

It has always been difficult for me to find touchstone texts to use with my students that fulfill the last two of Nia's criteria. Most essays by published authors cannot easily be analyzed and emulated when students craft their own writing. Although they are excellent pieces of writing, the writers possess abilities beyond those of my best writers and are difficult to read, and therefore too difficult to productively analyze. There most certainly is a time and place for students to internalize the workings of more demanding writing, but struggling with reading does not allow students to be "writerly readers"—readers who can easily internalize the structural frame and conceptual underpinnings of the pieces. I have discovered that writing that is within student reach can often be found in strong, edited pieces written, in fact, by other students. Studying peer-written pieces can begin to close the gap between student and published writers.

Excellent peer writing is appropriately scaffolded for student writers. It is writing that students can reasonably be expected to write because it can be easily understood with only minimal support. Once understood, students can learn to use language to discuss the writers' moves—to become writerly readers, analyzing the reasons why their peers chose certain ideas and placed them in specific parts of an essay. It is this "use of language to talk about language use" that is most helpful to student writers because the talk describes the characteristics of good writing that they will need to apply themselves.

Model student writing is also particularly riveting for students. Most often topics are of mutual interest, and students are curious to see how their peers address an essay topic that they, too, have chosen. Many times ideas found in one student's essay appear recycled a bit in another's. This is not copying; we expand our thinking by melding parts of others' thoughts with our own. Students also feel empowered when student writing is showcased, knowing that if another person with similar skill level and life experience can write something excellent, so can they.

A Treasured Essay from the Past

One of my touchstone texts for the personal essay was written by a Deaf adult coming back to school after years of full-time work. This student's "senior" status is easily recognized by the maturity of his thinking and his ability to reflect and make sense of a difficult time. He wrote his essay in response to "In the City of the Deaf," a piece by Martin Sternberg (1994) that was published in the *New York Times*. Sternberg's essay chronicled the trials and tribulations of being Deaf in New York City. I asked students to reflect upon their own experiences growing up Deaf in a hearing environment. This particular response, the best I have ever worked with, was revised four times. It more than fulfills all of Nia's (1999) criteria for selecting touchstone texts, and I use it as a model of superior narrative writing because of all that it has to teach us, despite the fact that narrative essays are no longer part of the writing curriculum.

Stranger in the Nest

My childhood was more or less like a fairy tale. I lived like a prince but always alone . . . an outsider in my own family.

I lived in a mansion located in a posh section of a town called _____, in _____, which is often called the "_____ Beverly Hills." I always had five maids to take care of everything, a chauffeur to take me to school, a gardener to take care of our acres of garden and a pool maintenance man.

But all this wasn't sufficient to fulfill my life which felt like the empty cocoon of a caterpillar.

I just wanted to be a part of my family, but I knew it would be impossible to be a "full member" because I am deaf and have always felt excluded from daily family business. Not being able to follow conversations made me a stranger in their nest.

My hell began when I was 5 years old. I figured out that I was different from my brothers, sisters, and cousins because of my "funny voice" and the hearing aid in my chest pocket which attached to my ears with yellow wires and always made tiny noises around my head. I discovered that I was deaf after being separated from my brothers and sisters by my parents' order . . . as if I had some disease. They thought I would limit my younger brothers' and sisters' oral communication skills. When my parents got divorced, my mother left with four of her five children, leaving me, "the deaf one" all alone in the mansion to face the big and ferocious lion that was my father. Since father was always traveling for his business, he hired a nanny to take care of me who I named "Murder Eyes" because of her rigid discipline. I felt ostracized by my own family after the divorce . . . as if I was a cancerous growth which needed to be extricated from their skin. But nothing was more humiliating for me than . . . .Wednesday night dinner.

I always attended Wednesday night dinner at my grandparents' house with about 30 members of my family. I never wanted to be with them because I was tired of being a "ghost" at their dinner table. But one time I let myself be convinced by my grandparents that they would mouth for me what every member of my family said. They needed me to be there because I am their first grandson and my presence is important. I thought to myself how much I hated the idea of being with them at that dinner table . . . how much frustration I had to endure again and again. But when Wednesday night arrived, I went to my grandparents' house. Yeah, I let myself be deluded for one more time.

I sat at the front of the big table with several members of my family. They started to have their usual conversation, and I was hoping one of my family members would see me as a living person. I was hoping to see that my grandparents would keep their promise.

They did keep their promise, but only for five minutes. After that, I was forgotten.

This incident was sufficient to kill my rare happiness. I felt myself lost in the middle of a flock of talking parrots . . . blah, blah, blah. It made me an invisible person since their eyes never so much as looked at mine. I didn't open my mouth to complain. I just tried to make some noise to get their attention by tapping my fork on the table. Nobody noticed. I thought to myself, "Why don't I leave this damn nest of parrots."

I left and went home without saying good-bye . . . and, of course, they didn't care about my leaving.

I don't have any more illusions about being a part of my family because of the old Chinese saying, "You can't change the color of flies' eyes." I can't change my family's feelings toward me . . . to have them accept me. As members of the upper class, they blindly follow society's demand for perfection. This is common among the best families in _____. It is impossible to change their minds . . . impossible. I rarely use this word because I have always been a positive person, but when I was with my family, the limiting word just landed on my tongue.

On my way home, while driving my car, I looked at my face in the small mirror. I realized that I would always be a stranger in the nest.

And I noticed that I was happier being alone than being with them.

There is rarely a dry eye in the room when students finish reading this essay. All are moved by it. All have had similar experiences, thoughts, and feelings that they need time to share. We start to study carefully how this writer achieves the effect he does, just exactly what makes this writing great writing. We now put on our writerly-reader hats and studiously read into this piece of writing. Here are some annotations that I share with my students over a period of time.

Stranger in the Nest

My childhood was more or less like a fairy tale. I lived like a prince but always alone . . . an outsider in my own family.

> *I sense the **tension** immediately and I'm hooked. A prince yet an outsider? I want to know why. Interesting **similes**---a childhood like a fairy tale and he living like a prince.*

I lived in a mansion located in a posh section of a town called _____, in _____, which is often called the "_____ Beverly Hills." I always had five maids to take care of everything, a chauffeur to take me to school, a gardener to take care of our acres of garden, and a pool maintenance man.

> *He doesn't live in just "a big house" in a "rich" part of town—**word and phrase choices** such as " mansion," "posh," and "acres of garden" are beginning to **stir my emotions**. The **comparison** to Beverly Hills is effective. Now I have an **image** of where he lived. But he continues to "colorize" this image with reference to all the people who worked for him—and he doesn't just say, "A lot of people worked for me"; **he specifies, with titles**. Notice also how the workers and their respective jobs are written as **parallel structures** and separated by commas. This use of grammar makes me realize there were a lot of people working for him because it looks like a **list**.*

But all this wasn't sufficient to fulfill my life which felt like the empty cocoon of a caterpillar.

> *This **single sentence set off on its own** says it all. We are led to believe that he should feel like a prince, but we are abruptly told otherwise. The sentence is almost a stop sign—stop thinking he was a prince! The use of a **simile**, "like the empty cocoon of a caterpillar," makes me realize that he is comparing his life to an empty shell. His*

metaphorical use of the word caterpillar makes me wonder if he, like a caterpillar, will soon change into something different.

I just wanted to be a part of my family, but I knew it would be impossible to be a "full member" because I am deaf and have always felt excluded from daily family business. Not being able to follow conversations made me a stranger in their nest.

*Here is the point of the essay, its **thesis**. He didn't want to be "empty"; he wanted to be "full," a part of the family "nest." Note the **symbolic** use of nest: meaning not just the family, but also the closeness that is experienced by being in a small, circular home. Note where **the title of the essay is pulled from**: the essay's central point.*

My hell began when I was 5 years old. I figured out that I was different from my brothers, sisters and cousins because of my "funny voice" and the hearing aid in my chest pocket which attached to my ears with yellow wires and always made tiny noises around my head. I discovered that I was deaf after being separated from my brothers and sisters by my parents' order . . . as if I had some disease. They thought I would limit my younger brothers' and sisters' oral communication skills.

*The organizational plan here is to start with some **background information**, letting us know when the feeling of being a stranger first started. **Another way of referring** to his life—"my hell"—offers an emotional transition. Note the **descriptive details** used to describe his hearing aid: where it stayed, what it looked like, and what it sounded like. Another **simile** juxtaposes being deaf with having a disease, and the last sentence of the paragraph clearly establishes the real reason his parents separated him from his siblings. As **the last sentence**, it **lingers** with us, **emphasizing its importance**.*

When my parents got divorced, my mother left with four of her five children, leaving me, "the deaf one" all alone in the mansion to face the big and ferocious lion that was my father. Since father was always traveling for his business, he hired a nanny to take care of me who I named "Murder Eyes" because of her rigid discipline. I felt ostracized by my own family after the divorce . . . as if I was a cancerous growth which needed to be extricated from their skin. But nothing was more humiliating for me than . . . Wednesday night dinner.

*Notice how he distances himself from his mother and siblings. His mother didn't leave with his brothers and sisters, but with four of **her children**. He is no longer a member of the family, but "the deaf one." By not using words that show sibling relationships, we sense that there were no relationships among him and his brothers and sisters. He was left not at home, but at "the mansion" because that was not a home. . . and left alone with a ferocious lion—a **metaphor** for his father. Can you imagine what the nanny was like? Saying that she was strict just wouldn't do; he gives her a **new name**. The disease **simile**, carried through to this next paragraph, has now become the metaphor of a cancerous growth, not in need of being removed but in need of being extricated—**a strong and vivid verb**. Here comes the **clincher**, saved for last because it is the most important piece of evidence for feeling like a stranger that he can remember. I am sensing some **impending conflict** because of the phrase "nothing was more humiliating . . . than," but I'm not rushed into it. He's making me so curious.*

I always attended Wednesday night dinner at my grandparents' house with about 30 members of my family. I never wanted to be with them because I was tired of being a "ghost" at their dinner table. But one time I let myself be convinced by my grandparents that they would mouth for me what every member of my family said. They needed me to be there because I am their first grandson and my presence is important. I thought to myself how much I hated the idea of being with them at that dinner table . . . how much frustration I had to endure again and again. But when Wednesday night arrived, I went to my grandparents' house. Yeah, I let myself be deluded for one more time.

> *The evening takes on significance by the **background details** that are provided. The ghost **metaphor** is especially appropriate here where we can almost picture an empty chair among the 30. He is **slowing down the details** to let us know that this is an important scene, using the **repeating phrase** "how much" to emphasize how distasteful the whole idea of the visit was, **letting us in on his thinking**. He ends by **alluding** to what happened at one Wednesday night dinner, "I let myself be deluded" —preparing us for what is to come.*

I sat at the front of the big table with several members of my family. They started to have their usual conversation, and I was hoping one of my family members would see me as a living person. I was hoping to see that my grandparents would keep their promise.

They did keep their promise, but only for five minutes. After that, I was forgotten.

This incident was sufficient to kill my rare happiness. I felt myself lost in the middle of a flock of talking parrots . . . blah, blah, blah. It made me an invisible person since their eyes never so much as looked at mine. I didn't open my mouth to complain. I just tried to make some noise to get their attention by taping my fork on the table. Nobody noticed. I thought to myself, "Why don't I leave this damn nest of parrots."

I left and went home without saying good-bye . . . and, of course, they didn't care about my leaving.

> *Talking parrots are an appropriate **metaphor** because they talk without moving their mouths. Being unable to lip-read his family members, they might as well have been parrots. We can "listen" to his **interior monologue** as he decides to leave the small, circular home that has been established only for parrots. The nest **theme is threaded through** right up until the end. A **single sentence set off on its own**—the fact that his grandparents mouthed only for five minutes and his leaving without saying goodbye—signal its importance to the final outcome of the essay.*

I don't have any more illusions about being a part of my family because of the old Chinese saying, "You can't change the color of flies' eyes." I can't change my family's feelings toward me . . . to have them accept me. As members of the upper class, they blindly follow society's demand for perfection. This is common among the best families in _____. It is impossible to change their minds . . . impossible. I rarely use this word because I have always been a positive person, but when I was with my family, the limiting word just landed on my tongue.

On my way home, while driving my car, I looked at my face in the small mirror. I realized that I would always be a stranger in the nest.

And I noticed that I was happier being alone than being with them.

> *This conclusion is* **enlightening**, **circular** *and above all,* **emotional***. We see the author realizing that his experiences were, in addition to being a personal account, a sign of some deeper issue in the society he grew up in. Here he was* **generalizing** *beyond the boundaries of this essay to reach some greater significance. The* **personal revelation** *that he will most likely always be "a stranger in the nest" is made particularly forcefully as he confronts his own image in his car mirror. He has come full circle realizing that any chance of breaking into the nest will be impossible. And even though he might be happier with this understanding as seen in his final* **single set-off sentence***, his audience probably isn't, and this is where our emotional chords are tugged.*

Granted, this piece is a personal essay, but look how full and rich it is with elements to teach that might be attempted in more academic writing. I could just refer to a particular craft ("try a more general statement in your conclusion," "thread your thesis through at this point," "add some background information here," "how about making me see this image more clearly?" "circle back to your introduction," "slow this down") and students would easily recall the section of this piece that houses the suggested craft element, regardless of the fact that this is a narrative and they are writing beginning academic essays—elements of good writing cross rhetorical modes and, like academic writing, this piece has a major point. And because this piece is so emotional, it becomes exceptionally memorable. Students will forget elements of good writing if they cannot remember the contexts in which they are embedded. It is the context, by which I mean an entire piece and not just a representative introduction or conclusion, that allows them to see and remember how individual elements of craft relate to and work with other elements of craft to create a whole that has had life breathed into it. Understanding the *reasons* why the author chose to use particular elements can only be accomplished if the stage that they play out on is in full view and relationships among them are discernible. By studying how great writing is created, and with lots of individual support and practice, studious readers will start to internalize craft elements that they can try out in their own writing, making writing easier for them, and just plain better.

Justine's Argument about Immaturity

In the academic essay below, Justine, a more typical student, argues that the main characters in Joanne Greenberg's *In This Sign*—Abel and Janice, undereducated Deaf newlyweds—react immaturely to the prospect of parenthood in chapter 5 of the novel. Justine was shocked by the reaction of the two Deaf adults and wanted to explore it a while longer. The essay was revised three times. The signposts of good essay writing that I walk my students through are written below the excerpts.

Immaturity

Up until Chapter 5 in *In This Sign* by Joanne Greenberg, Abel and Janice, as a Deaf married couple, have to work to earn money to pay off their debts. Now, in Chapter 5, with the impending birth of their daughter, they don't know what to do about their economic situation. They react with panic and immaturity.

> *Justine **lets us know what piece of literature she is referring to and who wrote it**. She offers **just enough summarizing story or background information** to give a bit of history to the reader so that the reader understands the context of her argument. We await to read supporting information about Abel and Janice's immature reaction—**Justine's point** for writing this paper or **her thesis**.*

Janice is ignorant about her monthly bleeding. Her work friends, Barbara and Mary, who are deaf, suspect that Janice has probably a baby in her womb. They told her that she is pregnant and asked her if, in the morning, she feels sick and throws up. Janice says no, but adds that she feels dizzy and tired. Her friends ask her if she knows about the monthly bleeding. Janice doesn't. Her friends say, "Oh, you are dumb! The monthly." Janice wonders, "What did the monthly bleeding have to do with having a baby? Didn't babies come from a man's Thing?" Can you imagine? She is about 23 years old and doesn't know about the monthly bleeding and thinks that babies come from a man's Thing. Her friends say, "How can you forget when you bled last? Don't you know enough to remember that?"

> *We know that this paragraph will show that Janice is immature because as an adult, she still doesn't know about the connection between lack of menstruation and pregnancy--**Justine sets this topic up in the first sentence**. Then, through a combination of **brief summarizing** and **direct quotes**, she lets us in on how Janice is perceived by her friends. Justine uses Janice's **interior monologue** which allows us to hear Janice questioning the connection between menstruation and becoming pregnant, corroborating for us that Janice is indeed clueless about the connection. Justine's subsequent **interpretation** is in the form of **a question** (Can you imagine?) to us—she **speaks directly to us** about her incredulity considering Janice's age, further fortifying her theme of immaturity while simultaneously inviting us into her piece by making us feel part of her discussion.*

Janice isn't prepared to give birth to her daughter, Margaret Ryder. When she arrives home from work, suddenly, she starts labor. She wasn't prepared to bring towels and a pot of hot water. **Her landlady and midwife bring the pot of hot water and newspaper. They encourage Janice to spread her legs, but** "she [Janice] didn't know a thing about having a baby; she fought them and thrashed here and turning and fighting until they thought she would kill herself." **Janice didn't know how to behave during labor, and she should have listened to the landlady and midwife because they probably have more experience with labor than she does.**

> *We see that lack of preparedness for childbirth is the **topic of this paragraph** and note that the paragraph is written in the style of a **"sandwich"**—there is the **lead-in or summarizing story or background information** (a first "slice of bread," highlighted in the first boldfaced text) that leads to a **quote that perfectly proves the point of the paragraph with language so striking that the reader needs to read it** ("the meat," highlighted by underlining); the quote is followed by Judy's*

interpretation of its significance in light of the topic of the paragraph (the second "slice of bread," highlighted in the second boldfaced text). In this last part of the sandwich, Justine explains why the quote she chose is important to her point. (The idea of teaching students to frame quotes from a text as if they were making a sandwich comes from my colleague Marian Arkin.)

Abel shows his immaturity by being willing to give up Margaret instead of paying the landlady and the midwife for their services. Abel doesn't have money to pay them for helping Janice give birth. The landlady and the midwife demand that he pay them right away. Abel doesn't know what to do for money and "thought that maybe he could give her the baby for all the money it took to get it out of Janice." One problem is he had bonus money from his work and he was selfish to keep this money and not pay the landlady and the midwife. He kept the money for food for himself and didn't share it with Janice and Margaret.

> *Justine summarizes from the chapter to add support to the claim she is trying to establish—that Abel is just as immature as Janice. She fortifies her argument with **some background information** about Abel—that there would have been plenty of money to pay the landlady and midwife had he not used it on himself. Notice how **the vivid quote** shows how desperate Abel is to not be financially responsible for the baby—**it was a good choice of words from the text to document his immaturity**.*

I believe that Abel and Janice are ignorant about their parental responsibilities and sex. This isn't their fault because Deaf institution teachers didn't teach them independent living skills. Also they didn't teach them about sex because in past years, the institutions didn't believe it was their responsibility. Teachers didn't realize that most Deaf students were ignorant about sex. They should have taught them about sex before they faced real life. However, Janice should have known more because she probably witnessed the birth of her twelve siblings. Abel should have known about labor from watching the birth of baby animals on his farm. Abel and Janice should stop resisting parenthood and take up their responsibility for Margaret.

> *We see Justine here **raising another issue** about Janice and Abel's immaturity— that it perhaps was not their fault. This **sets the discussion into a larger context** and leaves the reader with something to think about. She refutes this possible reason, however, **drawing upon additional story information**. Finally, she ends her piece with **a strong call for action** which circles back to her beginning, giving the reader a sense of closure.*

My file of touchstone texts includes both the essays analyzed above as well as a whole host of other edited student essays. The bulk of my teaching about writing comes from this file and transpires in front of the class where, through the use of my document camera, projector, and whiteboard, I write notes on and alongside our touchstone texts, naming the craft moves of the student writer whose essay we are analyzing. Students copy this information into their packet of touchstone texts, creating a collection of annotated models they can refer to again and again. This is extraordinarily helpful for my students, and it doesn't stop here. It is in conferences with students on a one-to-one basis where the teaching of craft is put to most effective use. In conference, students see how what they learned about the craft of essay writing applies to their own essays, when they are in need of a particular craft or crafts to make their own creations better. *There is no better teaching time than the time used in conferencing.* Examples of what typically transpires during writing conferences are what we turn to next.

Reading into Writing: Becoming Responsive Readers of Writing

I have been thinking lately about the relationship between craft and content in the teaching of writing. When I write, I have an idea—what I want to say—but, most often, not a very detailed one. Rather typically, what comes out at first is clearly not great. So, I put on my reader's cap and say, "Okay let's see what I have here." I read each line slowly to see if a couple of them make sense together. If they do, I continue on. If not, I am back thinking again, *trying to figure out the details of what I am trying to say and how to go about saying them well*. I can go back and forth with a couple of lines for quite a long time, even come back to them days, weeks, and even months later and continue to read and make changes. It is a kind of dance that I do, moving back and forth until I've crafted the content in ways that are satisfactory to me. This, of course, seems all well and good except for one small sticking point: There are times when I am satisfied with what I have written and think, "I've got it now," when, really, I haven't. I know this from the reaction of my readers.

My students, who are considerably less invested in their writing than I, tend to complete their writing quickly with substantially fewer rereads. Their first drafts, similar to most writers', are typically in need of much revision. They soon realize that the hard part of writing has only just begun. This is the part that requires the careful reading of writing by a writer who wants his meaning conveyed clearly and well with no chance of confusing his readers. This is the reading of a writer who writes with his readers in mind to ensure that what he wanted to write, or should have wanted to write, gets written. Unfortunately, it is the rare developmental writer who writes with his readers in mind. But this is where good teaching comes in. Just as students need to be taught to read like a student of writing, they need to be taught how to read as an interested and responsive reader.

"Stranger in the Nest" and "Immaturity," the two student essays analyzed in this chapter, were final drafts of essays written four and three times, respectively. A substantial number of hours were given to the first two drafts of each essay by a responsive reader. I was the reader for these essays because they were written at the beginning of a semester, but typically, after much modeling during the first few weeks of class, students become their own responsive readers. This is the goal, for them to develop inner conversations between themselves and their own texts so that they can judge whether their meaning is conveyed as clearly and effectively as possible—but before this can happen, students need practice responding to each other's writing.

Becoming a responsive reader of Deaf student writing is one of the areas of writing instruction that needs the most attention. It is much easier and less time-consuming for a teacher to do a surface read of a piece and make corrections based on what she or he assumes is the student's intended meaning than to take the time and make the effort to make a piece better by "talking" with the writer in the margins of his paper in order to clarify his intent. This entails trying to discern a student's line of reasoning, which many times is not apparent if thoughts are not yet fleshed out and if there are basic misconceptions about content. Even though students answer guide questions and annotate their readings, and even though they take notes from discussion and think in chunks about these notes prior to writing, most first drafts are still not in good shape. The additional challenge of working with Deaf student writers is that lexical disfluencies make smooth readings of first drafts even more problematic. Such disfluencies generally stem from incorrect word choices, word-form errors, and inexperience with how words partner with one another (see chapter 3), but teachers need to make the effort to read through them in order to piece together a student's line of reasoning.

Becoming a first-draft responsive reader means letting the writer know if her first-attempt ideas for a particular writing assignment make sense, and if they are compelling. We deal, at this stage, strictly with ideas. As much as we are tempted to correct phrasing and grammar, we need to remember that the writer is still only partially coming to terms with the concepts she is asked to write about. If we take what she has written as set in stone, we cut off the possibility of having her either expand or tighten her thinking. This will result in writing that is not worth reading. When we place a premium on early correction of error, students' thinking is prematurely stopped.

Jack's First Draft about Stereotyping

When I take on the role of responsive reader, I comment on the essay in the margins and then conference with the student to go over my comments. The student takes brief notes as we talk so he will remember what to revise.

As an example of the process, here is the complete first draft of an essay by one of my students. For this assignment, Jack responded to a question about stereotyping in two short stories, "What My Mother Knows," by Carole Glickfeld, and "Cathedral," by Raymond Carver. In order to follow Jack's points, it will help to know a bit about each story. In "What My Mother Knows," Ruth, a young, hearing girl explains that despite being Deaf, her mother knows just about everything about her neighbors and the comings and goings on her city street. She is also an exceptional mother. Ruth's friend Frankie's mother, however, refers to Ruth's mother as the "little deaf-and-dumb lady." In "Cathedral," a man meets a blind person, a friend of his wife's named Robert, for the first time. The husband (whose name is never mentioned in the story) comes to know and get used to Robert after seeing firsthand how Robert lives and learns. He is particularly impressed with the way Robert learns what a cathedral looks like—by holding his hand over the husband's as the husband draws a cathedral and as Robert feels its shape.

This was Jack's fourth essay of the term, written for an audience of his peers as well as for members of the English Department who may review students' writing portfolios.

> **In "What My Mother Knows" by Carole Glickfeld and "Cathedral" by Raymond Carver, a Deaf person (Ruth's mother) and a blind person (Robert) are stereotyped by people who do not know them. Have you, like Ruth's mother or Robert, ever been stereotyped? Citing examples from each of the stories, show how your experience is either similar to or different from Ruth's mother's and Robert's experiences. Why do you think you have or have not been stereotyped?**

1. I had read two stories about "What my Mother Knows" by Carole Glickfeld and "Cathedral" by Raymond Carver. The stories show stereotypes first "What my Mother Knows" Ruth's mother is deaf and her friend Frankie mother insult Ruth's mother that she is deaf-dumb, [but Frankie told his mother to stop saying that word.] "Cathedral" the blind man old friend of husband's wife. The husband think so much negative that he is so creepy to him. He stereotype to the Blind man. [The blind man change the husband personal and his way attitude because he asked him to draw for him to know what look like a Cathedral.] I have some experience almost relative to these two stories.

I think you're telling us too much story information here

2. Ruth mother is deaf, full deaf and she always know where Ruth is. Ruth is hearing and she know her mother really smart. Ruth's mother has lots of common senses and she is really smart woman. [She always after her to make sure everything all right.] Ruth has friend, Frankie. Frankie's mother was the meanest to Ruth's mother because she called her deaf-dumb, which mean she can't hear, useless, or anything. Frankie Mother say "With your mother, the little deaf-and-dumb lady, right? I really admire the way you talk with our fingers" [Frankie mother does not knows anything about deaf way. She think Ruth's mother can't care or able to communication with Ruth. This is reason why she called deaf-and-dumb. I know some hearing people don't have the taste of experience with deaf people.] [Once they understands the deaf ways, I am sure they will love to learn how to sign language, and face express.]

If you can give me a specific example of how Ruth's mother is smart, your reader would believe your argument

Very nice interpretation so far!

But what would they learn about deaf people?

3. This is my first time read the story called Cathedral and I was shocked that the husband changes his personal by the blind man, Robert. Robert good friend with husband's wife. The husband never has experience with the blind people. First time met with the Robert that his wife introduces him. He felt creepy because his eyes looked pale and [probably he is disability.] The husband

We already know this

kept saying negative thing and he insult Robert. Also he said, "They'd married, live and worked together, slept together—had sex, sure—and then the blind man had to bury her. All this without his having ever see what the woman looked like." [This is really not nice what the husband said.] At the end

What was the stereotype here? What didn't the husband consider about Robert's relationship with his wife?

of the story, Robert asked the husband to gather all the paper and pencil to bring to him. He showed the husband and together they drew. The husband started to like the idea, because he teaches him and shows the image with draw. [I know some people always have to be like that, but it not true. Because they hate blind or deaf people that they are disability. They also called

Is this about hate? What did the husband learn?

stereotype, which is not true. It's important to get knows the experience with blind people. That how the husband change his personal.]

4. I have lots experience the past. Last year I worked as staff at School Settlement Association in Brooklyn. I worked there for 3 years every summer, and I work to take care for the summer that the parents won't able to take care of the kids. So we Staff, take care of them kids around age 4–13 years old. I work with them age 8–13 boys group. [I had fun, but the fact is sometimes kid pain in ass that they always label my back. For example, they

turn on their low voice make me think I am deaf and can't hear any words.] *Nice example!*

[And sometime they make fun of me with my hearing aids, but I wasn't hurt and I had to report their parents that they were in deep trouble. This is how I reaction to them. However, sometime I tell them to stop playing around and do as I tell, they just pretend to said "huh."] [I was mad with them and report to their parents to the kid's behavior.]

What were these kids only seeing about you?

We already know this

5. The stories I read, it almost the same thing with my experience, [Ruth's mother is not dumb and of course she had lots of her mind sometime will happen in the city.] The blind man probably knows the husband not usually with him. So he chill chat him to get use to him and later on, [he told the husband to bring pencil and paper to make him more interesting to the blind man.] I prove the kids that I am not stupid and they think I can't report.

See my comment for paragraph 2. This idea needs to be discussed there before you use it in your conclusion.

We already know this

[In fact, I did what I had to and the kids learned their lesson and from now on, they start to like me because they change their attitude. Believe me disability people can prove the normal people. I will give u another example how disability people prove them, the lady with short arms and short leg. She have a car and she can drive by two woods below her legs, and if she want to turn signal left or right, she use the head hit on the right or left button to turn on the signal light.] [I am disability and I can prove them.] The two stories showed they prove and not stereotype.

Wow!

What exactly can you, Ruth's mother, and Robert prove?

*Jack -
Lovely first draft with lots of insight into how the stories spoke to you. I heard your voice throughout... look forward to draft 2!
Sue*

In considering my comments on this first draft, it is important to note first that I keep my responses to a reasonable number, and that my responses are a combination of questions, comments, suggestions, and accolades. We neither want to overwhelm students with what they tend to consider negative criticism nor do we want them to think that nothing that they have written is very good. There are a few unclear ideas that I leave alone in the first reading but will come back to in the next draft; I prefer to tackle the more serious issues first. Also note that I bypass all phrasing and grammatical mistakes that just need correction but are perfectly understandable as they incorrectly stand. The goal of this reading is to see Jack's thinking and to ascertain if, and how, he has addressed the essay topic.

In the first paragraph, Jack does a fairly good job of establishing the stereotyping he will discuss, signaling that he has understood *the requirements of the essay question*. He attempts an answer, but it is a bit too general—"the stories show stereotype"—and his explanation quickly turns into the inclusion of too much story information. Jack needs to learn that for the purposes of class essays, he needs to analyze *only certain parts of the readings to address the essay question* rather than summarize the entire "what happened" of the stories.

In the second paragraph, as a reader I need *more proof* that Ruth's mother was smart. Just taking Jack's word for it isn't convincing enough. He will have to dig back into the story to find supporting information. Also, Jack's comment that if people understand Deaf ways, "they will love to learn how to sign language, and face express" shows that he is not *staying on track* and will have to revisit this point. While there is no doubt that hearing people would gain joy in learning how to sign and use facial expression, the more important reason for learning sign language is missing—that hearing people would come to know Deaf people for their competencies, much like Frankie's mother would come to know those of Ruth's mother. Jack and I discuss this key understanding in conference.

In the third paragraph, because he already explained that Robert is blind, Jack doesn't have to say that "probably he is a disability"—he needs to eliminate such *writing that is unnecessary or repetitive*. The *significance of the quote* "They'd married, live and worked together, slept together—had sex, sure—and then the blind man had to bury her. All this without his having ever see [sic] what the woman looked like" is missing and I am left wondering why he chose to include the quote. I ask Jack to answer my "so what?" and explain why he chose the quote as something important to share, and we discuss that the husband is forgetting that there are other senses aside from sight that can be used to know and love a person. Jack's final interpretation in the last four sentences of the same paragraph signals that there is a misconception that needs some clearing up. We discuss the role of hatred as opposed to ignorance and fear in each of the stories.

Jack starts to make nice connections between the victims of stereotyping in the stories and himself in the fourth paragraph. However, he really does not penetrate the possible reasons that he is a victim of stereotyping. I show him that his charges equate being Deaf with "easy to fool" and "easy to mock" until the end of the essay where he says, "I prove the kids that I am not stupid and they think I can't report. In fact, I did what I had to and the kids learned their lesson and from now on, they start to like me because they change their attitude." We discuss how it would make this very important point of his essay clearer if he presented these reasons at the time he relates his story of being stereotyped. Jack needs to make *tighter connections* between his kids' behavior and his interpretation of it.

Jack ends his first draft by referring once again to similarities between the stories and his own experience. He attempts to briefly summarize each of the stories' points in light of what he has written, but he adds new information about the first story that was not explained in the essay: "Ruth's mother is not dumb and of course she had lots of her mind sometime will happen in the city." He is making the point that Ruth's mother, while Deaf, knew exactly what was happening on her city street just by gazing out the window of her apartment, solely by using her eyes. Jack and I discuss that *concluding statements* (other than totally new but related ideas, as we'll see at the end of his essay) need to *refer to, in a general way, or expand upon already explained ideas*. I explain that his reference to "sometime will happen in the city" will leave his readers puzzled because they won't know what actually did happen from the window of Ruth's mother's apartment. I remind Jack that this information is exactly what was missing from his second paragraph, so he needs to think about *shifting* that point to the front of the piece. I point out that Jack's reference to the use of pencil and paper in the second story, while referring to what was already explained, is *too repetitive* because he already used that exact idea and wording in his third paragraph. I compliment Jack on *concluding his piece with a related but new reference* to a woman with a disability who can drive a car with short arms and legs and explain that this strengthens his argument because he has found proof from a different source, making his essay more *generalizable*. We still need to know, in a general way, what exactly it is that the disabled people mentioned in the piece can prove. The ending cries out for a *call for action*.

Notice that my responses to Jack alongside the margins of his paper are, for the most part, genuine questions about the content of his essay. They are conversational in tone yet directive in that they request very specific information that is all related to either the stories or Jack's personal experiences. They speak to the need for the essay to present ideas more deeply and coherently, keeping its controlling idea in mind throughout, with suggestions so that Jack can approach the second revision knowing exactly what to do. As a lifelong reader of essays, I have internalized the craft elements of essay writing, and they stay in the back of my mind as I do a first read for meaning (just as they stay in my mind as I write when my mind is primarily focused on saying something). As I read Jack's draft, I note where and why I start to have trouble understanding the point and flow of the essay—its content. Through dialogue between Jack and me, as these trouble spots are discussed more thoroughly, an essay starts taking shape, driven primarily by a search for more and better ways of expressing ideas that address Jack's essay topic. As we talk about the questions and comments alongside the margins, I contextualize the language of craft (the italicized terms and phrases) by using the content of the stories so that Jack can start to internalize this new vocabulary and use it in subsequent conversations with himself as he writes other essays. Content and craft, then, work together for us; while content drives craft, craft gives us a way to abstract the essentials of good essay writing so that we can use these pointers to manage Jack's content for this essay and hopefully for those down the road.

Jack's second draft was considerably better. However, although most of the ideas that we discussed in conference were incorporated into this second draft, the essay continued to call out for more information and stronger interpretations. We take a look at my response to this second draft next.

Chapter 3

Reading and Writing to Link Lexis and Grammar–I

How does the conversation with Jack along the margins of his first draft become incorporated into subsequent drafts to shape clearly written prose? Our conversation guides Jack in working the essay where its content requires more crafting. At this point, it also gives Jack the English phrasing that he needs to say what he wants to say. While students do lean on the phrases that emerge from their deeper thinking about readings during writing-into-reading activities, as discussed in chapter 1, they need more focused assistance with English phrasing because they are expressing original thought. I do not expect Jack to approach his next draft knowing the English phrasing he needs for two reasons. First, he is still refining the ideas he is trying to express in his essay, so we must continue our conversation about the points he wants to make. Second, he has not yet mastered English, either orally/aurally or visually, and he is still in the process of internalizing this language through his reading and writing. He is just learning how to read and write about the ideas related to stereotyping in the two short stories he was assigned. Although his thinking and conversing about the stories become clearer with each draft, he still must work on putting his thinking into print and on arranging his ideas logically and spelling them out clearly, so that readers can understand his good points.

Not all students are ready to work on their phrasing at this stage. My less-experienced writers typically need more time to think more deeply about the points they are making, so a response at the second and third draft might still resemble my response to Jack's first draft, with questions that come to mind as I read the revision that need to be addressed. The number of drafts students need to complete in order to arrive at a satisfactory essay is a tangible way for students to see how their writing is progressing. There is little need for a test of their writing abilities—if it takes them more drafts to complete a piece of writing, they know that more work is necessary. I discuss this kind of progress assessment further in chapter 5.

Much of my thinking about how to approach subsequent drafts of student writing comes from the work of Michael Lewis (1997, 2000). In his introduction to *Teaching Collocation: Further Developments in the Lexical Approach*, Lewis comments about the nature of native English speakers' mental lexicons:

We now recognize that much of our "vocabulary" consists of prefabricated chunks of different kinds. . . . If native speakers store large amounts of language in chunks, what strategies should language teachers adopt if they are to help learners build mental lexicons which are similarly phrasal? . . . . We now recognize that the principal difference between intermediate and advanced learners is not complex grammar, but the greatly expanded mental lexicon available to advanced learners. (8)

Lewis makes it clear that an advanced language user is not someone who knows more words or grammatical rules, but someone who knows more phrases, or chunks of language, and how to use them accurately. He and his colleagues refer to these phrases as *collocations* and define them as "common combinations of words" (127), or groups of words that are regularly found together. These word patterns are not arbitrary, but, quite the contrary, rather predictable. They are the "company that words keep" (Hill 2000, 48) and cover many different kinds of multiword items. Here are some examples Lewis (2000) offers:

a huge profit	(adjective + noun)
heavy rain	(adjective + noun)
submit a report	(verb + noun)
radio station	(noun + noun)
examine thoroughly	(verb + adverb)
completely soaked	(adverb + adjective)
revise the original plan	(verb + adjective + noun)
speak through an interpreter	(verb + preposition + noun)
the fog closed in	(noun + verb)
to put it another way	(discourse marker)
a few years ago	(multiword prepositional phrase)
aware of the problems	(adjective + preposition + noun)
an apple a day keeps the doctor away	(fixed expression)
see you later/tomorrow	(semifixed expression) (50–51, 130–134)

Collocations include fixed and semifixed expressions and groups of words whose meanings are more or less predictable from their component parts; for example, students are more likely to understand how a profit can be huge (a more predictable combination) than how rain can be heavy (a less predictable combination). Collocations can be combinations of strictly lexical items (nouns, verbs, adjectives, and adverbs) as in *submit a report* or they can combine lexical words with a grammatical word such as *of* in *aware of the problems*. Collocations are found in naturally written and spoken texts. In the last fifteen years, huge amounts of computer-generated corpora have been statistically analyzed for frequency of occurrence in these contexts. Corpus linguists, who analyze and describe collections of natural text, now have authentic descriptions of the way English is really spoken and written. And, as a result, "It is only recently, through the rise of corpus linguistics that the extent of the fixedness of much language has become more widely recognized" (Hill 2000, 50). Recurring word patterns need to be brought to students' attention, and the most effective way to do this is to incorporate them into meaningful reading and writing assignments. Students begin to see how the words they need to use demand the company of other words—how words partner, or *collocate*, with one another—and they learn to use these phrases to express their ideas clearly and correctly.

Collocation and Grammar in Jack's Second Draft

Because Jack's essay is about stereotyping, it makes sense for him to learn how the concept of stereotyping collocates within the context of his essay. In Jack's introductory paragraph, he must learn to write more specifically about the concept of stereotyping as it relates to the two stories.

1. I had read two stories about "What my Mother Knows" by Carole

2. Glickfeld and "Cathedral" by Raymond Carver. The stories [show
        of disabled people]
3. stereotypes ∧ first "What my Mother Knows" Ruth's mother is deaf
                                                    [by stereotyping her as
4. and Ruth's friend Frankie's mother insult Ruth's mother, ∧ ~~that she is~~ Deaf and
                                              [meets the husband of an old friend] [for the first time]
5. Dumb.] "Cathedral" the blind man ~~old friend of husband's wife~~. The husband
            [and stereotypes him as
6. think so much negative ~~that he is~~ so creepy] to him. I have [some experience
            related
7. ~~almost relative~~ to] these two stories.

In line 3 I add the phrase *of disabled people* to give specificity but call Jack's attention to the wider phrase, *show stereotypes of disabled people*. Since Jack is familiar with traditional parts of speech, we discuss that *stereotypes* here is a noun surrounded by a verb to the left and a prepositional phrase to the right. I am showing Jack "the syntactic constraints on the use of lexis . . . moving out from the word to uncover the particular syntactic pattern[s] associated with it" (Woolard 2000, 44). Jack will be more likely to remember the collocation because I have him focus on how the chunk is used: the noun *stereotype* explains *what* the verb shows and the prepositional phrase explains *who* the stereotypes are about. In line 4, I show him how the idea of stereotyping collocates after his verb "insult" by substituting the phrase *by stereotyping her as Deaf and Dumb* for the words "that she is." I explain that the phrase *by stereotyping her* uses *stereotyping* as a verb that describes *how* Frankie's mother insults Ruth's mother and the word *her*, to the right, refers back to Ruth's mother, or *who* was stereotyped. The last part of the phrase, "Deaf and Dumb," specifies *what* the stereotype is through the use of adjectives. In line 6, we see that Jack is in need of a similar pattern as that in line 4 where *stereotypes* here is a verb in the pattern *stereotypes him* as "creepy."

Moving beyond collocations for stereotyping, in line 5 I remind Jack that it is important for his readers to know that the blind man was only meeting his friend's husband for the first time, and I show him how to phrase that. In lines 6–7, I explain to Jack that his experiences are definitely related to the characters he read about and that instead of "almost relative" a better phrasal choice is *related to* or *similar to*. I expand the phrase to *some experience related to/similar to*.

Whether or not the phrases I have chosen to recommend to Jack are true collocations, in the sense that they appear in statistically significant ways in language corpora, matters less than the fact that with them I have helped Jack to categorize his text into chunks or patterns that he can remember and use again with some automaticity. When Jack revises his essay, he will reread and rewrite the correct language. When he prepares his essay for presentation, he will reread the correct language three more times. (That is my requirement.) When he sees these phrases in his reading of other texts, he will notice and understand them, and the more he notices them, the more likely it is that he will begin to write them independently.

8.   This is my first time read the story called Cathedral and I

          [in the story]   *attitude about*

9.   was shocked that the husband ∧ changes [his ~~personal by~~ the blind

10.   man, Robert.] The husband never has experience with the blind people.

11.   He felt creepy because his eyes looked pale. The husband kept saying

          [by stereotyping his marriage as pitiful]

12.   negative thing and he insult Robert. Also he said, "They'd married, live ∧

13.   and worked together, slept together—had sex, sure—and then the blind man

14.   had to bury her. All this without his having ever see what the woman

15.   looked like." This is really not nice what the husband said. ∧   *[because he didn't understand how people know things by feeling]*

In line 9, Jack must first situate the husband for his reader by adding the phrase *in the story* and then change the word "personal"—his attempt at the word *personality*—to refine his meaning. Notice that I do not just change the word "personal" to *attitude* but include *attitude* in its syntactic frame, which Jack already partially specifies: "his attitude about the blind man, Robert." In line 12, I give Jack the phrase that collocates again with the verb *insult, by stereotyping his marriage as pitiful*. This phrase will also serve as the "bread" for Jack's "quote sandwich" (see chapter 2), to introduce the quote. Jack ignored the question I posed on his first draft, which asked him to extend his thinking about the quote that he chose (line 15). Since this is a critical point that will hold the piece together, we go back to the question, discuss it, and add the necessary idea.

Like most basic writers, Jack forgets that although he knows everything that happens in the stories he writes about, his readers do not. The next section of Jack's text could have been much clearer had he provided the missing phrases that appear in the first three brackets at lines 17, 18, and 20.

16. At the end of the story, Robert asked the husband to gather all

17. the paper and pencil to bring to him. He showed the husband ^ *[how to draw while his hand was on top]*

18. and together they drew with pencil on paper to give the blind man [image *of a cathedral]*

19. The husband started to like the idea, because he teaches him and shows

[of a cathedral by drawing]
20. the image ~~with draw~~. The husband learned that blind man can't see,
    ^

21. he can learn to feel what it look like. The husband always [stereotyped ~~to~~ the

    being so   about
22. blind man] and now he stop [~~making~~ negative ~~of~~ him.] It's important to get

23. knows the experience with blind people. That how the husband

    attitude
24. change [his ~~personal.~~ *about Robert.]*

The phrases added to lines 17–20 explain *what* specifically was drawn and *how* it was drawn. By now, Jack understands that in line 21, *stereotyped* as a verb would not partner with *to*, and that just mentioning who was being stereotyped would be enough. In line 22, rather than "making negative of him," Jack needs to learn the collocation *being so negative about*. In line 24, Jack can tighten the essay by adding that he is referring to the husband's attitude toward Robert.

The lexical issues that cause problems in the next excerpt start with the use of the phrase "label my back" in lines 25–26. There, and in line 28 where Jack writes "report their parents," Jack does not mean what he writes.

                                                                    me behind
25. I had fun, but the fact is sometimes kid pain in ass that they always [label my
                                                                           ^

    [profoundly
26. back.] For example, they turn on their low voice make me think I am deaf]
                                                                    ^

27. and can't hear any words. And sometime they make fun of me with my

    them to
28. hearing aids, but I wasn't hurt and I had to [report their parents] that they
                                                 ^

29. were in deep trouble. This is how I reaction to them. However, sometime

    say
30. I tell them to stop playing around and [do as I ~~tell,~~] they just pretend to said

31. "huh." They ignore me because maybe they think I am ~~cheap~~ ~~staff~~ ~~but~~ [powerless and] not

strict.]

I show Jack how to expand the phrases to include the missing information—label and report *who?* In line 26, if Jack is Deaf, why doesn't he think he is Deaf? Jack's point is that while he considers himself hard of hearing, when his charges "turn on their low voice" he feels as if he is *profoundly Deaf*—a useful collocation for him to learn. In line 30, he learns that the expression is *do as I say* as opposed to *do as I tell*. I am confused by the phrase "cheap staff but not strict" in line 31. While I understand that in Jack's lexicon *cheap* means *powerless*, I see this characteristic, as well as *not strict*, as similar rather than different. We discuss the use of the word *and* to establish this equivalence.

In the last excerpt from Jack's essay, the verb *prove* appears five times.

32. Ruth's mother is not dumb. The blind man probably knows the husband

33. not used to him. So he chill chat him to get use to him. I [prove ^*to* the kids]

34. that I am not stupid and they think I can't report. In fact, I did what I had to

35. and the kids learned their lesson and from now on, they start to like me

36. because they change their attitude. Believe me disability people can prove *[their competence]*

37. ~~the~~ ~~norma~~l people.] I will give u another example how disability people *[to non-disabled*

38. [prove ^ ~~them~~, I was reading a newspaper about one lady with short arms *their competence]*

39. and short legs. Some people said she can't drive ^ too impossible] because *[because it would be*

40. short arms and legs. But she can drive she used two woods below her legs,

41. and if she want to turn signal left or right, she use the head hit on the right

42. or left button to turn on the signal light. Ruth's Deaf mother, the blind man

43. and I are disability and we [can prove ^ ~~them~~ that they are wrong. We [can prove *to non-disabled people]*

44. ^*to* them] that we are not stereotype.

Jack needs to learn the correct phrasing that *prove* requires in each instance. In line 33 and then twice in line 43, *prove* needs *to* after it as part of its lexical frame. In lines 36–37 and 38, *prove* is missing the noun object that explains *what* was proved and, in line 37, to *whom* it was proved. Another missing chunk of language is the *because* phrase in line 39.

Stepping back for a moment and reviewing our work at this particular stage, we can see that Jack requires different kinds of phrasal assistance. There are phrases that must be substituted one for the other, such as *being so negative about* for "making so negative of" and *do as I say* for "do as I tell." There are phrases that must be added to make Jack's meaning more specific, as in *an image of a cathedral* as opposed to just "image" and *the husband in the story* as opposed to just "the husband." The draft is missing information that will carry Jack's point or thesis through the essay; for example, he must add *because he did not understand how blind people know things by feeling.* While Jack is responsible for correcting these phrases, I really want him to focus on the phrases he attempted the most and were therefore central to his thinking. Here is what I rewrite for Jack at the bottom of this draft:

      V   *Ref*   *Adj*
stereotypes him as creepy

      V   *N*
stereotyped [the blind man]

    V   *V*   *Ref*   *Adj*
insult . . . by stereotyping her as deaf and dumb

    V   *V*   *N*   *Adj*
insult . . . by stereotyping [his marriage] as pitiful

   V   *N*   *N*
show stereotypes of [disabled people]

We then roll up our sleeves and further analyze the grammar of these phrases. I call Jack's attention to the "word grammar" of *stereotype*, showing him how *stereotype* as a verb can have a variety of forms (*s, ed, ing*) but most seem to partner with either a noun box ("the blind man," "his marriage") or referent ("him," "her"). (I discuss boxes and referents in chapter 4.) We notice that in three instances the word *as* is used right before an adjective. We approach the use of the verb *prove*, also used frequently and a key idea in Jack's essay, in a similar manner:

    V   *N*
proved to [the kids]

    V   *N*
prove to [non-disabled people]

    V   *Ref*
prove to them

   V   *N*
prove [their competence]

I show Jack that *prove* collocates with *to* in three out of the four instances of the verb, when he writes about *to whom* disabled people would prove they should not be stereotyped. When he uses *prove* to write about *what* would be proved, there is no need for *to*.

Here I am asking Jack to first read and understand the collocations that will make his essay both clearer and much more college-level "sounding." To help him remember these collocations, he needs to see how they are constructed and the moves the verbs and their partners are allowed to make in these very specific contexts. Seeing these moves might be the most productive way for students to become comfortable with the notions of parts of speech with which they all struggle. Grammatically analyzing these lexical chunks will also help Jack identify these exact phrases in other reading contexts. Seeing them again and again incidentally, but this time understanding how they are built, Jack will begin to use them productively in his own writing. Jack must become not only a studious rhetorical reader, as advocated in chapter 2, but, in order to write grammatically, a studious grammatical reader as well. It will be incumbent upon Jack to do more than just notice the phrases he reads; he will have to understand how they work in his reading.

Here is the complete text of Jack's third draft. All phrasal changes are italicized.

I had read two stories about "What my Mother Knows" by Carole Glickfeld and "Cathedral" by Raymond Carver. The stories *show stereotypes of disabled people*. First "What my Mother Knows" Ruth's mother is deaf and Ruth's friend Frankie's mother insult Ruth's mother *by stereotyping her as deaf and dumb*. "Cathedral" the blind man *meets the husband of an old friend for the first time*. The husband think so much negative and *stereotypes him as creepy*. I have *some experience similar to these two stories*.

Ruth mother is deaf, full deaf and she always know where Ruth is. Ruth is hearing and she knows her mother really smart and she love her a lot. Ruth's mother has lots of common sense. She always after her to make sure everything all right because she was afraid there might happen outside and it could be dangerous for Ruth to go alone. Ruth is young girl, but it might could rape if she in alley alone. Ruth's mother said, "you run hide sneak. Not like . . . bad girl spanked . . . careful you." This is the quote from Ruth mother showed example that she do really take care of her lots. Ruth has friend, Frankie. Frankie mother was the meanest to Ruth mother because she called her deaf and dumb, which mean she can't hear useless. Frankie mother said, "your mother, the little deaf-and-dumb lady, right? I really admire the way you talk with your fingers." Frankie mother does not knows anything about deaf way. She thinks Ruth's mother can't take care or able to communication with Ruth. This is reason why she called deaf-and-dumb. I know some hearing people don't have the taste of experience with deaf people. Once they understands about deaf people, I am sure they would see deaf people are not dumb.

This is my first time read the story called "Cathedral" and I was shocked that *the husband in the story changes his attitude about the blind man, Robert*. The husband never has experience with the blind people. He felt creepy because his eyes looked pale. The husband kept saying negative thing and he insult Robert *by stereotyping his marriage as pitiful*. He said, "They'd married, lived and worked together, slept together—had sex, sure—and then the blind had to bury her. All this without his having ever seen what the woman looked like." This is really not nice what the husband said *because he did not understand how blind people know things by feeling*. At the end of the story, Robert asked the husband to gather all the paper and pencil to bring to him. He showed the husband *how to draw while his hand was on top* and together they drew on paper with pencil to give the blind man an *image of a cathedral*. The husband started to like the idea, because he teaches him and shows *the image of a cathedral by drawing with the blind man*. The husband learned that blind man can't see, he can learn to feel what it look like. The husband always *stereotyped the blind man* and now he stop *being so negative about him*. Its important to get knows the experience with the blind people. That how the husband *changed his attitude about Robert*.

Last year, I worked as staff at _____ in Brooklyn. I worked there for 3 years every summer, and I work to take care kids and their parents don't have time to care their kids and sometime they go to work. So, we staff, take care of the kids around age 4–13 years old. I work with them age 8–13 boy group. I had fun, but the fact is sometime kids pain in ass that they always *label me behind my back*. For example, they turn on their low voice make me think I am *profoundly deaf* and can't hear any words. And sometime they make fun of me with my hearing aids, but I wasn't hurt and I had to *report them to their parents* that they were in deep trouble. This is how I reaction to them. However, sometime I tell them to stop playing around and *do as I say*, they just pretend to said "huh." They ignore me because maybe they think I am *powerless and not strict*.

Ruth's mother is not dumb. The blind man probably knows the husband not used to him. So he chill with him to have him get used to him. I *proved to the kids* that I am not stupid and they think I can't report. In fact, I did what I had to and the kids learned their lesson and from now on, they start to like me because they change their attitude. Believe me, disability people can *prove their competence to non-disabled people*. I will give you another example how disability people can *prove their competence*. I was reading a newspaper about the lady with short arms and short legs. Some people said she can't drive *because it would be too impossible* because short arms and legs, but she can drive she used two woods below her legs, and if she want to turn on the signal right or left, she can use her head to hit on the right or left button to turn on the signal light. Ruth's deaf mother, the blind man and I are disability and we can *prove to non-disabled people* that they are wrong. We can prove to them that we are not stereotype.

I have loved the spirit of this essay right from its first draft, but this third draft says something to me, and to Jack, that was difficult to discern at its initial writing. Although there are still language issues that need to be addressed, this has become a very good essay, primarily through the addition and substitution of needed phraseology and continued crafting that we accomplished through discussion, rereading, and rewriting.

In *Teaching Collocation*, Jimmie Hill (2000) argues that helping students with phrasing assists them in conquering the "largest learning load" of students of English: the English lexicon. He writes:

> In ELT [English Language Teaching] we have grown accustomed to the idea that language—the content of what we teach—is a rule-governed system and if we could just learn the rules, we would acquire the language. We now know that this idea is so at odds with the way both first, and subsequent, languages

are learned that there is no point in hanging on to it as any kind of model for learning. To be efficient, learning must reflect the nature of what it is we are learning. Language is proven to be a mixture of the totally novel, the absolutely fixed, the relatively fixed, and all held together with fairly simple structures which we call grammar. The largest learning load and the one which is never complete—even for native speakers—is mastering the lexicon. (68)

Lewis (2000) adds that this lexical view of language turns conventional language teaching upside down. Whereas traditionalists value grammar rules and accuracy—presenting a grammar point and then encouraging correct practice of it to achieve language fluency—those who advocate the lexical approach see fluency as the product of an adequately large lexicon, and grammar "rules" as being acquired "by a process of observing similarities and differences in the way different chunks work" (173). Ultimately, accuracy is achieved "by breaking down chunks into components and [reassembling them] in novel ways. . . . [Here] accuracy is based on fluency, not, as was believed for so long, the other way round" (173–174). Instead of building up language grammatical brick by grammatical brick, we study and analyze the design of the bricks in already built-up language in order to know how to create new constructions.

Jack's third draft shows the benefits gained from working with the lexicon. The piece is mostly fluent, and we can be sure that continued reading and grammatically analyzing collocations will further develop his fluency. "Many applied linguists and most teachers believe that, at least to some extent, focusing learners' attention *explicitly on some aspect of the linguistic form* of the input is helpful in accelerating the acquisition process" (Lewis 2000, 160). Having had his attention called to these patterns in his writing, especially the way I broke down the chunks of language for him in our discussion of the words *stereotype* and *prove*—not only showing him the functions the words in the chunk serve (who, what, how) but also the way the words partner with other words (with nouns or verbs or adjectives) surrounding them—Jack will now notice these chunks in different reading contexts. Once he recognizes and understands them in his reading, Jack is likely to use them productively in new writing.

Chapter 4

Reading and Writing to Link Lexis and Grammar–II

When my students arrive at their third draft, they have already worked through the hardest parts of their writing. Among other things, they have

1. responded appropriately to the essay question with good points that include enough story information for the reader to understand the essay, without weighing it down;

2. eliminated repetitive, nonessential information and selected on-target quotes that accurately back up their points;

3. explained the significance of the quotes, the reasons why they were selected;

4. tied together ideas that support the appropriate response to the essay question logically and tightly without going off track;

5. added their voice so that their personality makes their writing interesting to read;

6. ended by giving the reader a sense of satisfaction that the response to the essay question is made well and forcefully; and

7. corrected phrasing.

Sometime during the fourth or fifth week of their writing course, it hits my students that crafting a well-written essay requires all of these elements. They had no idea of the amount of thinking that was involved!

But now we arrive at the point where I focus on the essay's remaining language issues. These are errors I have been bypassing since Draft 1, so they are not ones that interfere with meaning in major ways. That said, the errors still must be corrected, for four very important reasons:

1. My better students demand that they be corrected. One student, in her end-of-term letter to me, said, "I want my grammar to be good looking."

2. Learning how to correct these errors independently (which is very doable) will help them to grammatically analyze lexical chunks and remember them more easily.

3. Students should feel confident about their writing skills now that written communication has become essential and ubiquitous in the digital age.

4. Final drafts are treasured. They are signed in front of all class members and occasionally posted on the Web and compiled in books of model essays for subsequent classes to enjoy and learn from. So, they have to be correct.

Let's first categorize most of the remaining errors in Jack's third draft.

Verb Errors

time:	Some people said she *can't* drive
	from [then] on, they *start* to like me
verb forms:	she *do* really take care of her
	Frankie mother does not *knows*
	he can learn to feel what it *look* like
	Once they *understands* about
missing verbs:	she knows her mother ____ really smart
infinitive:	just pretend *to said*

Sentence Pattern Errors

conjoining sentences:	The husband learned that blind man can't *see, he* can learn to feel.
conjoining predicates:	she can't *hear useless.*
linking sentences:	I had to report them to their parents that they were in deep trouble. This is how I [reacted] to them. *However*, sometime I tell them to stop playing around . . . .
front shifters:	In fact, I did what I had to and the kids learned their lesson *and from [then] on*, they start to like me because they change their attitude.
end shifters:	but she [could] drive she used two woods below her legs
inserting extra information:	Ruth mother is *deaf, full deaf* and she always know where Ruth is

Errors Related to Nouns

words that introduce nouns:	Ruth is young girl, but *Frankie mother* was the meanest . . . The husband never [had] experience with *the blind people.*

words that refer to nouns: He felt creepy because *his* eyes looked pale.

(The noun referred to by the word *his* is unclear in context.)

Before we can help Jack learn to correct these errors of grammar, we should agree on what we mean by *grammar*. Here are some good working definitions that have lingered with me over the years:

> Grammar is part of the management of text rather than the focus of meaning-creation. This description emphasizes again that language is first about meaning, and meaning is primarily conveyed by lexis—words, collocations and fixed expressions—in a text; grammar, although important, plays a subordinate role. (Lewis 2000, 47)
>
> Language is . . . held together with fairly simple structures which we call grammar. (Hill 2000, 68)
>
> So we use learning to make corrections, in fact, only to make small corrections. We can use learning only for very simple rules, the ones that are easy to teach, easy to remember. Also we hypothesize that the things that we can consciously monitor are not very important for communication. They are the fine tuning. . . . [Learning] is only a corrector. It does not make things go. (Krashen 2002, 215)
>
> Grammar [begins] with, and continues with, a group of opposites . . . some are very familiar: one and many (which grammar calls singular and plural), negative and affirmative, past and present, active and passive, dependent and independent, question and answer. The grammar opposites are in every language even though they manifest themselves differently. (Kunz 2004, 5)

Culling from each of the linguists above, it seems that the reason we are able to understand Jack's third draft without too much difficulty is because his remaining errors are simple in nature. By emphasizing the crafting of content and lexis, we have clarified the more problematic parts of Jack's essay—the parts that Krashen might say make the piece "go." Jack now must learn a way of making simple corrections. He's going to have to learn some rules and then consciously monitor them in his own writing. Once his content has been decided, he will need to focus on his grammar—the management of his text with respect to use of time, agreement, verb forms, the linking of ideas, and the way he introduces and refers to nouns. How is Jack supposed to do this? To answer this question, we turn to the work of linguists whose conceptions of grammar teaching are in sync with my own.

One of my three most kindred spirits in the field of linguistics is Rei R. Noguchi. In *Grammar and the Teaching of Writing: Limits and Possibilities* (1991), Noguchi maintains that in order for grammar to improve writing instruction, principles of grammar must be streamlined to their bare essentials and integrated with content. He argues that only those grammatical principles that have the most relevance, determined by their utility in treating the most frequent writing errors, should be selected. This "bare bones" approach to grammatical instruction will open up more class time for actual writing instruction—the kinds of approaches exemplified in chapters 1 and 2 of this book—and will limit the unnecessarily abstract grammatical terminology that most students struggle to understand and find overwhelming. As Noguchi states in the last sentence of his book, "In the end, less is more" (121).

Noguchi explains that one of the reasons grammar instruction has been ineffectual in improving writing is because it is does not reveal to students the interlinked nature of language.

> To teach one grammatical category, teachers must often teach many. For example, to eliminate sentence fragments from their writing, students must understand what constitutes a sentence . . . but to understand what constitutes a sentence, they must understand what constitutes a subject and predicate. In order to understand the latter two concepts, they need some notion of noun phrase and verb, and on it goes. In other words, to teach one relevant grammatical category, teachers must often teach many, none of which are easy to grasp and any one of which, if inadequately learned, lends confusion to the whole chain of categories. (116)

I hear Noguchi saying that learning that the component parts of our language system are interlinked is important, but we, as teachers, have not found a way of clearly showing these linkages to our students in ways that will help them correct their grammatical mistakes. Instead, we have made learning grammar so disparate that students can't see the grammatical forest for the grammatical trees. We have been focusing too much time and energy on individual rules that don't seem to coalesce into larger, more helpful patterns that students can use to read and write better. We make grammar teaching unnecessarily harder than it needs to be. While we can describe our language, we seem to lack effective ways to teach students to use it.

Michael Lewis, the architect of the lexical approach discussed in chapter 3 and my next kindred-spirit linguist, warns against separating the domains of lexis and syntax. He claims that we sort language not just in lexical ways but in grammatical ways as well, and that grammar is the product of noted patterns of individual words and phrases. The teacher's role is to "facilitate the accurate observation by learners of appropriate parts of the input they meet . . . to [help them] search constantly for many different small patterns" (Lewis 2000, 185). Lewis advocates a melding of the traditional language teaching notions of vocabulary and grammar. His view is that language is fundamentally lexical in nature; however, it is grammar that assists in breaking down lexis. Students need teachers to help them notice these grammatical patterns and, thereafter, help them to grammatically chunk the kinds of text they are being asked to create. In this way, students examine the content or lexical patterns they need in light of grammar, making that language easier to remember for later use.

How can we do this? How can we teach students grammar in a way that is simple, that shows them the interlinked nature of language without unnecessary verbiage, and that gives them the language they need in memorable grammatical chunks? Is there a system that allows teachers and students to grammatically analyze *any* sentence housed in *any* text in ways that will help them see how real language actually works in real contexts? For the answers to these questions we turn to my third and final kindred-spirit linguist, Linda Ann Kunz.

Discovering X-Word Grammar

Linda, a colleague at LaGuardia Community College, taught me the basics of X-Word Grammar eight years ago, and I have used it in my teaching since then because, simply put, it works. Although it is not a panacea for all grammatical issues found in Deaf student writing, for the most part, students learn the system easily and, with continued practice, gain control of their written English and become much more accurate in their use of it. The system has been used for more than twenty-five years with ESL students, and primarily by the disciples of Robert Allen, a linguist who taught at Teachers College, Columbia University, in the early 1970s. Allen called his system of grammar teaching *sector analysis*, meaning a system of analyzing the syntax of written English, but gradually his graduate students, including Linda Kunz (and Alice Deakins and Robert Viscount, authors of *The Tapestry Grammar*, 1994), adapted it to fit the needs of teachers. I am told that the name of this adapted system, X-Word Grammar, came from a professor at Amherst College who, when discussing the following twenty words with his students, said "Oh, for now, just put an X over them." Others have said that the X stands for the X in the word *auXiliary*, as in *auxiliary verb*.

Here are the twenty X-words:

The DO Family:	do does did
The HAVE Family:	have has had
The BE Family:	is am are was were
The MODAL Family:	will can shall may must would could should might

In the remainder of this chapter I will introduce you to the workings of X-Word Grammar and show you how it fulfills the criteria we now expect of any smart approach to grammar teaching. I will use Jack's errors as examples of the kinds of errors most teachers find in their students' work at this stage of the writing process, and show you how to use X-Word Grammar to learn from and correct these errors with your students. My overview is based on Linda's work —found in her unpublished manuscripts *X-Word Grammar for Public School Teachers* (2004), *X-Word Grammar for ESOL Teachers* (2005), and *X-Word Grammar Intermediate: A Grammar Discovery Book* (2000), written with Laurie Gluck—and my adaptation of it for Deaf students in *Working Text: X-Word Grammar and Writing Activities for Students* is designed for students much like Jack, who have control over the syntax of English and have been exposed to English through reading and writing for many years. At this intermediate stage, as exemplified in the categorization of Jack's errors above, students need firm grounding in the English verb system, sentence patterns, and what we will refer to as *boxes*, or noun-centered structures.

I do not believe in stand-alone grammar courses, in which grammar instruction drives the writing in exercises such as "Write an essay using the simple present tense." Instead, teaching X-Word Grammar with the accompanying book *Working Text: X-Word Grammar and Writing Activities for Students* should be a small part of a real writing course, a course that teaches composition using strategies similar to the ones described in chapters 1 and 2 of this book. By "a small part," I mean perhaps only twenty-five minutes per class. What students learn accumulates from lesson to lesson and is applied to their own real writing at the appropriate time—primarily at the third draft, after most ideas have been thought through two or three times and the focus is on editing. Grammar is taught discretely, but in an organized and logical way, and then immediately applied to the kinds of writing required in the course. Students thus see how to use the grammar they are learning to express the meaning they intend—this is the intersection of grammar and lexis.

Similarly, because I did not want this book to be perceived exclusively as a book that assists Deaf students in writing correctly (albeit an important and absolutely necessary goal), I did not want the student book and accompanying teacher's guide to be distributed by themselves without a context within which to fit. Therefore, the teacher's guide to *Working Text: X-Word Grammar and Writing Activities for Students, X-Word Grammar for Deaf Students* appears at the end of this book as a supplement, so that those interested in learning how to teach grammar will read this book in its entirety to see the place that grammar teaching has in an English or language arts class.

Much of what this system asks of students is that they studiously analyze (i.e., read slowly and carefully) written English with the eyes of an X-word grammarian to discover how it works. The *Teacher's Guide* gives you the details of the system I outline in this chapter and over seventy-five activities that show you how to apply it—the same activities found in *Working Text: X-Word Grammar and Writing Activities for Students*—with the correct answers to the exercises, along with additional teaching tips. After you learn X-Word Grammar yourself, take the students through *Working Text: X-Word Grammar and Writing Activities for Students.* Project the activities for everyone to see as you work through the lessons. You can write the answers on a whiteboard with your students, or call on them individually to write the answers in front of their classmates. If you have a document camera, you can also project your students' completed workbook pages and ask the class to discuss if answers are right or wrong. There might be times when you will want to project the answers that appear in the *Teacher's Guide* as well.

As students learn the different components of X-Word Grammar, it is critical that they learn to recognize these components *in the kinds of writing that they will be required to do.* Three model student essays that have been grammatically analyzed appear in Appendix I. With your help, students will learn to read and grammatically analyze these essays—which appear unanalyzed as Appendix H in their workbooks—based on what they have learned, a little at a time. (If you assign different types of writing, you should collect excellent student models and analyze them grammatically with your students once you have studied the system and feel comfortable with it.) As the lessons accumulate, students must demonstrate their accumulated knowledge, as shown in the progression of analyses from the first essay in Appendix I to the third. Most often I assign this essential component of instruction for homework (a little at a time) and then check it the next day. Students are soon amazed to see that, yes, they have the knowledge to grammatically analyze any text. And so will you.

Most of the content I present here would work best taught in a writing course meeting approximately six hours a week over a fifteen-week semester. Jack, our model student, would be expected to correct only those elements he had been taught and had opportunities to read and analyze in other students' essays.

Learning About the Power of X-Words

Making Yes/No Questions

To introduce X-words to students, I use an expression from Linda Kunz: they are "little but mighty." They are little because they are spelled with few letters but mighty because they are the heart of English grammar. The game Twenty Questions demonstrates some of their might. In activity 1 students use the twenty X-Words listed to create questions that can only be answered with a *yes* or a *no*. I hide an object, such as a pair of scissors, in a bag and students ask me questions such as "Is it small?" or "Would I eat it?" to figure out what is in the bag. They notice that X-words are the first words in all their questions, which is enough for now. As students read the excerpted stories in the lessons, they will start to pick up the function of these X-words in context.

Discovering X-Words and Subjects

After the game is over and the hidden object is revealed (or guessed correctly before all twenty questions are used up), the students change all the questions that were true into statements. "Is it small?" was answered *yes*; to make that question into a true statement, move the X-word behind the subject, *it*, to make "It is small." The students then change all the questions they answered *no* to into negative statements in the same manner, by moving the X-word behind the subject but this time adding either NOT or N'T to the X-word, as in "Would I eat it?" to "I would not eat it" or "I wouldn't eat it" (activity 4). Students see the close proximity between X-words and subjects of statements, and I tell them that if they can find the X-word in any sentence, they can find the subject of that sentence just by looking to the left of the X-word (for a statement). I ask them to write an X over the X-words and to box the subjects. Everything from the X-word to the beginning of the sentence can be considered the subject of the sentence.

$$\boxed{\text{It}}\overset{X}{\text{ is small.}}$$

$$\boxed{\text{I}}\overset{X}{\text{ wouldn't eat it.}}$$

I want students to talk about subjects of sentences because they will reference this grammatical element as they continue to study more grammar. In activities 5 and 6, students practice finding X-words, labeling them by writing an X above them, and boxing all subjects. In just these few short lessons, students see that these mighty little X-words not only create yes/no questions, but also help to locate subjects of sentences. X-words also change true statements into negative statements by attaching to the word NOT or the contraction N'T.

Showing Time

In another lesson, I explain that X-words are also mighty because they can be placed into two time categories: BEFORE and NOW (see Appendix A). The X-words *has* and *have* are in between the BEFORE and NOW categories because they can mean both BEFORE and NOW time. They refer to events that happened before but continue up to now. We label them as NOW time. In activities 7–9, we add either an N or a B to the already labeled X-words.

       X-N

You can keep it.

     X-B   *X-B*

I could tell right then if Charlie's day had been all right.

Students notice that certain modals show NOW time and others show BEFORE time (as seen in *can* and *could* above), depending on the story they are telling in a text.

Showing How Many

Not only do X-words show time, they also show "how many." I tell my students they have two faces and can be put into two categories: ONE and MANY (see Appendix B). Notice how all the X-words that show ONE (*is*, *was*, *has* and *does*) end in *s*. This helps students to remember that these X-words are singular and will always match with subjects that show ONE and are singular. The modals in Appendix B show both ONE and MANY, as do all the BEFORE time X-words except *was* and *were*. To two new texts in activities 14 and 15, students add either an N or a B to show what time the X-words mean, as well as either a 1 or a 2 to show ONE or MANY, respectively. Students continue to box subjects.

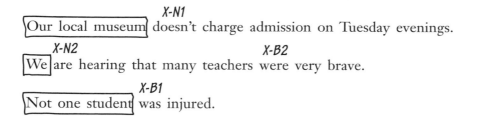

In just these few lessons, we see how X-words show basic grammar opposites: question and answer, affirmative and negative, now and before, and one and many. We notice the close relationship that X-words enjoy with subjects. Students also notice that subject boxes can be filled with one word or several words. Now Jack has to remember what he has been taught to correct the mistakes in his writing.

Applying X-Word Grammar to Jack's Essay–I

Jack has practiced correcting someone else's mistakes in editing exercises such as those in editing activities 17 through 19, but now he must show that he can self-edit. We nudge him along at the outset by indicating whether his mistake is due to a problem with TIME or HOW MANY or even with missing X-words, using X-Word Grammar correction symbols, listed in Appendix G. Later on, I might just draw a wavy line to signal that something in general is wrong and he should figure out what that something is from the totality of all the grammar he has been taught—but for now we go one or two grammar steps at a time with much support. We'll remove the training wheels down the road a bit.

I approach Jack's third draft by writing correction symbols for the errors above the errors themselves. Jack made TIME errors in X-words mostly because he was unaware of the BEFORE form for the modal *can't–couldn't*.

Time
Some people said she can't drive

Time
and they [thought] I can't report

Jack needs this form because this part of his essay relates a story he read in a newspaper and an incident that happened the year before, respectively. If he chooses to talk about experiences from his past, he must use BEFORE time in his X-words.

Jack had few problems with ONE and MANY in the X-words. I'd like to think that by the time Jack was at this fourth essay he had corrected these kinds of errors many times and was thus starting to understand how to avoid them. In the following sentence, Jack must substitute the singular form of *do–does* in order for it to match with his singular subject. He can find the correct X-word from the list in Appendix B.

S   X
She do really take care of her

Jack needs to think hard about which X-word to insert at the point indicated below — this thinking will get easier for him over time as his sense of grammar expands with the new grammatical concepts he encounters.

X?
She knows her mother really smart.
         ^

In this example, Jack must remember that he is describing Ruth's mother in general terms and her traits are displayed again and again, which calls for NOW time. Since the subject is ONE, *is* would be the appropriate X-word. We also point out that the word *smart* is an adjective and that BE-family X-words are most often used to describe what someone is like.

X-Words and Main Verbs

X-Word and Main Verb Match-Ups

We move on from examining the close relationship between X-words and subjects to look behind (to the right of) the X-word instead of in front of it. At about this time, students are noticing that sentences can have just one X-word or an X-word and a main verb. I love the way Linda describes the special relationship that X-words and main verbs enjoy: "Main verbs in English are a little complacent. They carry so much *content* (that is, meaning) in a sentence that they don't do much grammar work. . . . And as long as they have an X-word to do the work of the sentence for them, they don't even have to move out of their comfortable place in the predicate of the sentence" (103). We have seen how hard X-words work in the examples above, but they perform one more very important job: They dictate, 100 percent without exception, the form of the verb that follows them. English has only three main verb forms: the base form, in which verbs have no endings such as *s* or *ing* or *ed*; the *ing* form in which verbs end in *ing*; and the *D, T, N* form in which verbs end in either *d*, *t*, or *n*—and students learn that these forms are always, always found paired with the X-words found directly across from them as seen below. For example, the DO family X-words and the MODALS are always, always seen in the company of base form verbs. Similarly, the BE family X-words are always, always matched with *ing* form verbs. No exceptions. Students memorize the chart below (it also appears below activity 22 and in a slightly different form in Appendix C, and they do so willingly to try to trap me—because I tell them that if they ever find a two-word verb phrase (active, not passive) that violates the rules of this chart, I will exempt them from homework for the rest of the semester!

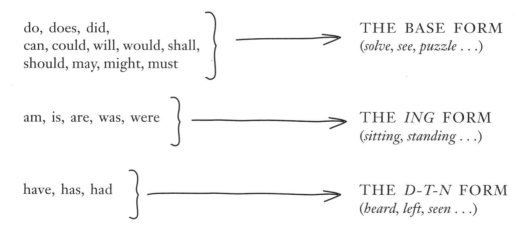

do, does, did,
can, could, will, would, shall,
should, may, might, must
⟶ THE BASE FORM
(*solve, see, puzzle . . .*)

am, is, are, was, were
⟶ THE *ING* FORM
(*sitting, standing . . .*)

have, has, had
⟶ THE *D-T-N* FORM
(*heard, left, seen . . .*)

Applying X-Word Grammar to Jack's Essay–II

Here is the correction symbol I use to show Jack that an X-word and a main verb are not matching in his third draft:

X   V
Frankie mother does not knows anything

Jack refers to his chart to see that because he uses the X-word *does*, he must change *knows* to its base form, *know*.

With more grammar concepts under his belt, Jack now understands why, in the following sentence taken from a different student's essay, the choice of an X-word is wrong, symbolized by the letters *WX*.

WX

It is clear that Comstock does impatient with Abel.

Since the X-word *does* appears only with a base form verb, it does not belong in this sentence because *impatient* is not a verb; it is an adjective and requires a BE-family X-word. Jack must think back to his prior lessons about TIME and HOW MANY in X-words to find the correct X-word to substitute. The time is BEFORE, and the HOW MANY in the subject (Comstock) is ONE. Therefore, the correct X-word is *was*.

Hidden X-Words

By now my students notice that not all sentences have X-words—or so they think. They are leery when I tell them that sentences in which you don't actually see an X-word still have an X-word hiding in them—but only one of three. Which three, and why can't they see them?

Only the X-words *does*, *do*, and *did*—the DO family—are given hiding privileges. They tuck TIME and HOW MANY inside main verbs, *does* and *do* for NOW time and for ONE and MANY, respectively. They tell us about general facts or repeated events that do not have any definite beginning or ending points. *Did* tells us about BEFORE time and ONE or MANY. I tell my students that they don't have to take my word for which X-word is hiding where, because I can prove it to them, as in these sample sentences:

Bob loves Mary.   Bob and Fred love Mary.   Bob loved Mary.

does is hiding in love*s*   *do* is hiding in love   *did* is hiding in love*d*

I have them look at the various endings of the verb *love*. It is no coincidence that each of the endings corresponds to the last letter of the X-word hiding inside. So, in the first example, the *s* at the end of "loves" signifies that *does* is hiding inside; no ending or O ending on "love" in the second example signifies that *do* is hiding inside; and the *d* ending on "loved" shows that *did* is hiding inside. But there is more proof.

I tell my students to suppose that their group of friends includes Bob, Mary, and Fred, and that some of their friends notice that Bob and Fred are interested in Mary. They want to know:

$$\overset{X}{Does} \text{ Bob } \overset{V}{love} \text{ Mary?}$$ or $$\overset{X}{Do} \text{ Bob and Fred } \overset{V}{love} \text{ Mary?}$$

You don't think so, so you respond:

No, Bob $\overset{X}{doesn't}$ $\overset{V}{love}$ Mary.   or   No, Bob and Fred $\overset{X}{don't}$ $\overset{V}{love}$ Mary.

But a friend disagrees—strongly. She says:

Yes, Bob $\overset{X}{does}$ $\overset{V}{love}$ Mary!   or   Yes, Bob and Fred $\overset{X}{do}$ $\overset{V}{love}$ Mary!

As it turns out, both Bob and Fred love Mary, but both can't handle the competition and both want out. They're done with Mary, and your friends want more answers:

$\overset{X}{Did}$ Bob $\overset{V}{love}$ Mary?   or $\overset{X}{Did}$ Bob and Fred $\overset{X}{love}$ Mary?

You respond:

Yes, sadly, Bob $\overset{X}{did}$ $\overset{V}{love}$ Mary.   or   Yes, sadly, Bob and Fred $\overset{X}{did}$ $\overset{X}{love}$ Mary.

The proof that *does*, *do*, and *did* hide inside main verbs is that they come out from hiding when they are needed to form questions, make statements negative, or state something emphatically. Students note that when these X-words show their faces, when they are pulled out of their main verb, they do so in a consistent manner. All of them match 100 percent with their main verb. No exceptions.

Applying X-Word Grammar to Jack's Essay–III

If there are no X-words visible in a sentence, Jack must make sure that his main verbs accurately hide them to show TIME and HOW MANY. This is the symbol I use to indicate that his verbs are missing the hidden X-word *does*, and need an *s* added to them:

$$\overset{V/XS}{}$$
He can learn to feel what it look like

$$\overset{V/XS}{}$$
and she always know where Ruth is.

Below, V/XO means that the main verb is missing the hidden X-word *do* or O (no) ending, so the *s* should be removed from "understands."

> *V/XO*
>
> once they understands about Deaf people.

Finally, in the next sentence, Jack needs to keep his main verbs in the past tense; he starts out doing so but loses track as he works his way to the end of his thought.

> In fact, I did what I had to and the kids learned their lesson and from [then] on,
>
> *V/XD*   *V/XD*
>
> they start to like me because they change their attitude.

While I work with Jack in conference, I call his attention to "unnecessary" X-words. First, two X-words will never be found back to back. So, in this sentence

>   X   X̸
>
> Ruth is young girl, [and someone] might could rape [her] if she in alley alone

one of the X-words has to be removed. We symbolize that with the letter X with a line drawn diagonally through it. Second, when we talk about BEFORE time, we can mean either some definite time in the past (hidden *did*) or some unspecified past time before another past time, by using the visible X-word *had* with the *D-T-N* verb form. All Jack's readers need to know at the outset of his essay is that he finished reading the stories, making the X-word *had* unnecessary here:

>   X̸
>
> I h̶a̶d̶ read two stories [about] "What My Mother Knows."

With the X-word left in, readers might ask, "What did you do before you read two stories?" I explain that this X-word is usually part of a sentence that has a hidden *did* in it so the two times can be contrasted, one being earlier than the other, as in *I had read the stories before I watched TV.* His unnecessary use is also symbolized with an X and a line through it.

Before we leave our study of X-words, I ask my students to make note of verbs that have the word *to* in front of them. In the little story about Bob and Mary (activity 30), students point out: *to eat*, *to treat*, and *to pay*. They see that these verbs are in the base form—and here they have just learned another helpful grammar tip: when a verb follows the word *to*, it is called an *infinitive*, and this verb must always be in the base form, with no endings such as *s* or *ing* or *d* or *tion* on the verb allowed. I symbolize that error by writing INF inside a circle that houses the infinitive error, as I do below with Jack's errors with infinitives.

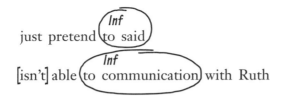

just pretend *Inf* (to said)

[isn't] able *Inf* (to communication) with Ruth

At this point, my students and I have accumulated some serious understanding about subjects and verbs. The eleven symbols they have learned thus far (see Appendix G for a complete list of all grammar correction symbols) will lead them to correct the mistakes they make with X-words, main verbs, and infinitives—and they make a lot of mistakes with these elements because the verb system in English is complicated, as it is in most languages, and not an easy system to master. How subjects match with X-words and how X-words match with main verbs will become more transparent. The more students studiously analyze these structures in their reading and correct them in their own writing, the more they will use them automatically when they write.

Sentence Patterns

Trunks (T)

X-Word Grammar posits seven sentence patterns that one can find in any text and use to edit sentence structure mistakes in student writing. In this system, a basic, simple sentence is called a *trunk* because as "the core of every written English statement or question, . . . it is as stable and crucial to the life of a sentence as a trunk is to a tree" (Kunz 2004, 22). A trunk does not include "leaves and branches," which can be considered extra information about when or why things happen. A trunk is composed of two positions: a subject position and a predicate position. Whatever is in the subject position tells us what the trunk is all about; whatever is in the predicate position tells us more about the subject. Trunks have only one X-word and/or main verb.

Crucial to understanding trunks is knowing how to identify whether a group of words can be considered a bona fide trunk or not. This is how we will identify a trunk: If a group of words can turn into a yes/no question, we can consider that group of words a trunk. Recall the game of Twenty Questions (activity 1), in which students asked yes/no questions that began with X-words to figure out what was hidden in a bag. We then made statements from those yes/no questions by swinging the X-word behind the subject (activity 3). Now we do the reverse. We test to see if a group of words can be made into yes/no questions by moving the X-word to the front and adding a question mark to the end. If doing this makes a good yes/no question, our group of words is a trunk. Remember, if you do not see an X-word, you must pull either *does*, *do*, or *did* out of hiding from inside the main verb shell. Be careful to include correct information about TIME and HOW MANY in the X-word you pull out. (Notice here how all our grammar knowledge thus far is being used again and again.) Here are some examples from activity 40.

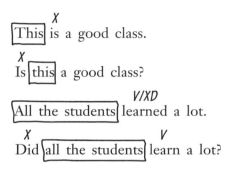

X
|This| is a good class.

X
Is |this| a good class?

V/XD
|All the students| learned a lot.

X   *V*
Did |all the students| learn a lot?

Since we have made two yes/no questions that look right and make good sense, we can safely assume that *This is a hard class* and *All the students learned a lot* are trunks. Let's try doing this with the following group of words:

I always homework

We can't begin to make this into a yes/no question because we cannot find a main verb. The group of words is not a trunk. Nor is this:

Can go later

because there is nothing to swing the X-word *can* around in front of. There is no subject. We will use this test for trunks later when we discuss sentence fragments but, for now, students learn that a trunk must have a subject and an X-word and/or main verb.

Trunk Plus Trunk (T,+T)

Students see that they can combine two trunks if both trunks have related ideas. If they are adding to a second trunk information that is new but related to the information in their first trunk, they can use the joiner *and*. If they are adding a contrasting idea or an unexpected outcome in the second trunk, they can add the joiner *but*. If they want to show that the second trunk is a result of the first, the joiner *so* would be appropriate. Or, if they want to add an additional choice to one already established in their first trunk, or if they want to express a possible result if whatever is supposed to happen in the first trunk doesn't happen, the joiner *or* should be selected. Here are examples of each T,+T pattern. Note how I place the label T above the verbs or X-words.

          T   *, +*   *T*
|Peter and Sue| decided to buy a new car, *and* |they| wanted to buy one quickly.

     T   *, +*   *T*
|They| wanted a regular car, *but* |their children| wanted an SUV.

$$T \qquad\qquad ,\; + \qquad\qquad T$$

[The cost of gasoline] was a concern, *so* [Peter and Sue] bought a Camry—a car with good mileage.

$$T \qquad\qquad\qquad ,\; + \quad T$$

[Their children] will get used to the Camry, *or* [they] can walk.

Notice how this pattern requires the following:

1. two trunks, each with a subject
2. a comma right in front of the joiner word
3. no capital letter on the second subject unless it is a specific name
4. each trunk is able to change into a yes/no question

I also explain that a semicolon (;) is fine to use instead of the joiner *and*. It will give their conjoined ideas the feel of two separate sentences but, at the same time, will tie them together even more closely than the joiner *and*.

$$T \qquad\qquad\qquad + \qquad T$$

[Peter and Sue] decided to buy a new car; [they] wanted to buy one quickly.

One Trunk with Two or More Predicates (T=)

For the next sentence pattern, T=, our students can be a little lazy. If they talk about the same subject in their second trunk as they do in their first trunk, they can drop their second subject—they do not have to repeat it. So, in the first example sentence above,

$$T \qquad\qquad\qquad ,\; + \qquad T$$

[Peter and Sue] decided to buy a new car, and [they] wanted to buy one quickly.

we see that the second subject *they* means the same as *Peter* and *Sue*. The pattern T= allows us to drop *they*, and, in this case, the comma as well, so the new sentence becomes

$$T \qquad\qquad\qquad\qquad =$$

Peter and Sue decided to buy a new car and wanted to buy one quickly.

Note that both main verbs apply to the one subject *Peter and Sue*.

There are no restrictions on the number of X-words or verbs a T= pattern may have. However, in a sentence that is composed of a series of X-words or verbs, commas must precede all X-words or main verbs:

$$\boxed{\text{She}}\overset{T}{\text{ missed her train, }}\overset{=}{\text{was late for work, and }}\overset{=}{\text{didn't}}\text{ show up for her first meeting.}$$

$$\boxed{\text{I}}\overset{T}{\text{ got home, }}\overset{=}{\text{walked the dog, }}\overset{=}{\text{made dinner, and }}\overset{=}{\text{collapsed}}\text{ on the couch.}$$

In this pattern, the T is placed over the first verb (or X-word), and then the equal sign (=) is placed over the remaining X-words or verbs.

Applying X-Word Grammar to Jack's Essay–IV

As Jack tried to combine two trunks, he typically left out either the joiner word or the necessary commas.

$$\text{The husband learned that }\boxed{\text{the}}\text{ blind man }\overset{T}{\text{can't}}\text{ see}\overset{,+}{,}\text{ he }\overset{T}{\text{can}}\text{ learn to feel.}$$

$$\text{Ruth }\overset{T}{\text{is}}\text{ hearing and she }\overset{,+}{}\overset{T}{\text{knows}}\text{ her mother }\boxed{\text{is}}\text{ really smart }\overset{,+}{}\text{ and she }\overset{T}{\text{loves}}\text{ her a lot.}$$

The correction symbols alert Jack to the fact that something is wrong at the point where his ideas are joining, and that he has to figure out how to fix the problem. In the first example above, he needs to add the joiner *but*; in the second, he could add two commas. However, adding commas to the second sentence makes it a bit repetitious—it has the look and feel of a runaway sentence. I offered an alternate sentence pattern. This signals to Jack that if he wants to, he can try a different combination of patterns. In this case, I suggest:

$$\text{Ruth }\overset{T}{\text{is}}\text{ hearing. She }\overset{T}{\text{knows}}\text{ her mother }\boxed{\text{is}}\text{ really smart and }\overset{=}{\text{loves}}\text{ her a lot.}$$

Being familiar with sentence patterns— what trunks are and how they combine—can help students tame potential run-on sentences.

Sometimes, what appears to be a totally incomprehensible sentence becomes understandable after a T= pattern is suggested:

she can't hear useless

becomes

$$\text{she }\overset{T}{\text{can't}}\text{ hear and }\overset{=}{\text{is}}\text{ useless.}$$

When I teach this pattern, it's as if a whole new world opens up before my students' eyes. Looking back from a second verb in a sentence to find its subject at the beginning of the sentence appears to never have dawned on them. (One wonders how this must have affected their reading all these years.)

Linkers and Trunks (LT)

Appendix D lists common *linkers*, which link the meaning of the sentence they begin to the meaning of the sentence just before it. Linkers can add information about time (*the next day*) or detail (*in fact*). They can signal a different idea (*on the other hand*) or an additional idea (*in addition*). They can explain things (*for example*) or offer an unexpected result (*however*) or a logical one (*therefore*). Here are some examples:

    T   L   T

It rained almost every day last summer. In fact, it was the rainiest summer on

record.

        T   L

There was a major loss of electricity in western Queens. Therefore, there were

no classes at LaGuardia Community College.

Applying X-Word Grammar to Jack's Essay–V

To see an instance where Jack's use of a linker does not quite work, we need to provide some context from his essay.

. . . they turn on their low voice [to] make me think I am profoundly deaf and

can't hear any words. And sometime[s] they make fun of me with hearing aids,

but I wasn't hurt and I had to report them to their parents that they were in

                         T   L   T

deep trouble. This is how I [reacted] to them. However, sometime[s] I [told] them

to stop playing around and do as I say, [but] they just pretend[ed] to [say] "huh."

They ignore[d] me because maybe they [thought] I was powerless and not strict.

The sentence Jack introduces with a linker is another instance of the abuse he had to endure as the counselor for a group of immature campers. He has already given two examples of their bad behavior, and he is onto his third. The linker *in addition* gets his meaning across more clearly because it signals that another display of bad behavior will be explained. *However* leads Jack's readers to believe that there might be a turnaround from the previous behaviors. This is the kind of mistake that my students make most often with linkers: They have a feel for the need for some connector, but they choose the wrong one, simply because they have not read enough to understand what the linker words actually mean. Many of these linkers are not used widely in casual conversation. They appear in more complicated text that developmental college students are only starting to read.

Front and End Shifters (FT and TE)

At this point our trunks are beginning to spread branches and leaves and take hold more firmly with a growing system of roots. Using this tree metaphor, I tell my students that if we want to convey more information in our sentences, we need to locate where to put this information, and the two most important places are outside the trunk, either in front of it (FT) or at the end of it (TE). X-Word Grammar calls these positions *shifter positions* for the simple reason that whatever you put in one of the positions must be able to shift to the other position and still look right. Here are some examples from Appendix E:

    F   *T*
While I was eating, I called my mother.

   T   *E*
I called my mother *while I was eating*.

   F   *T*
Because he was sick, he left school.

   T   *E*
He left school *because he was sick*.

Typically, shifters tell us when, why, where, how, and under what conditions. They add information about time, reason, place, method, and condition, and they show the unexpected. ("Although he was sick, he came to school.") Since their domain is the whole trunk, shifters are free to move back and forth without disturbing the inner meaning of the trunk; they offer information that applies to the whole idea of the trunk. Notice the difference between an FT and a TE: an FT has a comma after it (that is, unless it is just one word, and then you have a choice of using a comma or not); a TE has no commas. The emphasis differs as well. In the first sentence above, the emphasis is on the eating; in the second, it's on calling my mother. As Linda Kunz explains in *X-Word Grammar for ESOL Teachers*, "none of [the shifters] needs a comma in E position because TE is the 'natural' arrangement of things to an English speaker's ears: we state something and then give the when, where why, etc. When you put an adverbial element in FRONT SHIFTER position, it adds weight" (26).

Once again we return to our lessons on making yes/no questions. This time, with more grammatical knowledge, my students understand how to tell the difference between a fragment and a trunk using their skill of changing statements to questions. Activity 60 is a little passage about learning ASL. I ask my students to turn each of the groups of words into yes/no questions. If the resulting question looks right and makes sense, the group of words is a trunk. If the group of words looks weird or makes no sense when put into a yes/no question, the group of words is a fragment. Here is an example:

It isn't easy to learn American Sign Language.   <u>TRUNK</u>

YES/NO QUESTION: Isn't it easy to learn American Sign Language?

Because it's a foreign language.   <u>FRAGMENT</u>

YES/NO QUESTION: *Is because* it a foreign language?

Deaf students will not hear the difference between the sound of a trunk and the sound of a fragment, but they can easily see that the words *is* and *because* in the second sentence above do not look right together. I'm always pleased when students notice words placed together that don't look like they should, or when they tell me that they have never seen certain words together. Hearing students can say, "I've never heard that before"; Deaf students really can't. They can and do say, "I've never seen that before." Now I can explain why: Fragments will never turn into yes/no questions because they are not trunks. They might be shifters.

Applying X-Word Grammar to Jack's Essay–VI

Jack, like most of my students, has far fewer problems with fragments than he does with controlling his runaway sentences. I call Jack's attention to the fact that his first sentence below would have much more impact if it ended after the word *lesson*. I suggest the following patterns, written over his sentence first and then over the rewritten version.

   L   *T*   *, +*   *T*   *F*
In fact, I did what I had to and the kids learned their lesson and from

          T   *E*
[then] on, they star[ed] to like me because they chang[ed] their attitude.

   L   *T*   *, +*   *T*   *F*
In fact, I did what I had to, and the kids learned their lesson. From [then]

      T   *E*
on, they star[ed] to like me because they chang[ed] their attitude.
                                               LT,+T   FTE

I suggest this pattern because I believe Jack is explaining how reporting the campers' bad behavior to their parents changed things. It was right after the report that the change was noted, so emphasizing the time of the behavior change, by starting a new sentence with it ("from then on") would be important.

    The ideas in the sentence below, which tend to go on and on, are clearer once Jack gets some guidance in thinking through what part needs to be emphasized.

$$\overset{T}{\text{Some people said she}} \overset{}{\text{[couldn't]}} \text{ drive because it would be too } \overset{E}{\text{impossible}} \text{ because}$$

$$\overset{L}{\text{[she had]}} \text{ short arms and legs, but she} \overset{T}{\text{[could]}} \overset{E}{\text{drive she used}} \text{ two } \overset{}{\text{[pieces of wood]}}$$

$$\text{below her legs, and if she } \overset{F}{\text{want[ed]}} \text{ to turn on the signal right or left, she} \overset{T}{\text{[could]}}$$

use her head to hit on the right or left button to turn on the signal light.

$$\overset{T}{\text{Some people said she couldn't}} \text{ drive because it would be too } \overset{E}{\text{impossible}}$$

$$\overset{E}{\text{because}} \text{ [she had] short arms and legs. } \textit{However,} \text{ she} \overset{T}{\text{[could]}} \text{ drive } \overset{E}{\textit{because}} \text{ she used}$$

$$\text{two } \overset{}{\text{[pieces of wood]}} \text{ below her legs, and if she } \overset{F}{\text{want[ed]}} \text{ to turn on the signal}$$

$$\text{right or left, she} \overset{T}{\text{[could]}} \text{ use her head to hit on the right or left button to turn}$$

on the signal light.

       TEE LTE FT

Because Jack should emphasize the contrasting idea that yes, in fact, this woman could drive, a strong contrastive linker (*however*) would better get his intention across. This requires ending the sentence before introducing the new idea, so that the linker can get the attention it deserves.

Inserts (TI)

We now have arrived at the last of the basic seven sentence patterns, and the one that rarely appears in speech.

> Inserts are the darlings of journalists and academic writers because they really condense information and place it exactly where the writer wants it. Inserts add extra information . . . [but] they don't shift because they need to stay close to whatever it is they're adding extra information about. Inserts do us the favor of bringing along their own markers: double commas (i.e., commas on each side of the insert), a comma and a period, double dashes or a dash and a period [or] a pair of parentheses. (Kunz 2004, 26–27)

As seen below, inserts are found mostly before the predicate or at the end of a trunk.

$$\overset{T}{\text{George Washington,}} \overset{I}{\text{the first president of the United States,}} \text{ led American troops}$$

during the Revolutionary War.

$\overset{T}{\text{He}}$ solved many problems, especially $\overset{I}{\text{those}}$ that arose from forming a new

government.

Applying X-Word Grammar to Jack's Essay-VII

The idea of extra information staying close to whatever it is adding extra information about is also new to most of my students. They start off noticing the simple inserts and make approximations of them in their writing. Jack does this in the first sentence below but fails to add the necessary punctuation, in this case, a second comma indicated by an arrow, which sets the insert off from the rest of the sentence. In the second sentence, I explain to Jack that the stories he read were not about their titles. The titles really are the stories, and, therefore, the word "stories" and their titles need to sit tight right next to each other through the use of an insert and its proper punctuation, a comma, also indicated by an arrow.

Ruth[s] mother is deaf, full deaf and she always know[s] where Ruth is.

I read two stories "What my Mother Knows" by Carole Glickfield

and "Cathedral" by Raymond Carver.

Did you notice that most of Jack's errors with missing sentence joiners and punctuation, as well as his use of unwieldy and, at times, awkward sentences were due primarily to a lack of knowledge of sentence patterns? Knowing how trunks combine with other trunks, the flexibility that exists with attaching shifters, and the reasons for inserts offer Jack ways of correcting his errors simply and logically. All of this knowledge comes to life and becomes so much more understandable for Jack when we use it to crystallize and refine his ideas. We now turn to our last grammar unit: boxes and referents.

Boxes and Referents

Boxes: Nouns and the Words That Introduce Them

X-Word Grammar uses the term boxes to refer to the places where nouns "live." Nouns live in boxes with adjectives, possessive pronouns (*my, your, his*), possessive nouns (*Ann's*), and determiners like *a* or *the* or *a few* or *many*. Nouns are the most important words in the box. We spend some time finding nouns in boxes and starring them to show their importance.

She walked the [long road*] alone on [the second hottest day*] of [the summer*] with [her sister's dog.*]

My students begin to notice specific spelling patterns that signal nouns such as *ance, ees, ion, ity* and *ment*.

She had [the authority*] to give him [a promotion*] for [his excellent attendance.*]

We then look inside the boxes for clues as to ONE or MANY. The students understand that if there is an *s* on the noun, there can't be an *a* or *an* at the front of the box. If we find boxes where *a, an* or *s* appear, or if there are other determiners such as *another* or *each*, we say that the noun is *countable* (*a book, an idea, dolls, another lamp, each desk*) because we can show ONE or MANY of them—essentially, we can count them.

Finally, the word *the* also introduces nouns, but it does not say anything about ONE or MANY. Primarily, *the* shows readers special nouns or nouns readers already know something about from the context of the utterance.

Applying X-Word Grammar to Jack's Essay–VIII

Most often, Jack needs to be reminded to look at the noun in his box to make sure that if it is countable, this is shown. I call Jack's attention to this through the use of an arrow.

Ruth is [young girl*] but . . . .

The arrow helps Jack think through his problem. The sentence is about Ruth—one person—and "is" and "girl" are singular. Jack then understands that the arrow shows that some indication before "young" (because it is part of the box), must also show ONE since *girl* is a countable noun. He would know it's *a*. In the following sentence, the arrow reminds Jack that in the story he is writing about, the husband doesn't stop at one negative comment about Robert, the blind visitor, but has a whole list of stereotypical misconceptions about him. Jack therefore needs to indicate the idea of MANY on the word "thing."

The husband kept saying [negative thing.] ∧

Nouns that introduce other nouns (*possessive* nouns) inside boxes must show that the second noun belongs to the first, through the apostrophe signal.

[Frankie mother] was the meanest.
∧

Jack's errors with the introducer *the* are very common in Deaf-student writing. In the first example below, Jack uses "the" to introduce "blind people," making it specific rather than general. But he is not talking about a group of blind people that he already mentioned or a specific group of blind people; he means any blind person, and therefore *the* is not needed. Jack's next mistake is similar, except in the second example he is talking about one person and must use an introducer word that shows ONE, which in this example would be *a*.

The husband never [had] experience with [the blind people.]
∧

I was reading a newspaper article about [the lady] with short arms and short legs.
∧

When students study boxes, they quickly realize that they must "look left" inside their boxes as well as outside of them, down the sentence a bit, and out into the text, to be explicit about the meaning they are making about ONE or MANY or *a* or *the*. Although these decisions are grammatical, they are always based on the story thus far and what has happened and is happening. In almost all the examples above, the corrected noun or introducer depend on an idea expressed before it in order for its use to be accurate. We see this principle of looking left even more clearly in our lessons on referents.

Referents

It would make writing very boring if each time we wanted to talk about a box, we had to repeat the exact words in the box over and over again. Activity 81 presents a passage about a man who had six daughters and not enough money to realize his dream of sending them all to medical school. Here are the first few lines written with repeated boxes:

> Donald Thornton is a 52-year-old black man, a widower and a janitor. Donald Thornton has six daughters. And Donald Thornton had a dream for his six daughters. Donald Thornton wished that someday, his six daughters would all become doctors. (Inturrisi 1980, 114)

Have you heard the name "Donald Thornton" enough? How about "his six daughters"? Would the passage read better if it referred to Donald Thornton once and *he* thereafter and to his six daughters once and either *them* or *they* thereafter? I would think so. Words like *he*, *they*, and *them* are called *referents* because they replace or refer to boxes. Because referents can substitute for boxes, they must match their boxes in terms of ONE or MANY, and they must be spelled differently depending on whether they appear before the verb of the sentence they are in or after the verb.

Applying X-Word Grammar to Jack's Essay–IX

Jack's first draft used referents in ways that made his readers wonder who or what the referent was referring to. In the example below, we see a problem with the referent *it*. In explaining how the husband in the story starts to understand how Robert, the blind man, can learn what a cathedral looks like, Jack states:

and together they drew on paper with pencil to give the blind man an image of

a cathedral. The husband started to like the idea, because he teaches him and

shows the image of a cathedral by drawing with the blind man. The husband

learned that blind man can't see, [but] he can learn to feel what it looks like.

Here Jack learns that his referent *it* needs to be replaced by the box it references: "the image." He will not have difficulty "connecting the box" because, as in the last model essay of Appendix I, he has had lots of practice using arrows to connect referents to the boxes to which they refer. Extensive practice in grammatically analyzing other texts prior to correcting their own mistakes is crucially important for our students.

X-Word Grammar: Smart Grammar Teaching

Let's recall the questions I posed early in this chapter: "How can we teach students grammar in a way that is simple, that shows them the interlinked nature of language without unnecessary verbiage, and that gives them the language they need in memorable grammatical chunks? Is there a system that allows teachers and students to grammatically analyze *any* sentence housed in *any* text in ways that will help them see how real language actually works in real contexts?"

X-Word Grammar is just that system. X-Word Grammar clearly shows the interlinked nature of written English. We saw this throughout our discussion of the system, starting with the connectedness among yes/no questions, statements, and negative statements. We saw this in how subjects match with X-words, how X-words show TIME and HOW MANY, and how they match, 100 percent without exception, with verbs. We saw how three X-words (*does*, *do*, and *did*) hide inside verbs where they continue to show TIME and HOW

MANY and can be pulled out to form yes/no questions that offer proof as to whether or not a certain group of words can be called a trunk—which is our basic sentence. We saw that we can add trunks by looking left to discern the specific logical connector our thoughts require, and add more information to the beginning, ending, and middle of our trunks depending on the emphases we wish to create. We saw how punctuation is intimately tied to combining and adding to trunks—and we know that students cannot be expected to correct punctuation errors unless they have solid grounding in logical connectors and linkers and know how to shift and insert new ideas into their writing. We saw that looking left in boxes where our nouns reside helps us ensure they are coexisting well with their introducer words, and that looking outside the box reminds us of the nearby words to our left that might influence the countable nature of these nouns. Finally, we saw that our "look left" policy helps us decide when referents do not clearly specify the box they should refer to, and that referents can relate to boxes that appear sentences ahead. No word or phrase is an island, so to speak, in X-Word Grammar.

As students complete their study of X-Word Grammar, they are genuinely pleased to see that they can grammatically analyze any piece of writing. We have used a common set of terms that are not overwhelming, in an organized way that shows the systematic nature of the language, using just about twenty correction symbols (see Appendix G). All along, on models of the kinds of writing that will be expected of them, students have been labeling subjects, X-words, XV matches, hidden X-words, sentence patterns, and important words in boxes, and drawing arrows from referents to the boxes they refer to. At the same time, they have been correcting their errors, with the correction symbols gently nudging them along. They have been working text to see the relationships that lie within it. This combination of reading, grammatically analyzing the kind of text they are expected to write, and correcting their own errors places the emphasis on application, application, application, instead of on rules, rules, and more rules in the hope that all the rules will coalesce into better writing. But it is the conscientious reading of grammatically chunked meaning, again and again, and then again, that will serve our students best in their quest to write accurately. X-Word Grammar simplifies the basic grammatical tenets enough so that students can discover, and, most importantly, remember grammar's manifestation in chunks of real language.

Take a moment to imagine how X-Word Grammar might look if it were used across the curriculum. I envision content-area teachers talking about key concepts (chunks of information) in their discipline, and, as they are talking, writing key phrases on the board, quickly boxing those phrases that are noun boxes, starring the noun in the box, pointing out the adjectives within. They are boxing subjects and labeling X-words and verbs for agreement. Imagine, for homework, asking students to write a brief summary of what they learned during a particular lecture or devising some more creative writing assignment to cement new learning. With grammar overlaid on content language, with opportunities to understand the grammatical underpinnings of the phrases they need to know for courses in their majors, Deaf students would surely have an easier time writing in their respective disciplines.

Chapter 5

How Will Students Know When They Are Becoming Better Writers?

In chapters 1 through 4 I describe how students need to understand their reading, see their deeper thinking about their reading, study the craft of required writing, partake in conversation about their writing, and study their writing to see how lexical and grammatical changes can make it better. These activities answer the question "How do students learn to write?" and show us that learning to write well is hard, hard work. But hard work can be good for students. We want them to work at a piece of reading because we want them to know it well. We want them to be so set on getting their points across about this reading that they, like real writers, are willing to draft and redraft until they have said something worth reading and said it clearly and effectively. And because we want them to see that their hard work is paying off, we want them to understand how they are progressing as real writers and tell us that, yes, they feel this progress themselves as they look at their drafts over the course of an essay and over the course of a term or terms. If students see that they are making progress, it will motivate them to continue to learn, and this last component of the writing process is perhaps its most important.

Evaluation Rubrics

There are thousands of hearing students in basic writing courses at my college and all over the country. Providing a rubric to the faculty members who teach these courses streamlines the evaluation process and saves them precious time. A rubric gives everyone a common set of terms with which to talk about writing, and it forces everyone to think about a piece of writing in fairly simple ways with simple standards and simple rankings: superior, passing, or not yet passing. (See figure 1 at end of chapter for a sample rubric.) However, because writing is not simple, I believe there are more effective techniques for evaluating student writing than using rubrics.

I want to do more for my students than just tell them that their "organization" and "support" are or aren't passing, and, if they are not, leave the students on their own to figure out how to revise. For many of my students, their first, second, and most likely third draft would be scored "not yet passing" if they were evaluated after each turn; if I had to fail a student three times on an essay that I loved from the beginning before checking off the passing box, I would not have become a teacher of writing. Not only is this bad pedagogy, in my opinion, it is also unkind, and, what is most important, it does not help students learn.

Maja Wilson (2006), author of *Rethinking Rubrics in Writing Assessment*, has similar feelings about the use of rubrics as I do. In chapter 2 of her book, she delves into the history of rubric creation, explaining how a group of researchers/writers were commissioned to create a reliable rubric to evaluate college admissions essays and concludes:

> The authors' search for the clean categories of scientific thinking effectively stripped writing assessment of the complexity that breathes life into good writing. However, their reduction and categorization allowed for the consistent scoring necessary for ranking via standardization; if we all look at the same isolated aspects of a particular paper in the same way, we will produce the same score. (23)

Wilson's point is that while the general categories used in most rubrics might facilitate reliable scoring, the question remains if the scoring is valid. Does the measure actually tell us what writing abilities of students should be valued or does it merely sort and rank students in an efficient way?

Bob Broad (2003) in *What We Really Value: Beyond Rubrics in Teaching and Assessing Writing* states that the field of writing assessment does not have an adequate answer to this question: What do we value in students' writing? Quoting others to support his point, he writes:

> What we have instead are rubrics and scoring guides that "over-emphasize formal, format, or superficial-trait characteristics" of composition (Wiggens 132) and that present "generalized, synthetic representations of [rhetorical] performances . . . too generic for describing, analyzing, and explaining individual performances" (Delandshere and Petrosky 21) . . . . In the field of writing assessment, increasing demands for truthfulness, usefulness, and meaningfulness are now at odds with the requirements of efficiency and standardization. The age of the rubric has passed. (4)

Broad claims that since the 1990s, much more emphasis has been placed on using assessment as a way to support learning and teaching, and that assessment "must judge students according to the same skills and values by which they have been taught" (11). To actualize his thinking, Broad created a Dynamic Criteria Map (DCM), drawing on writing instructors' accounts of how they teach and assess writing in their classrooms. The DCM, which includes a host of textual and contextual criteria for evaluating writing specified by writing instructors, coordinates teaching and evaluation to better serve the needs of students and moves "beyond rubrics, traditionally the main obstacle to telling the full and true story of how writing is valued" (122).

Similarly, Brian Huot (2002) in *(Re)Articulating Writing Assessment for Teaching and Learning* asks us to move beyond the use of "stock phrases like unity, details, development, or organization [on] a chart or scoring guideline." He suggests ways that assessment can become an integral part of pedagogy in which "students can be helped to develop specific assessment criteria for each piece they write." In this way, "students can learn the power of assessment . . . within the context of their own work" (78). By making assessment more specific, and moving away from generic assessment categories, students will be more likely to understand what it is they have to do to become better writers. But how shall we make assessment more specific?

Reframing Assessment

A more appropriate way to assess a student's development as a writer is to take a serious look at how each piece has progressed over time. The context for the course is the student essay that is based on a reading or readings, and students argue for or against ideas that evolve from the reading or share an insight that they support with information from the readings. Because students' writing improves with practice in context-bound ways (Carroll 2002), we expect that students asked to demonstrate their knowledge of specific crafts of writing they have had opportunities to practice will see themselves developing as writers. They should know how to apply the crafting technique they have learned and be accountable for it in each of their specific writing tasks. This may seem to be the same idea as applying a rubric to student writing. But I am not talking about assessment categories; this is about the different ways students see and understand the implications of the kinds of questions and comments that are raised by responsive readers, such as in the dynamic discussion of ideas in the margins of Jack's first draft reproduced in chapter 2. Through this kind of response assessment becomes "an integral part of the writing process" (Wilson 2006, 63). Wilson continues:

> Our assessments and instruction should acknowledge the complexity of the writing process. In this acknowledgment, we make our assessment process transparent, talking and thinking through what goes on in our minds as we follow our students' words—a process we used to mask by focusing on how our students met the external standards of the rubric. Without the forced agreement of the rubric, we keep our minds open to new insights about writing, and encourage our students to do the same.(63)

To assist Jack in seeing where he is and where he needs to be as a writer, I have him sit down next to me and spread out all four drafts of his essay. (Yes, my students must save all their drafts.) As Jack and I discuss his first draft, my genuine questions and comments alongside the margins signal to Jack that many of his ideas and his ways of expressing them are to the point and interesting to read, but some need to be rethought, refined, recast, or removed. He sees firsthand how his writing affects me as a responsive reader, much the same way that most writers do when they reread their own work. As Wilson says, "All writers assess writing as we go, hesitating slightly as we make judgments about what word works best or what ideas should come next. Every writing choice we make springs from some assessment that we've already made" (89). My job is to help Jack understand what he hasn't yet done and what he needs to do to make his paper say something, to inspire the new thinking that should appear in his next draft. Essentially, then, if I am interpreting Wilson correctly, we can frame assessment as in-depth, organismic response. No preconceived categories are brought to the piece, only the desire to understand it and work it to make it better. Each new piece of writing that Jack does will have different responses based on what it needs from its inside (its purpose) to its outside (its readers). This will change with every draft and with every essay topic.

One Essay Over Time

Jack and I have the four drafts of his essay spread out in front of us. This is what he and I would discuss.

Draft 1 into Draft 2 Discussion

I show Jack how much better his second draft is because he lightened the amount of story information in his introduction and eliminated repeating information at different points in the essay. He sees that he didn't respond to my asking him to reflect on what the husband didn't consider about Robert's relationship with his wife and what the husband learned after drawing the shape of a cathedral with him—these are crucial points that address the essay topic and create a more tightly constructed draft. He learns that he needs to work on explaining the significance of his quotes in light of the essay topic.

Draft 2 into Draft 3 Discussion

I remind Jack of the several word partners that helped him express his good thinking about stereotyping; how *stereotype* can be used as a verb or a noun; and how *prove to* partners with REFERENTS or BOXES.

Draft 3 into Draft 4 Discussion

I show Jack that he needs to be mindful of the connector *but* that explains a different idea; that trunks require added shifters that explain why through the use of *because*; and how nouns that introduce other nouns inside of BOXES must have apostrophes.

This discussion does not go into great detail. Because Jack and I have already carefully reviewed each of my comments and questions one draft at a time during our conferences, this talk focuses on only the biggest issues in his writing and serves to remind him of what he learned as he actually looks at his trail of work. I find this process to be much more fruitful than handing him back a filled-out evaluation form that he may not read or even understand. Nevertheless, department policy asks me to complete and attach the "Evaluation of Essays in ENA099/ENG099" form (see figure 1) to Jack's last draft. I complete the form, but I do not score the Words and Sentences category; instead, I explain to Jack that this category should be viewed as a place where work is progressing, where improvement will be seen over time as he continues to notice and study lexical and grammatical choices in his reading, as he is taught more grammar, and as he applies his new learning to other writing contexts.

I will not fail Jack because I really liked his essay; he worked hard at revising it and had a good essay by the end of the fourth draft. He would get a grade of C+, which means to my students that they have produced good work in what I consider a reasonable amount of time. Ending up with a good essay in four drafts is an important indicator of writing progress. I know this because my less-skilled writers require five, six, and sometimes seven drafts before we sit down to have our end-of-essay discussion. (I further discuss the significance of numbers of drafts later in this chapter.) First drafts from these students show little effort or do not address the essay question. Many times students choose inappropriate quotes to back up their points or have difficulty with the craft of sandwiching (see chapter 2), because their lead-in to the quote is off the point of the quote, or their interpretation of the quote's significance is irrelevant to the point of the essay. This is where I know immediately that the final essay will not be finished in four drafts. Students producing first drafts such as these learn they will have to roll up their sleeves and get to the hard work of thinking through their points with me in conference, before we even approach collocational or grammatical issues. This is why, in assessing progress during the course, my students and I look long and hard at the conversation in the margins of the first two drafts to see how thinking is developing.

My assessment is my written commentary along the margins and my subsequent discussions with Jack, where he can "listen" to assessment language that is authentic and actually see his improvement from draft to draft with his own eyes. I hold strongly to my (and Maja Wilson's) belief that the best assessment happens during response. But can students assess themselves without any input from me? I have experimented over the years with asking my students to use the department's evaluation rubric to evaluate their own work and found that generic evaluation forms beget generic understandings about improvement as writers, as seen in these examples:

Jon: "I learned to make a good organization."
Jane: "My thesis is clear and effectively placed." (copied from the evaluation form)
        "I have improved my bodies."
        "My organization is little mess up."
Mary: "This essay seems to have good support."
Helen: "I improvement a lot on Introduction, 1st body, 2nd body and conclusion."
Alan: "My grammar wasn't well."

Students should be able to write about their improvement in more specific ways. I found they could do so most effectively when they reviewed their work across the term.

Drafts Across the Term

First Drafts Across the Term

My students see their progress as writers by looking at similarly numbered drafts across the term, given essay topics of similar levels of interest and difficulty.

Jane

In the first draft of her second essay of the term, on Chitra Divakaruni's short story "Mrs. Dutta Writes a Letter," Jane argues that Mrs. Dutta's decision to return home to Calcutta, after having moved to San Francisco to live with her son Sagar and daughter-in-law Shyamoli, is the right one. In her first body paragraph Jane writes:

> Mrs. Dutta doesn't like America's ways because some of men do laundry for women, but in India, there men never do that to do wash clothes. Mrs. Dutta want do wash clothes for Sagar instead he have to do because Mrs. Dutta don't want see him to wash clothes like India's ways. "Mother! Shyamoli said, "This is why Indian men are so useless around the house. Here in America we don't believe in men's work and women's work." She feels that is very horror for her.

Jane and I talk about the need for some general statement at the outset of this paragraph that would explain the point that she will make, that there are some cultural customs in America that Mrs. Dutta cannot get used to. There is some tangled language in the next sentence, but its essence is that Mrs. Dutta wants to wash Sagar's clothes. The quote selected is not from Mrs. Dutta, but from her daughter-in-law, Shyamoli, which throws the reader off because there is no lead-in that would prepare us for the switch in characters. We do not hear Jane's thoughts on why Shyamoli's ideas are so horrifying to Mrs. Dutta, and I ask her to extend her thinking about why she chose this quote.

In the first draft of Jane's fifth essay of the term, she compares the male protagonists in two short stories and argues that although both are obsessed with appearance and control, one is much more controlling than the other. She starts with Abboud in "Another Evening at the Club" by Alifa Riatt.

> I think Abboud is very unappealing. I just pick one example from "Another Evening at the Club." " 'Tell people you're from the well-known Barakat family and that your father is a judge,' and he went up to her and gently patted her cheeks in a fatherly reassuring gesture that he was often to repeat during their times together." Abboud told to Samia, it is his wife. I feel like that he want to tell everyone that his wife, she is without class. He doesn't want embarrassing that his wife's father works on a mere clerk at the Court of Appeal because Abboud is work in Inspector of Irrigation and earn big salary from job. He wants his wife to be beautiful wife and best life. When they are together, Abboud pay her to get new clothes look so classic. Also, he pays her to get jewelry like diamond bracelet and emerald ring. Abboud expects his wife to act with suitable dignity.

Here Jane makes more general statements at the outset of her paragraphs, and her quote is appropriately selected, spoken by the story character we expect to hear from. She lingers with the quote to explain its significance to the point of her essay and ends with a nice summarizing statement, using a sophisticated phrase (*to act with suitable dignity*) that she learned during class discussion of this story—I had written it on the whiteboard and it became part of her notes, in a process I discuss in chapter 1.

In her review of her own portfolio of work, Jane writes:

> I always struggle with the second essay [drafts] because I tend to repeat and there are not enough details. I am struggle with first and second body about pick the quotes and have to add. . . . But wow, I am writing first essays [drafts] are very simple information. I am learned to describe more.

While I hope that Jane, with time, will learn to describe her progress in even more specific ways, she understands that she is making progress in quoting the text accurately to support her points and in explaining the significance of her selected quotes.

Irene

Irene had problems with the first-draft conclusion of her sixth essay of the term. She compares her experiences with mainstreaming with those of a hypothetical deaf student in Christine Wixtrom's essay "Alone in the Crowd." Wixtrom makes the case that rather than being fully integrated with hearing classmates and the social life of the school, the hypothetical student was uninvolved and socially isolated from hearing students. Irene's point is that her experiences were both similar to and different from this student's.

> In conclusion, if is it a deaf child of most common hearing parents would rather to place the deaf child to mainstreaming school because parents not familiar so much about deaf culture. Unless, a hearing parents know about deaf culture then the deaf child able to be put to the school for the deaf. For in most common, a deaf child of deaf parents would send this deaf child to the school for the deaf. For example, in Maryland Scholl for the deaf there are almost more of many deaf children who have deaf parents to attend this school to be part of a deaf community in this area. In other situation of reasons, deaf parents would rather place the deaf child to mainstreaming school to get high levels of education to be like hearing students.

Based on Irene's thesis, I was hoping to hear in her conclusion whether her similarly negative experiences with mainstreaming outweighed her positive ones or vice versa, and, based on that analysis, if she could make some general statement about mainstreaming. Instead, she attempts to say that mainstreaming will work for Deaf students whose hearing parents are not familiar with Deaf culture; likewise, it would be better for Deaf students who have Deaf parents to go to a school for the deaf—but there are some Deaf parents who want their child to get a higher level of education, in which case they should put the child in a mainstream school. Whoa! Irene is drifting away from her own experience toward making some educational policy statement, a red flag that signals that Irene is not ending this essay as she should be. This was the sixth essay of the term, written close to the end of the term. By this point, Irene should know that for this essay, in her conclusion, she should generalize from her own experiences with mainstreaming to her own ambivalence about it, which I sensed was her true feeling.

As it happened, Irene had to repeat the course (she did not pass the departmental exit exam), but she hit the ground running the following semester. Here is the first-draft conclusion of her second essay, on de Maupassant's story "The Necklace." She argues that Madame Loisel, of all the characters in the story, is the most to blame for the ten years of misery she and her husband endure.

> From 10 years of everything, Madame Loisel made a lot of mistakes. If there is never happening then she should accept to use an old dress or insist not to go to the party. She could use flowers which are cheap price, instead of borrow the necklace. If she happened to borrow the necklace from Madame Forestier then she lost it, either of Monsieur or Madame Loisels should tell Madame Forestier the truth and then she would understand and ask them to owe her the worth only 500 francs, so they would to save 35,500 francs! It would be best for Madame Loisel to be less obsess about being rich. She needs to move on her life, such as find a job to save money in the bank, so she can spend her money something more important for her life needed.

Irene is thinking harder about her conclusions, and it shows in this first draft. The conclusion starts with a big statement that says her point and ties tightly to her thesis. Irene offers several options that Madame Loisel could have pursued instead of the one that caused her ten years of grief, and suggests that she rethink her values. The reflection on what could have spared Madame Loisel from her misery and the plea to "get real" indicate to me that Irene is learning how to work her conclusions.

Irene writes in her portfolio review:

> I think the essay is about mainstreaming that I was struggled with because I had to support my ideas and more specific examples for compare. In my conclusion seemed complex because it was too much information in different paths. I think I need to work on my conclusions to make better and impact on readers to more reflect and realize something like that.

Third and Fourth Drafts Across the Term

While I value and look for improvement in my students as writers in the way they think on paper and the way they see themselves thinking on paper, I simultaneously note progress in other arenas as well, namely with collocation and X-Word Grammar. I do not get rattled, however, if development in these areas is slow, because, as any teacher of writing will tell you, students need to be reminded over and over and over about grammatical details in the context of their own writing. Marc Ward (1997), director of the ESL program at Lehman College, views grammatical proficiency not as a prerequisite for college study, but as *a result* of four years of college study. He says, "Acquiring a first language is a complex process that takes years; the same is true of learning a second language. The time required to master any language, native or foreign, is one limitation of being human, and our attempt to shorten it is a fight against nature" (B8). In other words, we can expect college ESL writers to be better at writing accurately when they graduate than when they complete their ESL or basic reading and writing sequence of courses. As I emphasize in chapters 3 and 4, students will get better at collocation and grammar the more they read in grammatical chunks of lexis, which requires slow and purposeful reading of accessible text. It makes sense to look for grammatical accuracy to be a *developing* skill as opposed to one that is "finished" being learned after a sequence of developmental language, reading, or writing courses. By the end of four years, students will, hopefully, have interacted with volumes of text and had tons of practice reading and writing.

Still, my students want to see signs of progress with their grammar. They tell me this again and again:

> "I am thinking that I need to practice on my grammar. I just need to force on this than others."
> "More practice with grammar!"

They do see progress in several ways. When they see the correction symbols pointing out the same grammatical errors they make again and again, despite having learned the concepts, they literally hit their heads in frustration. When they start using the correction symbols more effectively and not repeating the same errors, they hit their heads less. That is definitely a sign of progress.

When a few sentences clustered together contain few, if any, errors, I make sure to point this out and congratulate the student. Justine's improvement is evident in this passage, in which she argues that Janice, wife of Abel in *In This Sign* by Joanne Greenberg (1970), is changing for the worse:

> When Abel arrives from his work, he notices Janice doesn't clean the dishes and when Janice arrives home from her work, she sleeps on her bed with her clothes on. Abel is angry because Janice doesn't clean [up] and he feels that "it was her job to do that—the wife's job."

By my praise for this well-written passage, Justine knows she is making progress. Sometimes just seeing how well they are coming along spurs students on with more vigor and effort because they see that all their hard work is not in vain.

Finally, I look to see how the students self-assess their grammatical progress over time. The more specifically they write about what they need to pay attention to, the more likely they will be conscious of these elements as they self-edit in subsequent drafts. Here is what students have said about their work with grammar:

> "My grammar have to be very carefully with V/XO, V/XD, T,+T and FT."
> "I shouldn't put on noun at end like *silence* [when I mean] *silent*."
> "I need to study hard with referents."

Counting the Drafts: 40, 80, 120

Sometimes I feel like the exercise instructor on the workout videos I use every morning, with my students playing my role. I look forward to my morning rendezvous with this instructor, because she makes hard work almost fun. She's soft-spoken but peppy and full of praise for her television audience (even though she can't see how I lose count and mix up legs!). The workouts are themed so I can focus on muscle toning one day and step aerobics the next, and if I work with her on a consistent basis, I notice an incredible difference in my fitness level over time. If I slack off, it takes me time and lots of workouts to regain that same fit level. No surprises here—success at anything is time on task.

I am not always soft-spoken and peppy, but I see my students responding to me in the same way. They improve as writers the more they write under my guidance, in an atmosphere that is supportive and encouraging. I often think of drafting, receiving response, and revising as one workout session (not all accomplished at once, of course). Those student-writers who are fairly "fit" before taking my writing course require 40 workout sessions, those not-so-fit 80, and those in dire need of fitness training 120 in order to pass the English departmental exit exam. Forty workout sessions is the equivalent, on average, of one writing course where ten essays are required, each one going through four drafts. Students in need of more time on task repeat the course, sometimes three times. (That's where the 120 workout sessions come from.) No one fails, except those who miss workouts or do not complete them consistently or in a timely manner.

Weaker students learn that they need more workout sessions before they notice a difference in their feeling of fitness—they need to go to a fifth and sixth draft before a piece is ready to be attended to grammatically. If this workout pattern persists, students might need fifty or fifty-five or sixty drafts to complete the course requirement of ten essays. This, they begin to understand, is an indication of weak writing, and they see exactly why it would be in their best interest to continue working on their writing by repeating the course. Conversely, those students who sail through workouts one through four, or who may not even need to take their essays to a fourth draft—whose essays might be ready for collocational and grammatical work at the second draft—have tangible evidence that their writing is progressing well. My students see that it pays for them to sweat for the first two drafts, to say something important and well as early on as possible. Having read this book up until this point, you now know that this early sweating happens long before composing the first and second drafts.

Presenting the Final Draft

I don't believe in sticking completed work in folders and bringing them out for an airing only during portfolio review time. After all their hard work, students need to celebrate as many final essay drafts as we have time for. As part of our celebration my students present their pieces to the class, which requires translating them into ASL—which is yet another way for students to note how well they are progressing as writers. At the bottom of each final draft, I write: "Please prepare this for presentation: Read it slowly three times as you practice interpreting it into ASL." Being able to move from English to ASL smoothly means that the students must know the signs for all the new vocabulary they learned during the writing of the essays, as well as where to chunk the stream of English so that interpretations look like ASL instead of meaningless sign-for-word matches. I encourage weaker signers to meet with stronger signers until they are confident in all the signs they need. During the presentation, a student places his or her final draft on the document camera and stands to the left of the projected text up at the front of the room, body angled a bit so that he or she can see text and audience simultaneously as much as possible. We are all eager to see the final product and the students' skill in interpreting it. These presentations are rather magical for me. The students see that what they project and share look like college-level essays. Not wanting to be embarrassed in front of their friends, their signing is practiced and good. I notice that the audience members read each projected line like hawks, catching signs out of the corners of their eyes, enjoying seeing sign interpretation and English text side by side primarily because, being familiar with the readings for the essays, they understand the presentation in full.

Students know they are becoming better writers when they can tell us in specific terms what they are doing in their writing that shows good thinking and is therefore making it better. Through discussions along the margins and in conference, students learn what is expected of their writing in contextualized and understandable ways. From these discussions, they extract the elements of the craft of essay writing that they will soon be able to apply to other essays, about more complicated topics that will call for even more tightly organized text and specialized vocabulary. They learn that writing well requires hard work, but that the rewards are well worth it. Listen in on what I have caught my students signing: "lots of sweat," "not easy," "takes time and focus," "big difference," "looking better," and, perhaps most important, "feeling better" about themselves, ready to take on the rigors of freshman composition and future college-level writing assignments, with teachers who, I hope, will help them continue to develop as writers.

Essays written in ENA099/ENG099 must be at least 300 words and judged at least "passing" in all of the following categories in order to pass. The standards apply to all essays written in the course, including the exit exams.

OVERALL RESPONSE TO THE ESSAY:

Please work on:

_____

I. MAIN IDEA: The main idea, sometimes called the thesis, is clear and effectively placed.

___SUPERIOR   ___PASSING   ___ NOT YET PASSING

II. ORGANIZATION: Your essay has a clear beginning, middle, and end and avoids repetition. The development from idea to idea, and paragraph to paragraph, is clear.

___SUPERIOR   ___PASSING   ___ NOT YET PASSING

III. SUPPORT: In this essay, you use examples and analysis to support your main idea. You also make effective use of course readings and ideas to fully develop your thesis. You introduce and elaborate on new ideas using specific details, vivid language, powerful expressions and original thought.

___SUPERIOR   ___PASSING   ___ NOT YET PASSING

IV. WORDS AND SENTENCES: You express your thoughts clearly and effectively. Although errors may still exist, your subjects and verbs are generally appropriate. You show, through punctuation, where sentences begin and end.

___SUPERIOR   ___PASSING   ___ NOT YET PASSING

Figure 1. Evaluation of essays in ENA099 and ENG099.

Chapter 6

Best Practices: Not Just for Hearing Students

Is teaching writing, along with the theory and practice described in this book, to Deaf students so very different from teaching it to hearing students? In November of 2004, the Writing Study Group of the National Council of Teachers of English (NCTE) Executive Committee created a document entitled "NCTE Beliefs about the Teaching of Writing" (updated on the Web at http://www.ncte.org/positions/statements/writingbeliefs). I would like to examine highlights of these beliefs in light of what I have advocated in *Working Text*, emphasizing the essence of my thinking and showing where, if at all, theory and practice might differ between Deaf and hearing students. Here then, with my commentary, are nine principles that NCTE believes should guide effective teaching practice.

1. *Everyone has the capacity to write, writing can be taught, and teachers can help students become better writers.*

By "everyone," NCTE makes it clear that there is ample evidence that anyone can get better at writing. Their position statement makes reference to developing writers and states that these writers require support that comes from carefully designed writing instruction: "Teachers of writing should be well-versed in composition theory and research. . . .When writing teachers first walk into classrooms, they should already know and practice good composition" (1). I find this particularly important. It is clearly in line with my thinking that teachers of Deaf students should expand their notion of teaching so that they are not just teaching language or English alone but also how to compose something of substance. And one does not have to come before the other; teachers should not wait until sentences, in the air or on paper, are correct before they ask students to create a thoughtful piece of writing in response to readings. Good form will eventually derive from good thought if this thought is worked, as exemplified throughout this text.

But how will teachers become prepared to walk into classrooms knowing and already practicing good composition? With the educational-standards movement now infiltrating schools for Deaf students, teachers of Deaf students should receive the same training in writing instruction that teachers of hearing students receive. Prospective teachers of Deaf students should not only take courses in composition theory and practice, but also learn how to assist students in reading the texts from which they should be asked to gather their ideas. Here the strategies I explained in chapter 1 (in the section "Writing into Reading") in which students learn how to dig into their readings through the assistance of guide questions, to mark their text, to respond to focused reading notes, and to use a dictionary are crucially important. Of course, these strategies would be considerably helpful for hearing readers as well because they are not just fundamentally good teaching practices, but they are essential for unpracticed readers.

2. *People learn to write by writing.*

The NCTE guidelines state, "As is the case with many other things people do, getting better at writing requires doing it—a lot" (1). I don't think that requiring students to write approximately ten, sometimes eleven, essays during a seventy-two-hour term (12 weeks × 6 hours per week) is excessive. These essays, as I explain in chapter 5, are written four, five, sometimes six times each. That can mean upwards of eighty drafts if a student must repeat a writing course, which for many of my students is the norm. Students "draft, rethink, revise, and draft again" (1), and with each draft they are making their writing better. In the context of learning to write well, for all students, but perhaps especially for Deaf students, more is better.

3. *Writing is a process.*

When NCTE speaks of writing as a process, it speaks to the "complex actions that writers engage as they produce texts" (2). These actions are in no way "a formulaic set of steps [because]. . . . Experienced writers shift between different operations according to tasks and circumstances" (2). We saw these actions in chapters 1 and 2, in which students learn to come to terms with their reading, to write to see their deeper thinking about reading, to study the craft of exceptional pieces of the kind of writing they will be required to do, and to become responsive readers of writing. In chapters 3 and 4 we learned ways of engaging students with editing, first for key phrasing and then for grammatical principles already taught. Finally, in chapter 5, we saw how students prepare and present their pieces for a wider audience than just their teacher. Let me be very clear in saying that these actions cannot be turned into a writing curriculum in lockstep fashion. Given the constraints of time and the need to do lots of writing, these aspects of the writing process blend into one another rather seamlessly throughout the twelve-week period. So, at about mid-term, some students might be working on four or five different essays at the same time. One student might be working on essay 4A (first draft of the fourth essay) as well as essay 3C (third draft of the third essay) and 2D (fourth draft of the second essay). This is because we do not wait to finish one essay to begin the next and because each student works on his/her essays according to the neediness of his or her writing. Some students need more time to shape their essays in ways that make them as clear and correct as possible. Others require fewer drafts to arrive at a piece that is presentation-ready. What remains absolutely inviolate, however, is that for each piece of writing, students have enough time to come to terms with the ideas in the readings they will be using to compose from, and enough time to gather their thinking about the ideas in these readings, as discussed in chapter 1 in the section "Writing to See Our Deeper Thinking about Reading." For Deaf students then, we might say that the writing process should be stretched a bit, not made any differently, just slowed, to ensure that students can articulate and present their ideas as thoughtfully as possible.

4. *Writing is a tool for thinking.*

The notion that writing is a medium for thought is important in several ways. It suggests a number of important uses for writing: to solve problems, to identify issues, to construct questions, to reconsider something one had already figured out, to try out a half-baked idea. This insight that writing is a tool for thinking helps us to understand the process of drafting and revision as one of exploration and discovery, and is nothing like transcribing from pre-recorded tape. . . . but of finding more and more wrinkles and implications in what one is talking about. (3)

I mentioned in the introduction to this book that although Deaf students may be competent oral language users, their skills in those language contexts will not be helpful in writing contexts. I explained that this is because each modality abides by its own set of rules and that writing is visible and permanent and speaking/signing is not. Because of these latter advantages, writing allows us to re-see or re-view our ideas, again and again, and gives us the opportunity to explore and discover new meaning. In writing we save temporary thinking and come back to it as many times as necessary, to add, discard, reorder, or tweak.

I once observed my husband, Peter, dictating a legal brief into a tape recorder. He had a few sparse notes lying around on the kitchen table, but absolutely no prewritten text, not even an outline. I couldn't believe it! With my limited knowledge of legal briefs, I knew that the finished product had to be somewhat like an essay, with points of law used to back up a particular stance on a legal issue. Peter dictating instructions to his secretary was one thing, reminders to himself another, but a legal brief? How could he see the patterns of his thinking and cross out what wasn't working, as I do almost once every minute as I sit at my computer writing this book? How does he scroll to the top of a paragraph, a page, the whole text to see if what he is writing makes sense or even just to see where his thinking is taking him? How does he know where to fit in his points of law and how to check to make sure that he is not repeating himself or saying nothing or saying something so convoluted that no judge would understand? In essence, how was he planning to reread and re-see what he wrote?

My shock subsided when I remembered that Peter doesn't know how to type. He speaks little sound bites at a time into his recorder then drops the tape off with his secretary who listens to it, types up what she hears, and gives the copy to him to revise. So begins a drafting process that, at times, has taken twenty-seven turns between the two of them for one brief. (This particular secretary was very loyal.) Peter does reread—and often. Pressing him a bit further, I wanted to know if he rereads with the same purpose that I do. Did his ideas grow bigger each time he reread? Did he find better ways of saying something each time he reread? Did he see relationships to other ideas that never dawned on him until he reread what he wrote? Yes, yes, yes—he had to think about his ideas again and again, and each time he thought about them, his ideas got better and were said better as well.

Educators of Deaf students must heed the NCTE principle that writing is a tool for thinking. This belief has been "back-burnered," if you will, for far too long, because teachers have been overly concerned with form as opposed to substance in writing. Therefore, we should no longer consider asking Deaf students to sign their compositions onto video and then transcribe the sign composition into written English while viewing the video (Bello, Costello, and Recane 2008, 186), either as a means to assess writing skill or as a strategy for teaching writing, because, simply put, compositions cannot be talked. They need to be built. For Deaf students, writing well must mean writing in English right from the outset, as it does for hearing students, with the support of all the bridging work exemplified in this book. It is the interaction of thought and written English worked across drafts that is key for Deaf students learning to write, not seeing how the "talk" of one language translates into the written form of another. Comparative linguists might be interested in knowing how surface structures between two languages differ, but real writers are not. They are much more interested in creating a line of reasoning.

5. *Writing grows out of many different purposes*

Guideline number 5 states that writing is not just one thing and that "within academic settings, the characteristics of good writing vary among disciplines; what counts as a successful lab report, for example, differs from a successful history paper, essay exam, or literary interpretation" (4). While most academic writing, often referred to as critical writing, requires some form of argument, different writing tasks call for different ways of presenting the argument. As examples, in my writing course, students must use text-based support in arguing their points to pass their exit exam, but they also have to pass the CUNY/ACT writing test, which asks them to select one of two different proposals to improve their school or their community and to argue in support of the selected proposal based on their own experiences. Each writing task embodies its own set of rhetorical structures or craft elements that students must master. For the exit exam, students need to know how to create a thesis statement in the introduction and to quote from text with interpretations of the quotes that explain their significance to the students' argument. For the CUNY/ACT test, students need to master an introduction that presents two proposals, with reasons why one is preferred over the other. They also learn how to set up a second body paragraph as a counterargument. How do they learn these elements? From writers who have written well in these genres before. A very big part of writing instruction, as we have seen in chapter 2 in the section "Reading into Writing: Becoming Studious Readers of Writing," is for students to study the craft of exactly what it is that they are required to write. They do this through the judicious use of excellent student-writing, writing that exemplifies the exact craft elements the students need to learn. Using student models is particularly beneficial for Deaf students because it is very likely that students can read the compositions of their peers independently. This is crucial because students need to study the way pieces are constructed—not just to get a gist of their meaning but to understand exactly what each student writer did to create an excellent essay. This can only happen through reading deeply into writing that is at their level.

6. *Conventions of finished and edited texts are important to readers and therefore to writers.*

Addressing the notion of correctness, NCTE states, "writers need an image in their minds of conventional grammar, spelling, and punctuation in order to compare what is already on the page to an ideal of correctness." Although there is no further explanation of what is meant by "an image in their minds," this brings to my mind essentially what I have advocated throughout this book: Students must be able to visually recognize and remember lexical and grammatical patterns. We have seen how students need to attend to the collocations of words that express key ideas in their essays, how X-Word Grammar principles can be recruited to overlay grammatical patterns on written text, and how students learn to identify relationships between and among these patterns. It is not grammatical rules that students remember, but the incidences of these rules as expressed in words and phrases that they remember seeing, again and again. The patterns inherent in X-Word Grammar make it much easier to visually remember words and phrases.

Within this same principle, NCTE advises teachers to teach without using "excessive linguistic terminology" but not to shy away from using terminology that might be necessary to teach particular kinds of usage. Similarly, as discussed in chapter 4, we want Deaf students to talk about the reasons one would use front shifters (FTS) instead of end shifters (TES) or why certain verbs require the hidden X-word *does* and others the hidden X-word *do*. Finally, NCTE's mention that "all of the dimensions of editing are motivated by a concern for audience" (5) speaks to the need to give students a real reason to write. I get the best work from students when I tell them that their work will be posted on the Internet or selected to be read at an end-of-term party for department members or just to their fellow classmates. Many of them are quite stunned by the quality of their finished products and are proud to show off their good, hard work.

Of course a major difference between the grammatical-editing work required of Deaf students and that required of hearing students is the level of intensity that the former do seem to benefit from. This is not to say that the same level of detail wouldn't benefit ESL students, because I believe it would. But for comparative purposes, NCTE does not mention the use of a grammar teaching methodology even though it does state that "Teachers need to . . . be excellent at teaching conventions to writers" (5). I am left wondering how this can be expected of teachers without formal training in teaching grammar to make writing better.

7. *Writing and reading are related.*

Principle 7 states, "reading is a vital source of information and ideas. For writers fully to contribute to a given topic or to be effective in a given situation, they must be familiar with what previous writers have said" (5). Over the eight years that it has taken me to write this book, I have given several talks about teaching writing to Deaf students. At particular points in my writing, I went back and reread all of these talks and found ideas that I wanted to think about again, especially after having read other authors who write about teaching writing. Although my original ideas were sound and worthy of inclusion in this book, more elaborated ideas, more refined ideas grew from additional information that infiltrated my thinking. I don't think that I can emphasize this point enough. Better writing begins and ends with good ideas that are well said, and good ideas come primarily from reading, rereading and thinking about other texts. These are the texts that other people have thought long and hard about and now invite us to add to what is being discussed. Once we have formulated our own ideas and worked our text until our ideas are clear and engagingly said, we will have produced something worth reading for a next writer to think about and take to a next level of thought. This, as I mentioned in chapter 1, is why I like to assign full texts for students to read and write about over time, chapter by chapter, or to assign more than one reading on a particular topic—because students will have more opportunities to think about more ideas and to see relationships among them. Their creative juices will flow more easily if they have more material to work from.

8. *Writing has a complex relationship to talk.*

NCTE'S metaphor for the relationship between writing and talk is stated as, "writing exists in a nest of talk" (6). They explain, "Writers often talk in order to rehearse the . . . content that will go into what they write, and . . . they sometimes confer with teachers and other writers about what to do next, how to improve drafts, or in order to clarify ideas and purposes" (6). I don't think I enjoy any part of the writing process more than conference time, specifically the time in between the first and second drafts where talk has its best and most important impact. Here is where my students and I talk about their ideas in relation to the big picture that they are trying to create, which most often means that we are talking about some heavy topics, straightening out confusions from assigned readings, or jumping off to talk about how ideas written about can be seen in or applied to everyday life. When I conference with students, I push back my chair, wrap my arms back behind my head, stretch out my legs and look off into the distance because I really need to think about ideas that they might consider incorporating into their next draft. Yes, I give away ideas—lots of them. In fact, I am always asked this question by adjunct teachers: "Is it okay to suggest ideas about content when I review a draft with the students?" In their fear to usurp students' thinking, these adjuncts fail to understand how crucial it is for teachers to open up as many avenues as possible for students. I answer this question with: "For this assignment, whom else will our students learn from more than you?" I remind our adjuncts that unlike hearing students, because of communication barriers, Deaf students have limited choices of people to turn to for help with their work. This does not mean that they can't help one another, and time is allotted for students to discuss their thinking about their writing with their peers, but, most often, the thinking that gets pulled and pushed happens during conferencing with teachers. And, it has to absolutely happen through the expert use of ASL (for students who sign) because the language has grammatical ways to clearly express complex meaning. So, here then is the connection between language through the air and writing: it is through talking about ideas that writing becomes better, and this talk needs to be deep, proactive and conceptually clear. As teachers, we must not rush this talk, which is what I fear happens in our haste to correct before we've pushed and pulled students' thinking.

9.   *Assessment of writing involves complex, informed, human judgment.*

NCTE starts its discussion of assessment by stating that assessment occurs for different purposes. There is assessment that is continuous where judgments are made in process, and there is assessment that makes final judgments about the quality of student work. Additionally, "sometimes an entity beyond the classroom assesses a student's level of achievement in order to say whether they can go on to some new educational level that requires the writer to be able to do certain things" (8). At LaGuardia, we have all three different forms of assessment, but the one I think is most valuable is the one that I focus on in chapter 5—ongoing, in-process judgments about what students know. This is where the students and I assess how well we are approaching the course goals, to get better at writing text-based essays and the language used to express these kinds of essays. Students see their progress over time because as each piece of writing is brought to closure, it leaves a trail of work behind it that can be uncovered. The trail of work is the responses to the writing that have been written along the edges and at the ends, the corrections in the text, and the revisions done from draft to draft and from essay to essay over the course of the term. Studying this trail of work in conference with me, my students see how they are progressing as writers, and they see that if an essay can be considered presentation-ready in three or four drafts, they are moving along nicely.

Another form of assessment is an exit exam, which many departments require of their writing students. For this exam, in my experience, teachers create writing top- ics based on readings they have reviewed with the students. Exam topics grow out of coursework, so students write about what they have been reading through the course or have been asked to read for the exit test—but the topic must be one they have not yet written about. I much prefer that students write about issues they have been discussing for a while and ideas with which they have developed a certain comfort level with writing about, as well as a tuned-in grammatical eye for words and phrases they have been using for a while as well. Student writing on topics for which there has been no preparation is not an accurate assessment of progress. This is true for all students, but it is all the more so for Deaf students, and we will come back to this point later. Exit exams that require students to complete timed writing tasks on new topics fail to reflect the heavy emphasis teachers place on drafting and redrafting all during the term and essentially ask students to do a very different type of task than what they have been practicing all term. And many exit exams are pass/fail, meaning that a student who has been doing well all term but fails the exam may still have to repeat the course. In this case, I might present work from the student's portfolio, typically an essay packet with a trail of three drafts that I believe show that he or she is ready for freshman composition, and the department may agree to pass the student.

The third method of assessment discussed by NCTE—in my opinion moving from best to worst—is assessment done by an entity beyond the classroom. Students in virtually all school systems have to pass a standardized test to prove that they are competent to move on to a next level of writing instruction; in my case, it is the CUNY/ACT test. In this exam, students are given general topics such as "Would you prefer to upgrade the computer lab or the book store?" and they must think quickly on their feet. There is no reading to help stimulate thinking or to lean on in a response. Deaf students have not had the opportunity to learn the phrasing for these essays—they are unlikely to have overheard people talking about such topics as the need for computer labs or book stores or read about them with understanding. Whereas hearing students have plenty of opportunities to borrow ideas that they have heard about from others; Deaf students' access to this information is restricted.

For final judgments about the quality of student writing, students' writing skills should be put to the test on something they have studied and have had opportunities to discuss. Although a portfolio review would be the ideal way for colleges to assess movement from level to level, an exit test with a flexible appeals procedure is acceptable, especially when the procedures have been honed over the years, essays are read by faculty, and, most important, students can study for the exam by knowing the readings it is based on inside and out. Testing what has been taught makes the most sense for hearing, and, especially, Deaf students. It views the assessment of writing similarly to the assessment of content, and that is fair.

The NCTE principles about the teaching of writing for hearing students hold true for the teaching of writing for Deaf students, with some tweaking of practice. And so, in answer to the question I posed at the beginning of this chapter, "Is teaching writing to Deaf students and the theory and practice described in this book so very different from teaching writing to hearing students?" I would have to say no, it is not. In the conclusion to the first chapter of my 1997 book *Rethinking the Education of Deaf Students*, which addressed the need to use American Sign Language and written English to teach the mainstream curriculum, I wrote:

Regardless of their language or hearing status, then, students learn in much the same ways. Differences arise only in the language(s) used, the degree to which context needs to be facilitative and, perhaps, the time required to digest understandings that might come more quickly for those students who have been immersed in the language of instruction, reading, and writing as their first language. (18)

In the twelve years since I wrote *Rethinking the Education of Deaf Students* we have, for the most part, come to accept the use of ASL in classrooms for Deaf students, but we still need to work on making learning contexts more facilitative and building in more time within these instructional contexts. As for the teaching of writing, then, we must make sure to assign readings with some way of guiding students through them; to choose readings for studying the craft of writing that are accessible to our students; to devote more time to being a responsive reader of student writing; to give considerably more attention to the teaching of grammar for writing; and to assess writing in ways that reflect how students have been doing reading and writing up until the assessment. These suggestions would of course benefit hearing students in their quest to become better writers, but they are essential for Deaf students who depend primarily on their eyes to learn.

References

Angelillo, Janet. 2003. *Writing about Reading.* Portsmouth, NH: Heinemann.

Anzaldúa, Gloria. 1991. "Lifeline." In *Connections*, ed. Sarah Lanier Barber, 23–25. Dubuque, IA: Kendall/Hunt.

Bean, John. 1996. *Engaging Ideas.* San Francisco, CA: Jossey-Bass.

Bello, Michael, Patrick Costello, and Suzanne Recane. 2008. "Participating in the Massachusetts Comprehensive Assessment." In *Testing Deaf Students in an Age of Accountability*, ed. Robert C. Johnson and Ross E. Mitchell, 186. Washington, DC: Gallaudet University Press.

Broad, Bob. 2003. *What We Really Value: Beyond Rubrics in Teaching and Assessing Writing.* Logan: Utah State University Press.

Brueggemann, Brenda Jo. 1999. *Lend Me Your Ear.* Washington, DC: Gallaudet University Press.

Carroll, Lee Ann. 2002. *Rehearsing New Roles: How College Students Develop as Writers.* Carbondale: Southern Illinois University Press.

Carver, Raymond. 1981. "Cathedral." In *Raymond Carver Stories*, 209–28. New York: Random House.

Chafe, Wallace L. 1980. "The Deployment of Consciousness in the Production of a Narrative." In *The Pear Stories: Cognitive, Cultural, and Linguistic Aspects of Narrative Production*, ed. Wallace Chafe, 9–50. Norwood, NJ: Ablex.

Chorost, M. 1985. "Print Is My Native Language." In *Removing the Writing Barrier: A Dream?: National Conference Proceedings: Innovative Writing Programs and Research for Deaf and Hearing-Impaired Students*, 191–97. New York: Lehman College: The City University of New York.

Clay, Marie M. 1982. *Observing Young Readers.* Exeter, NH: Heinemann Educational Books.

Crook, David. 2007. A Profile of Native and Non-Native English Speakers at CUNY. Paper presented at the Conference on Teaching, Language, and the CUNY Student, New York.

Deacons, Alice, Kate Parry, and Robert R. Viscount. 1994. *The Tapestry Grammar.* Boston: Heinle.

de Maupassant, Guy. 1907. "The Necklace." In *The Short-Story: Specimens Illustrating Its Development*, ed. Brander Matthews. New York: American Book Company. Retrieved on July 15, 2007, from www.bartleby.com/195/20.html.

DeSena, Laura Hennessey. 2007. *Preventing Plagiarism.* Urbana, IL: National Council of Teachers of English.

Dorris, Michael. 1989. *The Broken Cord.* New York: HarperCollins.

Esquivel, Laura. 1989. *Like Water for Chocolate*. New York: Bantam, Doubleday, Dell.

Fjeldstad, Mary. 2006. *The Thoughtful Reader*. Boston: Thomson Wadsworth.

Glickfeld, Carole. 1991. *"What My Mother Knows."* In *Connections*, ed. Sarah Lanier, 98–102. Barber. Dubuque, IA: Kendall/Hunt.

Greenberg, Joanne. 1970. *In This Sign*. New York: Henry Holt.

Harris, Joseph. 2006. *Rewriting: How to Do Things with Texts*. Logan: Utah University Press.

Harklau, Linda, K. M. Losey, and M. Siegal, eds. (2003, October). ERIC Clearinghouse on Languages and Linguistics. *Generation 1.5 Students and College Writing*. Retrieved on August 12, 2007, from www.cal.org/resources/Digest/0305harklau.html.

Hill, Jimmie. 2000. Revising Priorities: From Grammatical Failure to Collocational Success. In *Teaching Collocation*, ed. Michael Lewis, 47–69. Hove, England: Language Teaching Publications.

Hirvela, Alan. 2001. Connecting Reading and Writing through Literature. In *Linking Literacies: Perspectives on L2 Reading-Writing Connections*, ed. Diane Belcher and Alan Hirvela, 109–34. Ann Arbor: The University of Michigan Press.

Hout, Brian. 2002. *(Re)Articulating Writing Assessment for Teaching and Learning*. Logan: Utah State University Press.

Inturrisi, Louis. 1980. The Ways of Written English. New York: Language Innovations.

Kennedy, Robert F. 1969. *Thirteen Days*. New York: NAL Penguin.

Krashen, Stephen. 2002. Theory Versus Practice in Language Teaching. In *Enriching ESOL Pedagogy*, ed. Vivian Zamel and Ruth Spack, 211–28. Mahwah, NJ: Lawrence Erlbaum.

Kunz, Linda. 2004. "X-Word Grammar for Public School Teachers." Photocopy, The English Language Center, LaGuardia Community College, The City University of New York.

———. 2005. "X-Word Grammar for ESOL Students." Photocopy, The English Language Center, LaGuardia Community College, The City University of New York.

Kunz, Linda, and Laurie Gluck. 2000. "X-Word Grammar Intermediate." Photocopy, The English Language Center, LaGuardia Community College, The City University of New York.

Lewis, Michael. 1997. *Implementing the Lexical Approach*. Hove, England: Language Teaching Publications.

———, ed. 2000. Teaching Collocation. Hove, England: Language Teaching Publications.

Livingston, Sue. 1997. *Rethinking the Education of Deaf Students: Theory and Practice from a Teacher's Perspective*. Portsmouth, NH: Heinemann.

National Council of Teachers of English. 1998–2009. *NCTE Beliefs about the Teaching of Writing.* Retrieved on July 28, 2009, from http://www.ncte.org/positions/statements/writingbeliefs.

Newbury House Dictionary of American English. 2004. Boston: Heinle.

Nia, Isoke Titilayo. 1999. "Units of Study in the Writing Workshop." *Primary Voices K-6* 8 (1): 3–11.

Noguchi, Rei R. 1991. *Grammar and the Teaching of Writing.* Urbana, IL: National Council of Teachers of English.

Ray, Katie Wood. 1999. *Wondrous Words.* Urbana, IL: National Council of Teachers of English.

Santini, Rosemarie. 1990. "An American Dream." In *Side by Side: A Multicultural Reader*, ed. Harvey S. Wiener and Charles Bazerman, 24–29. New York: Houghton Mifflin.

Sternberg, Martin. 1994. "In the City of the Deaf." *New York Times*, August 21.

Tannen, Deborah. 1982. "Oral and Literate Strategies in Spoken and Written Narratives." *Language* 58 (1): 1–21.

Thomason, Tommy, and Carol York. 2002. *Absolutely Write!* Norwood, MA: Christopher-Gordon Publishers.

Ward, Marc. 1997. "Myths about College English as a Second Language." *The Chronicle of Higher Education*, September 26, B8.

Wilson, Maja. 2006. *Rethinking Rubrics.* Portsmouth, NH: Heinemann.

Wong, Elizabeth. 1990. "The Struggle to be an All-American Girl." In *Side by Side: A Multicultural Reader*, ed. Harvey S. Wiener and Charles Bazerman, 32–34. New York: Houghton Mifflin.

Woolard, George. 2000. "Collocation: Encouraging Learner Independence." In *Teaching Collocation*, ed. Michael Lewis, 28–46. Hove, England: Language Teaching Publications.

Part 2

Teacher's Guide and Supplement to
Working Text: X-Word Grammar and
Writing Activities for Students

Based on the work of Kunz and Gluck 2000.

To the Teacher

This teacher's guide further exemplifies the principles of grammar teaching presented in chapter 4 of this book that have worked well for me as a teacher of developmental writing to Deaf students at LaGuardia Community College of the City University of New York over the past eight years. As discussed in that chapter, grammar instruction is a small but necessary part of good writing instruction. With X-Word Grammar, teaching and learning grammar happens

1. not as a stand-alone course, but *concurrently* as a small part of a course that teaches composing;

2. without the use of overwhelming grammatical terminology;

3. by having students work with *chunks* of language;

4. by showing students the *interlinked* nature of language;

5. through the *accumulation* of learning from lesson to lesson;

6. by studiously grammatically analyzing models of the kind of writing that is required to become improved *noticers* of grammatically correct chunks of written English; and

7. by applying what is learned to students' own writing, again and again and again, *after* the hard, hard work of composing has been accomplished.

With Part 1 of *Working Text* and this teacher's guide in hand, I am confident that you, like your students, can *discover* the elements of X-Word Grammar without difficulty. This guide offers mini-lessons that walk you through the major elements of the grammar with the answers to the lesson activities right there for you to study. Here are some teaching tips for you to keep in mind:

1. Teach a lesson or two from *Working Text: X-Word Grammar and Writing Activities for Students* and assign the practice exercises that follow each lesson for in-class work *and* for homework.

2. Read all story excerpts within lessons aloud to the students first to ensure that they understand the vocabulary and phrases they will be asked to grammatically analyze.

3. Let students work in small teams as they do each lesson. Have the teams compete, and assign winning points to those team members who can not only get the right answers, but can explain why the answer is correct, using the language of X-Word Grammar (e.g., "It's wrong because this X-word does not match with its main verb"). Encourage argument and disagreement as this is how students learn best, but before the competition begins, members within each team should agree on one correct answer.

4. After a lesson or two and after the practice exercises, have students grammatically analyze, using X-word correction symbols (see Appendix G), excellent models of the kind of writing you will expect of them. I have included three models of the kind of writing expected of my students, but your required assignments will perhaps differ. They should analyze these model essays for only what they have been taught—a little bit at a time.

5. At the appropriate point in the writing process, use the X-word correction symbols to indicate errors in the students' own writing as shown in chapter 4 and in the Practice Editing sections of this book.

6. Remember that learning needs to accumulate, so when grammatically analyzing model essays, students need to carry over onto those essays all that they have already been taught as seen in the progression of grammatical analyses in the essays in Appendix I. These analyses are for you to study and to eventually learn from so that you can analyze any type of written text you require your students to do.

Included in this guide are four quizzes with answers that, of course, do not appear in the student text. There is also occasionally more explanatory information at the top of each lesson to help you along with your discovery of the grammar. Other than that, the teacher's guide and student activity books are the same. Wherever possible, the Practice Editing pages are composed of examples of actual errors made by Deaf students. For the most part, I've tried to keep all the editing and practice exercises as full texts so that students can see how grammar plays out over expanses of language--in its most authentic setting.

Students who would get the most benefit from this book are those who have some understanding of basic syntax. My thinking is that students in upper middle school through college would feel very comfortable using X-Word Grammar.

I highly recommended that students see all the correct answers in writing. The best way to accomplish this is to project the student text onto a whiteboard and to write the answers right over the text on the whiteboard after the teams of students have fought the answers out with each other.

Have fun—yes, it will be fun! Please email me with any questions at SLivings@lagcc.cuny.edu.

Section 1

- **Discovering X-Words and Subjects**
- **How X-Words Show Time**
- **How X-Words Match with Subjects**
- **Editing Practice**

Key teaching points:

X-words are powerful.

They show time and how many in the subject.

They have two faces.

ACTIVITY 1   Using X-Words: 20 Yes/No Questions

Place a pair of scissors or another small object in a bag without students seeing. Have the students use the X-word chart in activity 2 to help them think of questions that can only be answered with a "yes" or a "no" to help them discover what is in the bag. Fill in the chart with the students first. Have them notice that each question begins with an X-word. They should not repeat X-words. They will need assistance with phrasing and with ideas, so help them by writing their questions on a whiteboard. (These are only suggested questions, and anything can be placed in the bag.)

1. Is it small? _____ Yes

2. Would I eat it? _____ No

3. Could I play with it? _____ Yes

4. Does it smell nice? _____ No

5. Can I take it to school? _____ Yes

6. Must I be careful with it? _____ Yes

7. Do students use it at home? _____ Yes

8. Might it be used in college? _____ Yes

9. Has it been used in kindergarten? _____ Yes

10. Have babies used it? _____ No

11. Will I find it in a store? _____ Yes

12. Should I use it by itself? _____ No

13. Did it require practice to use? _____ Yes

14. Am I good at using it? _____ Yes

15. Was it ever harmful to people? _____ Yes

16. Are people afraid of it? _____ No

17. Shall I use it in just one way? _____ No

18. Were people using it a long time ago? _____ Yes

19. May I use it everyday? _____ Yes

20. Had I ever used it to cook? _____ No

ACTIVITY 2 Make an X-Word Chart

Have the students memorize the X-words in their families as shown below. Test them on these the next day. Don't worry about defining modals just yet. It will be better to explain what they mean in the context of the 20 Yes/No Questions activity and in the excerpted stories the students will read in activities 5 and 6. When you explain the modals in context, students will understand them better and thereby remember what they mean.

The DO Family	**Do**	*Does*	*Did*		
The HAVE Family	**Have**	*Has*	*Had*		
The BE Family	**Is**	*Am*	*Are*	*Was*	*Were*
The MODAL Family	**Will**	*Can*	*Shall*	*May*	*Must*
	Would	*Could*	*Should*	*Might*	

ACTIVITY 3   **X-Words and Subjects: Statements**

Show the students what was in the bag.

After discovering what was in the bag, change your questions to statements only if they are true. This means that each X-word will move to the right of the subject, and you will remove the question mark and replace it with a period. When you have finished, put an X on top of each X-word and draw a box around each subject.

X
1. It is small.

X
3. I could play with it.

X
5. I can take it to school.

X
6. I must be careful with it.

X
7. Students do use it at home.

X
8. It might be used in college.

X
9. It has been used in kindergarten.

X
11. I will find it in a store.

X
13. It did require practice to use.

X
14. I am good at using it.

X
15. It was harmful to people.

X
18. People were using it a long time ago.

X
19. I may use it everyday.

ACTIVITY 4   **X-Words and *Not* and *n't*: Negative Statements**

Point out that X-words hug tight to not *and* n't.

Now change the remaining questions (the ones you answered "no" to) to *negative statements*. This means that you will need to add the word *not* or the letters *n't* to each X-word. When you have finished, put an X on top of each X-word and draw a box around each subject.

       X   X
2. [I] would not/wouldn't eat it. _____

        X   X
4. [It] does not/doesn't smell nice. _____

          X   X
10. [Babies] have not/haven't used it. _____

         X   X
12. [I] should not/shouldn't use it by itself. _____

           X   X
16. [People] are not/aren't afraid of it. _____

        X
17. [I] shall not use it in just one way. _____

         X   X
20. [I] had not/hadn't used it to cook. _____

Finding X-Words and Subjects:
Making Yes/No Questions #1

Mark each X-word in the passage below and draw a box around its subject. There are 17 X-words for you to find. (*Hint*: Don't miss X-words that are shortened to contractions like *it's* for *it is*.) Words that look like X-words after the word *to* (e.g., *to do* in this story excerpt) are not X-words. When you are finished, change sentences 1–5 into yes/no questions. Use your own paper for that.

From **"Pencils"** in *Wayside School Is Falling Down*
by Louis Sachar, pp. 66–67

Jason borrowed a pencil from Allison. When he gave it back to her, **X** [it] was full of teeth marks.

Allison held the pencil by its point. "Yuck!" she said. "You chewed on it."

Jason felt awful. **1.** **X** [It] is very embarrassing to borrow somebody's pencil and then chew on it.

"Sorry," he said. "[I] didn't mean to chew it on purpose."

"[You] can keep it," said Allison. She dropped the pencil on Jason's desk, then raised her hand.

"Mrs. Jewls, can [I] go to the bathroom? [I] must wash my hands. Jason slobbered all over my pencil."

Everybody laughed.

Jason turned red. "[I]'m sorry, Allison," he said. **2.** "[It]'s a disgusting habit. [I] just can't help it." . . .

3. [Jason] was so mad at himself. He broke the chewed up pencil to bits.

4. [That] wasn't a smart thing to do.

"Everybody take out a pencil and a piece of paper," said Mrs. Jewls. "[It]'s time for our

spelling test."

Jason slapped himself on the forehead. "[I]'m so stupid!" he thought. "Rondi, may [I] borrow a

pencil, please?" he asked.

Rondi made a face. **5.** "[All my pencils] are new. How do [I] know [you] won't eat them?"

Finding X-Words and Subjects:
Making Yes/No Questions #2

Mark each X-word in the passage below and draw a box around its subject. There are 21 X-words for you to find. (*Hint*: Don't miss X-words that are shortened to contractions like *he'd* for he *had*.) When you are finished, change sentences 1–5 into yes/no questions. Use your own paper for that. (*Hint*: If a sentence has two X-words, only the first X-word gets moved.)

From *A Letter to Mrs. Roosevelt*
by C. Coco De Young, pp. 1–2

I never used to pay much attention to the dark. Well, except for the nights when I sat on our front

porch swing, counting the stars and waiting. **X** [I] would find a patch of stars caught between the rooftops

across the street and swing and count, and count and wait.

One night my best friend's mother called to me from her porch next door, "Margo, go inside. *X* [It]'s

raining. *X* [There] are no stars for you to count."

"Thank you, Mrs. Meglio, but *X* [I] can still see the stars from last night," I called back. *X* [I] didn't tell

her that *X* [my eyes] were closed tight and *X* [I] was trying to remember them.

1. *X* [Nighttime] was my friend back then, keeping me company while I waited for the trolley car to

bring Mama and Papa home. *X* [I] could hear the clatter as it crossed over the First Street Bridge and

turned right onto Maple Avenue. 2. *X* [Papa] would climb down the steps, then hold out his hand to

Mama. 3. *X* [I] could tell right then if [Charlie's day] *X* had been all right.

4. [Charlie] *X* had been kicked in the knee when [he]'d *X* tried to break up a fight between two boys

during a game of kickball. [He]'d *X* convinced Mama and Papa that [it] *X* was an accident, but [I] *X* was not sure.

5. [I] *X* can remember hearing Charlie groan during the night. When the doctor visited, he told Papa to

get Charlie to the hospital immediately.

[I] *X* was seven. The hospital rules posted in the front lobby said [I] *X* was too young to visit my brother.

So, I stayed home, although [Sister Cecilia] *X* did sneak me up to the third-floor children's ward to see

Charlie one time.

In "Pencils" (activity 5) some X-words are used to talk about BEFORE time and some X-words are used to talk about NOW time. Go back and write B over the X-words that talk about BEFORE time and N over the X-words that talk about NOW time. (See Appendix A for a complete list of BEFORE and NOW X-words to help you.)

Have students memorize Appendix A and test them on it after they do this exercise.

From "Pencils" in *Wayside School is Falling Down*
by Louis Sachar, pp. 66–67

X-B

Jason borrowed a pencil from Allison. When he gave it back to her, it was full of teeth marks.

Allison held the pencil by its point. "Yuck!" she said. "You chewed on it."

X-N

Jason felt awful. It is very embarrassing to borrow somebody's pencil and then chew on it.

X-B

"Sorry," he said. "I didn't mean to chew it on purpose."

X-N

"You can keep it," said Allison. She dropped the pencil on Jason's desk, then raised her hand.

X-N   *X-N*

"Mrs. Jewls, can I go to the bathroom? I must wash my hands. Jason slobbered all over my pencil."

Everybody laughed.

X-N   *X-N*   *X-N*

Jason turned red. "I'm sorry, Allison," he said. "It's a disgusting habit. I just can't help it." . . .

X-B

Jason was so mad at himself. He broke the chewed up pencil to bits.

X-B

That wasn't a smart thing to do.

X-N

"Everybody take out a pencil and a piece of paper," said Mrs. Jewls. "It's time for our

spelling test."

X-N   *X-N*

Jason slapped himself on the forehead. "I'm so stupid!" he thought. "Rondi, may I borrow a

pencil, please?" he asked.

X-N   *X-N*   *X-N*

Rondi made a face. "All my pencils are new. How do I know you won't eat them?"

X-Words and Time #2

In *A Letter to Mrs. Roosevelt* (activity 6) some X-words are used to talk about BEFORE time and some X-words are used to talk about NOW time. Go back and write B over the X-words that talk about BEFORE time and N over the X-words that talk about NOW time. (See Appendix A for a complete list of BEFORE and NOW X-words to help you.)

From *A Letter to Mrs. Roosevelt*
by C. Coco De Young, pp. 1–2

I never used to pay much attention to the dark. Well, except for the nights when I sat on our front

X-B

porch swing, counting the stars and waiting. I would find a patch of stars caught between the rooftops

across the street and swing and count, and count and wait.

One night my best friend's mother called to me from her porch next door, "Margo, go inside.

X-N   **X-N**

It's raining. There are no stars for you to count."

X-N   *X-B*

"Thank you, Mrs. Meglio, but I can still see the stars from last night," I called back. I didn't tell

X-B   *X-B*

her that my eyes were closed tight and I was trying to remember them.

X-B

Nighttime was my friend back then, keeping me company while I waited for the trolley car to

X-B

bring Mama and Papa home. I could hear the clatter as it crossed over the First Street Bridge and

X-B

turned right onto Maple Avenue. Papa would climb down the steps, then hold out his hand to Mama.

X-B   *X-B*

I could tell right then if Charlie's day had been all right.

X-B   *X-B*

Charlie had been kicked in the knee when he'd tried to break up a fight between two boys during

X-B   *X-B*   *X-B*

a game of kickball. He'd convinced Mama and Papa that it was an accident, but I was not sure.

X-N

I can remember hearing Charlie groan during the night. When the doctor visited, he told Papa to get

Charlie to the hospital immediately.

X-B   *X-B*

I was seven. The hospital rules posted in the front lobby said I was too young to visit my brother.

X-B

So, I stayed home, although Sister Cecilia did sneak me up to the third-floor children's ward to see

Charlie one time.

X-Words and Time #3

Mark each X-word in the passage below and draw a box around its subject. There are 33 X-words for you to find. Write B over the X-words that talk about BEFORE time and N over the X-words that talk about NOW time. (*Do* in *to do* is not an X-word.)

Words that look like X-words after the word to *(e.g.,* to do*) are not X-words. The X-words* has/have *indicate the action is possibly continuing into NOW time.*

"My Parents"

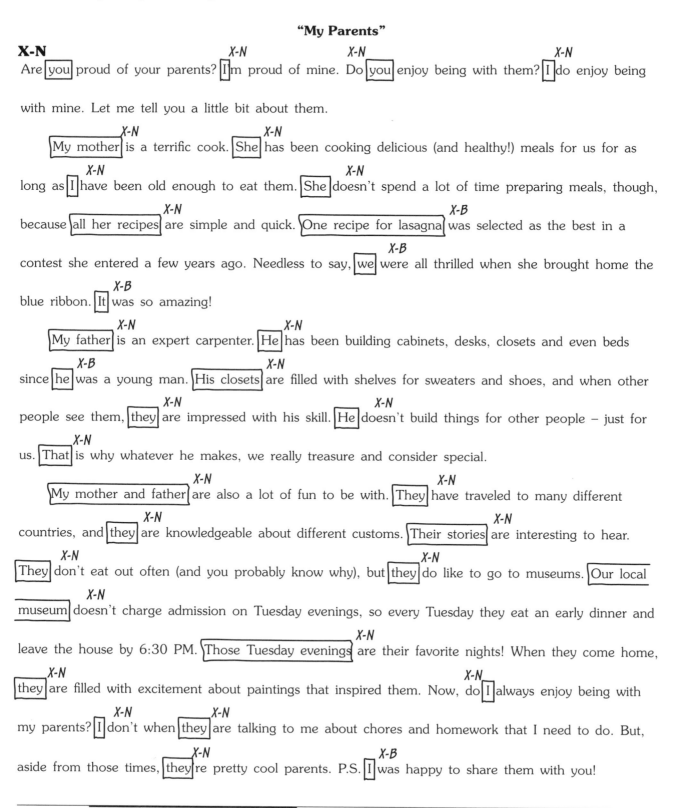

Subject and X-Word Match-Ups #1

On the lines below each set of X-words, write the subjects from "My Parents" (activity 9) that match-up with the X-words. Do not use the subject *I* and do not repeat subjects.

I̲s̲ Wa̲s̲ Ha̲s̲ Doe̲s̲

My mother	She	One recipe for lasagna	It
My father		He	That
Our local museum			

Are Were Have Do

You	all her recipes	we
His closets	they	My mother and father
Their stories	Those Tuesday evenings	

➡ What letter does the first group of X-words end with? __s__

Can that letter mean *singular* or 1 subject? Yes! *You* will always match with 2 or many.

Show students how the second group of subjects shows 2 or many.

Which family of X-words is missing on this page? Check Appendix B to see if you can figure this out, and the reason for it.

The modals are missing. They match with subjects that are 1 or 2 or many.

Subject and X-Word Match-Ups #2

Which is the only subject from "My Parents" (activity 9) that matches with all of these X-words?

DO   WAS   AM   HAVE

I *is the only subject that matches with all of these X-words.*

ACTIVITY 12 X-Words and Time #4

Mark each X-word in the passage below and draw a box around its subject. There are 35 X-words for you to find. Write B over the X-words that talk about BEFORE time and N over the X-words that talk about NOW time. *The X-words has/have indicate the action is possibly continuing into NOW time.*

"On the Evening of September 11th, 2001"

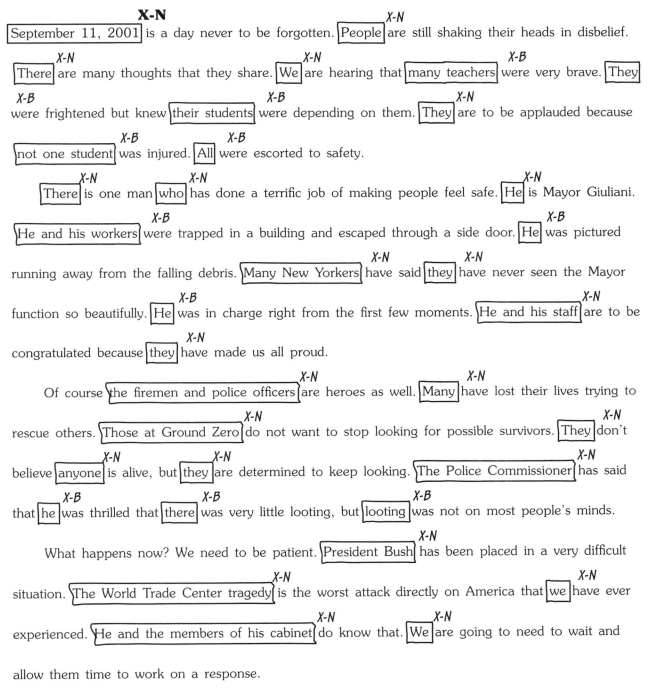

[September 11, 2001] **X-N** is a day never to be forgotten. [People] **X-N** are still shaking their heads in disbelief.

[There] **X-N** are many thoughts that they share. [We] **X-N** are hearing that [many teachers] **X-B** were very brave. [They]

X-B were frightened but knew [their students] **X-B** were depending on them. [They] **X-N** are to be applauded because

[not one student] **X-B** was injured. [All] **X-B** were escorted to safety.

[There] **X-N** is one man [who] **X-N** has done a terrific job of making people feel safe. [He] **X-N** is Mayor Giuliani.

[He and his workers] **X-B** were trapped in a building and escaped through a side door. [He] **X-B** was pictured

running away from the falling debris. [Many New Yorkers] **X-N** have said [they] **X-N** have never seen the Mayor

function so beautifully. [He] **X-B** was in charge right from the first few moments. [He and his staff] **X-N** are to be

congratulated because [they] **X-N** have made us all proud.

Of course [the firemen and police officers] **X-N** are heroes as well. [Many] **X-N** have lost their lives trying to

rescue others. [Those at Ground Zero] **X-N** do not want to stop looking for possible survivors. [They] **X-N** don't

believe [anyone] **X-N** is alive, but [they] **X-N** are determined to keep looking. [The Police Commissioner] **X-N** has said

that [he] **X-B** was thrilled that [there] **X-B** was very little looting, but [looting] **X-B** was not on most people's minds.

What happens now? We need to be patient. [President Bush] **X-N** has been placed in a very difficult

situation. [The World Trade Center tragedy] **X-N** is the worst attack directly on America that [we] **X-N** have ever

experienced. [He and the members of his cabinet] **X-N** do know that. [We] **X-N** are going to need to wait and

allow them time to work on a response.

Subject and X-Word Match-Ups #3

On the lines below each set of X-words, write the subjects from "On the Evening of September 11th, 2001" (activity 12) that match-up with the X-words. Do not repeat subjects.

I̱s Wa̱s Ha̱s Doe̱s

September 11, 2001	There	Who	He
The Police Commissioner		looting	not one student
The World Trade Center tragedy		President Bush	
anyone			

Are Were Have Do

People	There	We	teachers	They
Their students		All	He and his workers	
Many New Yorkers		He and his staff		
The firemen and police officers		Many		
Those at Ground Zero				
He and the members of his cabinet				

ACTIVITY 14 Subject and X-Word Match-Ups #4

In "My Parents" (activity 9) some X-words are used to talk about 1 and some X-words are used to talk about 2 or many. Go back and write a *1* over the X-words that talk about 1 subject and a *2* over the X-words that talk about two or more subjects. Do not label the subject *I* for 1 or 2. (See Appendix B for a complete list of X-words that show 1 or 2 or many to help you.)

X-N2   **X-N**   **X-N2**   **X-N**
Are you proud of your parents? I'm proud of mine. Do you enjoy being with them? I do enjoy being

with mine. Let me tell you a little bit about them.

     X-N1   *X-N1*
My mother is a terrific cook. She has been cooking delicious (and healthy!) meals for us for as

X-N   *X-N1*
long as I have been old enough to eat them. She doesn't spend a lot of time preparing meals, though,

X-N2   *X-B1*
because all her recipes are simple and quick. One recipe for lasagna was selected as the best in a

X-B2
contest she entered a few years ago. Needless to say, we were all thrilled when she brought home the

X-B1
blue ribbon. It was so amazing!

X-N1   *X-N1*
My father is an expert carpenter. He has been building cabinets, desks, closets and even beds

X-B1   *X-N2*
since he was a young man. His closets are filled with shelves for sweaters and shoes, and when other

X-N2   *X-N1*
people see them, they are impressed with his skill. He doesn't build things for other people – just for

X-N1
us. That is why whatever he makes, we really treasure and consider special.

X-N2   *X-N2*
My mother and father are also a lot of fun to be with. They have traveled to many different

X-N2   *X-N2*
countries, and they are knowledgeable about different customs. Their stories are interesting to hear.

X-N2   *X-N2*
They don't eat out often (and you probably know why), but they do like to go to museums. Our local

X-N1
museum doesn't charge admission on Tuesday evenings, so every Tuesday they eat an early dinner and

X-N2
leave the house by 6:30 PM. Those Tuesday evenings are their favorite nights! When they come home,

X-N2   *X-N*
they are filled with excitement about paintings that inspired them. Now, do I always enjoy being with

X-N   *X-N2*
my parents? I don't when they are talking to me about chores and homework that I need to do. But,

X-N2   *X-B*
aside from those times, they're pretty cool parents. P.S. I was happy to share them with you!

Subject and X-Word Match-Ups #5

In "On the Evening of September 11th, 2001" (activity 12) some X-words are used to talk about 1 and some X-words are used to talk about 2 or many. Go back and write a 1 over the X-words that talk about 1 subject and a 2 over the X-words that talk about two or more subjects. (See Appendix B for a complete list of X-words that show 1 or 2 or many to help you.)

X-N1   X-N2

September 11, 2001 is a day never to be forgotten. People are still shaking their heads in disbelief.

X-N2   *X-N2*   *X-B2*
There are many thoughts that they share. We are hearing that many teachers were very brave. They

X-B2   *X-B2*   *X-N2*
were frightened but knew their students were depending on them. They are to be applauded because

X-B1   *X-B2*
not one student was injured. All were escorted to safety.

X-N1   *X-N1*   *X-N1*
There is one man who has done a terrific job of making people feel safe. He is Mayor Giuliani.

X-B2   *X-B1*
He and his workers were trapped in a building and escaped through a side door. He was pictured

X-N2   *X-N2*
running away from the falling debris. Many New Yorkers have said they have never seen the Mayor

X-B1   *X-N2*
function so beautifully. He was in charge right from the first few moments. He and his staff are to be

X-N2
congratulated because they have made us all proud.

X-N2   *X-N2*
Of course the firemen and police officers are heroes as well. Many have lost their lives trying to

X-N2   *X-N2*
rescue others. Those at Ground Zero do not want to stop looking for possible survivors. They don't

X-N1   *X-N2*   *X-N1*
believe anyone is alive, but they are determined to keep looking. The Police Commissioner has said

X-B1   *X-B1*   *X-B1*
that he was thrilled that there was very little looting, but looting was not on most people's minds.

X-N1
What happens now? We need to be patient. President Bush has been placed in a very difficult

X-N1   *X-N2*
situation. The World Trade Center tragedy is the worst attack directly on America that we have ever

X-N2   *X-N2*
experienced. He and the members of his cabinet do know that. We are going to need to wait and

allow them time to work on a response.

ACTIVITY 16   A Brief Word about Most *WH-* (information) Questions

Go back to activity 3 and ask for more information about the 20 yes/no questions that you answered "yes" to. Pick *WH-* questions (WHEN, WHERE, WHY, and HOW) that make sense. Be sure to make up brief answers to your questions that make sense, too. (Your answers do not have to be full sentences.) What do you notice about the X-words?

In WH- information questions, the X-word most often comes after the WH-word. Have students notice that WHEN questions require a TIME response; WHERE questions require a PLACE response, and WHY questions require a REASON response most often shown by the word BECAUSE.

1. *Why is it small?   Because that's the way it was made*

3. *How could I play with it?   By using it to cut out shapes from paper*

5. *When can I take it to school?   Anytime*

6. *Why must I be careful with it?   Because you could cut yourself*

7. *How do students use it at home?   To cut articles from the newspaper*

8. *Where might it be used in college?   In classrooms and labs*

9. *Why has it been used in kindergarten?   To teach young children how to cut*

11. *Where will I find it in a store?   In the school supplies area*

13. *Why did it require practice to use?   Because it´s hard to do at the beginning.*

ACTIVITY 17 **Practice Editing I**

Edit the following sentences using the correction symbols to the right of each sentence to help you find the errors.

Review the correction symbols that appear below using the X-Word Grammar Correction Symbols (see Appendix G). Review the X-word chart in activity 2 as well and explain that to correct errors of TIME and matching (SX), students should look in the same family group that houses the incorrect X-words. They do not have to "jump across family groups" to correct errors of TIME and matching (SX). Explain that the excerpt is part of a story—if you know the famous story "The Necklace," briefly summarize it for the students. Have the students read through the excerpt before they begin correcting the mistakes to get a feel for how time is used in it.

Adapted from **"The Necklace"**
by Guy de Maupassant

is
"What the matter with you?" asked her husband.   **X?**

do
"I . . . I . . . I did not see the necklace."   **Time**

were
They searched everywhere. They was unable to find it.   **SX**

had
"But if you have dropped it in the street, it should still be there."   **Time**

Did
"Yes. Do you take the number of the cab?"   **Time**

Did
"No. you take the number of the cab?"   **X?**

will   *can*
"No. I go over all the ground and see if I could find it."   **X? Time**

had
Her husband returned about seven. He has found nothing.   **Time**

was
"Tell your friend that the necklace were broken."   **SX**

will
"That give us time to look for it."   **X?**

didn't
They don't find the necklace.   **Time**

was
They bought a new necklace. It is worth $40,000 francs.   **Time**

were
They was allowed to pay $36,000 francs.   **SX**

ACTIVITY 18 Practice Editing II

Edit the following sentences using the correction symbols to the right of each sentence to help you find the errors.

Explain that the excerpt is part of a story. Have the students read through the excerpt before they begin correcting the mistakes. Review the X-word chart in activity 2 as well and explain that to correct errors of TIME and matching (SX), students should look in the same family group that houses the incorrect X-words. They do not have to "jump across family groups" to correct errors of TIME and matching (SX).

Adapted from *Charlotte's Web*
by E. B. White, pp. 1–3

is
"Where ~~are~~ Papa going with that ax?"   **SX**

                                          were
"Out to the lighthouse," replied Mrs. Arabel. "Some pigs are born last night."   **Time**

don't
"I didn't see why he needs an ax," continued Fern.   **Time**

                          is
"Well," said Mother, "one of the pigs was a runt."   **Time**

  is
"It very small and weak."   **X?**
   ^

              has
"So your father have decided to kill it."   **SX**

              is
"Just because it are smaller than the others?" shrieked Fern.   **SX**

                          is
"Don't yell, Fern!" she said. "Your father was right."   **Time**

                                          was
Fern pushed a chair out of the way and ran outdoors. The grass wet.   **X?**
                                                   ^

              were
Fern's sneakers are sopping by the time she caught up with her father.   **Time**

          don't
"Please didn't kill it!" she sobbed.   **Time**

  is
"It was unfair."   **Time**

                    must/should
"Fern," he said gently. "You learn to control yourself."   **X?**
                              ^

                          is
"Control myself?" yelled Fern. "This was a matter of life and death!"   **Time**

          couldn't
"The pig can't help being born small."   **Time**

ACTIVITY 19 **Practice Editing III**

Explain that the excerpt is part of a story. Have the students read through the excerpt before they begin correcting the mistakes. Review the X-word chart in activity 2 as well and explain that to correct errors of TIME and matching (SX), students should look in the same family group that houses the incorrect X-words. They do not have to "jump across" to correct errors of TIME and matching (SX).

Adapted from **Charlotte's Web**
by E. B. White, pp. 3–7

         will
"All right," he said. "You go back to the house, and I ~~would~~ bring the runt." **Time**

  was
When Mr. Arable returned to the house, Fern is upstairs changing her sneakers. **Time**

was
He were carrying a carton under his arm. **SX**

   was
The carton wobbled, and there were a scratching noise. **SX**

   was
There, inside, looking up, is the newborn pig. **Time**

  didn't
Fern doesn't take her eyes off the tiny pig. **Time**

   Doesn't
"Oh, look at him! Don't he look perfect? **SX**

    had
At this moment, Fern's brother, Avery, has come in the room. **Time**

 is
"What was that?" he demanded. **Time**

 is
"What Fern holding?" **X?**

Did
"Do you wash your face and hands Avery?" asked Mrs. Arable. **Time**

  is
"That pig no bigger than a white rat!" **X?**

    will
"Hurry and eat. The school bus would be here soon." **Time**

 do
"I does want a pig, too," said Avery. **SX**

  was
"No, Fern is up at daylight, and I only give pigs to early risers." **Time**

 couldn't   *had*
But Fern can't eat until her pig has had a drink. **Time** **Time**

  was
A minute later, Fern were sitting on the floor giving her pig a bottle. **SX**

was   *were*
She is teaching it how to suck, and her brother and mother was watching. **Time** **SX**

Explain that the excerpt is part of a story. Have the students read through the excerpt before they begin correcting the mistakes.

Adapted from: **"The Necklace"**
by Guy de Maupassant

When Madame Loisel took back the necklace to Madame Forestier, Madame	**Time**
Forestier does not open the box.	
From then on, Madame Loisel were very poor.	**SX**
Every month, the notes has to be paid.	**Time**
Madame Loisel became old. Her hair were grey, her skirts was old and her	**SX SX Time**
hands are red.	
One Sunday, Madame Forestier is taking a child for a walk.	**Time**
She is as beautiful as ever!	**Time**
Shall Madame Loisel speak to her?	**Time**
Yes! She tell all.	**X?**
Madame Loisel said, "Hello." Madame Forestier said,	**X?**
"But . . . Madame . . . I not know you."	
"No . . . I was Mathilde Loisel."	**Time**
"Oh . . . my poor Mathilde, how you has changed!"	**SX**
"Yes, and it are all your fault."	**SX**
"For the last ten years, my husband and I has been paying for your necklace."	**SX**

Edit the following sentences using the correction symbols to the right of each sentence to help you find the errors.

Adapted from: **"The Necklace"**
by Guy de Maupassant

When Madame Loisel took back the necklace to Madame Forestier, Madame **Time**

did
Forestier does not open the box.

was
From then on, Madame Loisel were very poor. **SX**

had
Every month, the notes has to be paid. **Time**

                      was   *were*
Madame Loisel became old. Her hair were grey, her skirts was old and her **SX SX Time**

were
hands are red.

was
One Sunday, Madame Forestier is taking a child for a walk. **Time**

was
She is as beautiful as ever! **Time**

Should
Shall Madame Loisel speak to her? **Time**

will/would
Yes! She ˄ tell all. **X?**

Madame Loisel said, "Hello." Madame Forestier said, **X?**

                   do
"But . . . Madame . . . I ˄ not know you."

am
"No . . . I was Mathilde Loisel." **Time**

                    have
"Oh . . . my poor Mathilde, how you has changed!" **SX**

    is
"Yes, and it are all your fault." **SX**

                   have
"For the last ten years, my husband and I has been paying for your necklace." **SX**

Section 2

- **X-Words and Main Verbs**
- **Hidden X-Words**
- **Editing Practice**

Key teaching points:

X-Words match 100 percent without exception with their main verb.

If you do not see an X-word, DOES, DO, or DID is hiding in the main verb.

ACTIVITY 20 **X-Word and Main Verb Match-Ups #1**

Put an X over the X-words in the sentences below. If an X-word has a main verb next to it, put a V over the main verb partner. There are 10 X-word and main verb match-ups.

"The King and the Bees"

One day, King Solomon was sitting on his throne, and his great men were standing around him.
         X   V   X   V

Suddenly, the Queen of Sheba entered the room.

                                                 X   V   X
"My dear King," she said, "in my country, far, far away, I have heard there was no puzzle you
X   V   X
could not solve." Then she held up in each hand a beautiful wreath of flowers that were so alike that
         X   V
no one could see any differences.

"Someone made one of these wreaths from flowers from your garden. Someone made the other

wreath from artificial flowers, shaped and colored by a skillful artist. Now tell me, dear King, which
X   X   X   V   X
is the true and which is the false wreath? I have heard that you are the wisest man in the world," she
                                     X   V
said, "so surely this simple thing should not puzzle you."

                                                                       X
Then the King remembered something. He remembered that close by his window there was a
                                   X   V
vine filled with beautiful sweet flowers. He remembered that he had seen many bees flying among these

flowers and gathering honey from them.

So, he said, "Open the window!"

The next moment, two bees flew eagerly in, and then . . . another and another. All flew to the

flowers in the Queen's right hand. Not one of the bees so much as looked at those in her left hand.
                                X   V
"Dear Queen of Sheba, the bees have given you my answer," said Solomon.
                              X
And the Queen said, "You are wise, King Solomon. You gather knowledge from the little things
                            X   V
which common men do not notice."

Now . . . Match up all the X-word and main verbs here:

X-WORD	MAIN VERB	X-WORD	MAIN VERB	X-WORD	MAIN VERB
was	sitting	could	see	have	given
were	standing	have	heard	do (not)	notice
have	heard	should (not)	puzzle		
could (not)	solve	had	seen		

X-Word and Main Verb Match-Ups #2

Put an X over the X-words in the sentences below. If an X-word has a main verb next to it, put a V over the main verb partner. There are 27 X-word and main verb match-ups.

Students will ask you if certain words are verbs. They will confuse adjectives with verbs. Explain that adjectives describe.

"Saving the Birds"

                X V   **X**

One day in spring, four men were riding on horseback along a country road. These men were lawyers,

    X V   **X V**   *X*

and they were going to the next town to attend court. It had rained, and the ground was very soft.

   X V   *X*

Water was dripping from the trees, and the grass was wet.

      X V

As they were passing through a grove of small trees, they saw something in the wet grass.

     X   *X*

"What's the matter?" asked the first lawyer, whose name was Speed.

     X   *X*   *X*

"Oh, it's only some old robins!" said the second lawyer, whose name was Hardin. "The storm has

V   *X*   *X V*

blown two of the little ones out of the nest. They're too young to fly, and the mother bird is making a

great fuss about it."

          X V   *X*

"What a pity! They'll die down there in the grass," said the third lawyer, whose name I can't

V

remember.

       X   *X*   *V*

"Oh, well! They're nothing but birds," said Mr. Hardin. "Why should we care?"

       X   *V*

"Yes, why should we care?" said Mr. Speed.

The three men, as they passed, looked down and saw the little birds fluttering in the cold,

wet grass. They saw the mother robin flying about, and crying to her mate. Then they rode on,

                                X   *V*

talking and laughing as before. In a few minutes, they'd forgotten about the birds.

                  X

But the fourth lawyer, whose name was Abraham Lincoln, stopped. He got down from

                                                           X   *V*

his horse and very gently took the little ones up in his big warm hands. They did not seem afraid,

           X   *V*   *X*

but chirped softly, as if they had known they were safe.

➡ **more on next page**

                                           X V

"Never mind, my little fellows," said Mr. Lincoln, "I will put you in your own cozy little bed." Then

                                X   V   X   X

he looked up to find the nest from which they had fallen. It was high, much higher than he could

V   X   V   X   V   X

reach. But Mr. Lincoln could climb. He had climbed many trees when he was a boy. He put the birds

softly into their warm little home.

                                    X   V

      Soon the three lawyers who had ridden ahead stopped at a spring to give their horses water.

                 X

      "Where is Lincoln?" asked one.

           X   V   X   V

      "Do you remember those birds?" asked Mr. Speed. "Very likely he has stopped to take care of them."

                                         X   V   X

      In a few minutes, Mr. Lincoln joined them. He had torn his coat on the thorny tree and had

V

gotten mud all over his shoes.

                                    X   V

      "Hello, Abraham!" said Mr. Hardin. "Where have you been?"

                             X   V   X   V

      "Gentlemen," said Mr. Lincoln, "I would not sleep tonight if I had left those helpless

little robins to perish in the wet grass."

Now . . . Match up all the X-word and main verbs here:

X-WORD	MAIN VERB	X-WORD	MAIN VERB	X-WORD	MAIN VERB
were	riding	should	care	had	ridden
were	going	had	forgotten	do	remember
had	rained	did (not)	seem	has	stopped
was	dripping	had	known	had	torn
were	passing	will	put	had	gotten
has	blown	had	fallen	have	been
is	making	could	reach	would (not)	sleep
will	die	could	climb	had	left
can't	remember	had	climbed		
should	care				

X-Word and Main Verb Match-Ups #3

Group the main verbs from "The King and the Bees" (activity 20) and "Saving the Birds" (activity 21) into the following categories. **Don't repeat verbs.**

The Base Form (no endings on the verb)	**The _ing_ Form** (_ing_ ending on the verb)	**The _D-T-N_ Form** (verb ends with _d, t_ or _n_)
1. solve	1. sitting	1. heard
2. see	2. standing	2. seen
3. puzzle	3. riding	3. given
4. notice	4. going	4. rained
5. die	5. dripping	5. blown
6. remember	6. passing	6. forgotten
7. care	7. making	7. known
8. seem		8. fallen
9. put		9. climbed
10. reach		10. ridden
11. climb		11. stopped
12. sleep		12. torn
		13. gotten
		14. been
		15. left

These main verb forms match <u>100% without exception</u> to the X-word families:

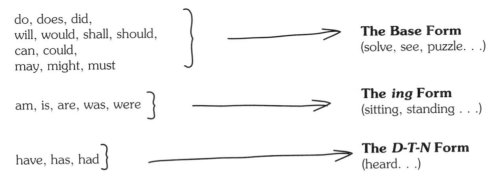

do, does, did,
will, would, shall, should,
can, could,
may, might, must
} ⟶ **The Base Form** (solve, see, puzzle. . .)

am, is, are, was, were } ⟶ **The _ing_ Form** (sitting, standing . . .)

have, has, had } ⟶ **The _D-T-N_ Form** (heard. . .)

Now . . . Check your X-word and main verb match-ups in activities 20 and 21 to see if they follow the 100% without exception promise!

This promise is for active verbs and not passive verbs, which are not covered in this book.

X-Word and Main Verb Match-Ups #4

Put an X over the X-words in the sentences below. Then use Appendix C (first three columns) to fill in each blank with the correct main verb form. Complete the chart below by putting all of the main verbs into their form groups.

From **"Angels and Other Strangers"** in *A Christmas Treasury*
by Katherine Paterson, pp. 57–58

Minutes after the letter came from Arlene, Jacob set out walking for Washington. He wondered how

X   *X*

long it would ___take___ him to get there. Before the truck died, he could ___*make*___ it in an hour, but

(TAKE)

X   *X*   *X*

he'd never ___*tried*___ to walk it. At sixty he knew that he didn't ___*have*___ the endurance that he had

(TRY)   (HAVE)

X   *X*

once ___*had*___, but he was still a strong man. Perhaps he could ___*get*___ there by morning if he kept

(HAVE)   (GET) *X*   *X*

a steady pace. Or if he could at least ___*reach*___ a place where there was a bus, he could ___*ride*___ as

(REACH)   (RIDE)

X

far as the few bills in his pocket could ___*take*___ him.

(TAKE)

X

Arlene needed him, so he would ___*go*___ to her if he needed to walk every step of the way.

(GO)

X

Arlene, his baby granddaughter, whom it seemed he had recently ___*stopped*___ bouncing on his

(STOP)

X   *X*

knee, was ___*going*___ to have a baby herself. She was alone and scared in the city and wanted her

(GO) *X*

granddaddy, so he had ___*put on*___ his dead wife's overcoat and then his own and started out. The

(PUT [ON])

X

two coats protected him from the wet snow, but his wife's was too small and cut under his arms.

X   *X*

"I'm ___*coming*___, Arlene baby," he said to the country road. "I'm ___*going*___ to be with you for

(COME)   (GO)

Christmas."

BASE FORMS	*take*	*make*	*have*	*get*	*reach*	*ride*	*go*	*take*
ING FORMS		*going*			*coming*		*going*	
D-T-N FORMS		*tried*		*had*		*stopped*		*put on*

➡ How many main verb base forms did you find?   8, I hope!

How many main verb *ing* forms did you find?   3, I hope!

How many main verb *d*, *t*, or *n* forms did you find?   4, I hope!

ACTIVITY 24   X-Word and Main Verb Match-Ups #5

Put an X over the X-words in the sentences below. Then use Appendix C (first three columns) to fill in each blank with the correct main verb form. Complete the chart below by putting all of the main verbs into their form groups.

"The Glass Dog"

An accomplished wizard once lived on the top floor of a tenement house and passed his time in

thoughtful study. He possessed all the books and recipes of all the wizards who had X __lived__ before
(LIVE)

him and even X had __invented__ several magic potions himself.
(INVENT)

People X were always __interrupting__ his studies to consult him about their troubles.
(INTERRUPT)

X
There would also __be__ loud knocks from delivery men that were very X __distracting__ .
(BE)   (DISTRACT)

X
These interruptions aroused his anger, and he decided he must __have__ a dog to keep people away
(HAVE)

X
from his door. He didn't __know__ where to find a dog, but in the next room lived a poor glass-
(KNOW)

X
blower who he had __known__ for several years. So, he went into the man's apartment and asked,
(KNOW)

X
"Where can I __find__ a dog?"
(FIND)

"What sort of a dog?" inquired the glass-blower.

X   X
"A good dog. One that will __bark__ at people and will __drive__ them away.
(BARK)   (DRIVE)

X   X   X
One that will __be__ no trouble to keep and won't __expect__ to be fed. One that doesn't
(BE) X   (EXPECT)

X
__have__ fleas and is neat in his habits. One that will __obey__ me when I speak to him.
(HAVE)   (OBEY)

X   X
"Such a dog is hard to find," said the glass-blower who was __making__ a blue flower pot with
(MAKE)

a pink glass rosebush in it.

X
Why can't you __make__ me a dog out of glass?" he asked.
(MAKE)

X   X
"I can," declared the glass-blower, "but it would not __bark__ at people, you know."
(BARK) X

X
"Oh, I'll __fix__ that easily enough," replied the other. "If I could not __make__ a glass dog
(FIX)   (MAKE)

X
bark, I would __be__ a very poor wizard.
(BE)

➡ **more on next page**

_____

Section 2 • X-Words and Main Verbs   131

BASE FORMS	be	have	know	find	bark	drive	be	expect
	have	obey	make	bark	fix		make	be

| ING FORMS | interrupting | | distracting | | making | |

| D-T-N FORMS | lived | | invented | | known | |

➡ How many main verb base forms did you find?   15, I hope!

How many main verb *ing* forms did you find?   3, I hope!

How many main verb *d*, *t*, or *n* forms did you find?   3, I hope!

X-Word and Main Verb Match-Ups #6

Put an X over the X-words in the sentences below. Then use Appendix C (first three columns) to fill in each blank with the correct main verb form. Complete the chart below by putting all the main verbs into their form groups.

After this activity, it will be helpful to give the students a few examples of wrong X-V match-ups and to ask them to correct the mistakes. Examples might be: will eaten, had drive, *and* was wait.

From: ***Red Scarf Girl: A Memoir of the Cultural Revolution***
by Ji Li Jiang, pp. 11–12

Principal Long was ⟨X⟩ _____**reading**_____ a newspaper. She raised her head and peered through her glasses
READ

to see who had ⟨X⟩ _____**interrupted**_____ her. "Principal Long, here is a note from my father." ⟨X⟩ I hurried
INTERRUPT ⟨X⟩

out of the office before she could _____**look**_____ at it or ask me any questions. I ran down the hallway,
LOOK

colliding with someone and running blindly on, thinking only that she must ⟨X⟩ _____**be**_____ very disappointed.
BE

My best friend, An Yi, and our homeroom teacher were ⟨X⟩ _____**standing**_____ outside the main building.
STAND

As soon as they saw me, An Yi shouted, "Where have you ⟨X⟩ _____**been**_____ ? Hurry up! You're ⟨X⟩ _____**going**_____
BE   GO

to be late."

I opened my mouth but couldn't ⟨X⟩ _____**say**_____ a word.
SAY

"I . . . I'm not ⟨X⟩ _____**going**_____ ." I bowed my head and twisted my fingers in my red scarf.
GO

I did not ⟨X⟩ _____**raise**_____ my head. I didn't ⟨X⟩ _____**want**_____ to see An Yi's face.
RAISE   WANT

I tried hard not to cry. Father wouldn't ⟨X⟩ _____**let**_____ me.
LET

BASE FORMS	*look*	*be*	*say*	*raise*	*want*	*let*
***ING* FORMS**	*reading*	*standing*	*going*	*going*		
D-T-N FORMS	*interrupted*	*been*				

➡ How many main verb base forms did you find?   6, I hope!

How many main verb *ing* forms did you find?   4, I hope!

How many main verb *d*, *t*, or *n* forms did you find?   2, I hope!

Hidden X-Words in Main Verbs:
The Powerful X-Word *Does* #1

V/XS
Bob loves Mary.

Where is the X-word? The *s* on the main verb *love* means that the X-word *does* is hiding inside it, ready to do lots of work.

Here is the proof:

Yes/No Question: Does Bob love Mary?

Negative Statement: Bob doesn't love Mary.

Emphatic Statement: Bob does love Mary!

Find the hidden DOES X-word in the sentences below and place a V/XS over it. Then change it to make a YES/NO QUESTION, a NEGATIVE STATEMENT, and an EMPHATIC STATEMENT with an X over the X-word and a V over the main verb. *Both sentences talk about NOW time and about one subject.*

V/XS
The teacher lives in Virginia.

Yes/No Question:	**X** **V** Does the teacher live in Virginia?
Negative Statement:	**X** **V** The teacher doesn't live in Virginia.
Emphatic Statement:	**X** **V** The teacher does live in Virginia!

V/XS
She works at the Maryland School for the Deaf.

Yes/No Question:	*X* *V* *Does she work at the Maryland School for the Deaf?*
Yes/No Question:	*X* *V* *She doesn't work at the Maryland School for the Deaf.*
Emphatic Statement:	*X* *V* *She does work at the Maryland School for the Deaf!*

ACTIVITY 27 Hidden X-Words in Main Verbs: The Powerful X-Word *Does* #2

Here is more practice with the hidden X-word DOES. Find the hidden DOES X-Words in the sentences below and place a V/XS over them. Then change each to make a YES/NO QUESTION, a NEGATIVE STATEMENT, and an EMPHATIC STATEMENT with an X over the X-word and a V over the main verb. The first two sets are done for you. **All sentences talk about NOW time and about 1 subject. The main verbs look like X-words, but they mean *to own something* (have) or *to physically do some action* (do). They are not X-words.**

Explain this concept to students by showing them that in ASL the main verbs are signed, but the X-words are not.

V/XS   (yes, *has* is the main verb here. It means "to own something.")
The boy has a lot of homework.

                        X   **V**
Yes/No Question: Does the boy have a lot of homework?

                        X   **V**
Negative Statement: The boy doesn't have a lot of homework.

                        X   **V**
Emphatic Statement: The boy does have a lot of homework!

V/XS   (yes, *does* is the main verb here. It means "to do something.")
He does his homework in the morning.

                        X   **V**
Yes/No Question: Does he do his homework in the morning?

                        X   **V**
Negative Statement: No, he doesn't do his homework in the morning.

                        X   **V**
Emphatic Statement: He does do his homework in the morning!

V/XS
The dog has an appointment with a vet for an x-ray.

                        X   *V*
Yes/No Question: *Does the dog have an appointment with a vet for an x-ray?*

                      X   *V*
Negative Statement: *The dog doesn't have an appointment with a vet for an x-ray.*

                      X   *V*
Emphatic Statement: *The dog does have an appointment with a vet for an x-ray!*

V/XS
The vet does the x-ray in his office.

                        X   *V*
Yes/No Question: *Does the vet do the x-ray in his office?*

                         X   *V*
Negative Statement: *The vet doesn't do the x-ray in his office.*

                        X   *V*
Emphatic Statement: *The vet does do the x-ray in his office!*

ACTIVITY 28 **Hidden X-Words in Main Verbs:**
The Powerful X-Word *Do* #1

V/XO
Bob and Fred love Mary.

Where is the X-word? No ending on the main verb LOVE means that the X-word DO is hiding inside it. Nothing (O) shows.
Here is the proof:

Yes/No Question: Do Bob and Fred love Mary?

Negative Statement: Bob and Fred don't love Mary.

Emphatic Statement: Bob and Fred do love Mary!

Find the hidden DO X-words in the two sentences below and place a V/XO over them. Then change each to make a YES/NO QUESTION, a NEGATIVE STATEMENT, and an EMPHATIC STATEMENT, with an X over the X-word and a V over the main verb. *Both sentences talk about NOW time and about 2 or many subjects.*

V/XO
The teachers live in Virginia.
                              X   **V**
Yes/No Question: Do the teachers live in Virginia?
                              X   V
Negative Statement: The teachers don't live in Virginia.
                              X   V
Emphatic Statement: The teachers do live in Virginia!

V/XO
They work at the Maryland School for the Deaf.
                         X   *V*
Yes/No Question: *Do they work at the Maryland School for the Deaf?*
                              X   V
Negative: *They don't work at the Maryland School for the Deaf.*
                            X   V
Emphatic Statement: *They do work at the Maryland School for the Deaf!*

ACTIVITY 29 Hidden X-Words in Main Verbs: The Powerful X-Word *Do* #2

Here is more practice with the hidden X-word DO. Find the hidden DO X-words in the sentences below and place a V/XO over them. Then change each to make a YES/NO QUESTION, a NEGATIVE STATEMENT, and an EMPHATIC STATEMENT with an X over the X-word and a V over the main verb. The first two sets are done for you. **All sentences talk about NOW time and about 2 or many subjects. The main verbs look like X-words, but they mean *to own something* (*have*) or *to physically do some action* (*do*). They are not X-words.**

Explain this concept to students by showing them that in ASL the main verbs are signed, but the X-words are not.

V/XO   (*have* is the main verb here. It means "to own something.")
The boys have a lot of homework.

                         X   **V**
Yes/No Question: Do the boys have a lot of homework?

                         X   **V**
Negative Statement: The boys don't have a lot of homework.

                         X   **V**
Emphatic Statement: The boys do have a lot of homework!

V/XO   (*do* is the main verb here. It means "to do something.")
The boys do their homework in the morning.

                         X   **V**
Yes/No Question: Do the boys do their homework in the morning?

                         X   **V**
Negative Statement: The boys don't do their homework in the morning.

                         X   **V**
Emphatic Statement: The boys do do their homework in the morning!

                   V/XO
Some children have problems getting along with their parents.

                       X   *V*
Yes/No Question: *Do some children have problems getting along with the their parents?*

                       X *V*
Negative Statement: *Some children don't have problems getting along with their parents.*

                       X *V*
Emphatic Statement: *Some children do have problems getting along with their parents!*

          V/XO
Parents do their best to raise good kids.

                       X   *V*
Yes/No Question: *Do parents do their best to raise good kids?*

                       X *V*
Negative Statement: *Parents don't do their best to raise good kids.*

                       X *V*
Emphatic Statement: *Parents do do their best to raise good kids!*

ACTIVITY 30 Finding Hidden *Does* and *Do*

Mark every X-word and X-V match as you have done before, but this time look for 9 hidden *does* and 6 hidden *do* X-words. Mark V/XS over the hidden *does* X-words and V/XO over the hidden *do* X-words. If you see the word *to* next to a base-form verb, circle the *to* and the base-form verb and label the circle *INF*, as shown below with *to save*, to mean *infinitive*. Remember to box all your subjects and label all X-V matches. List all V/XS and V/XO in groups. **The passage talks about NOW time and about things that happen in general every day.**

Bob and Mary

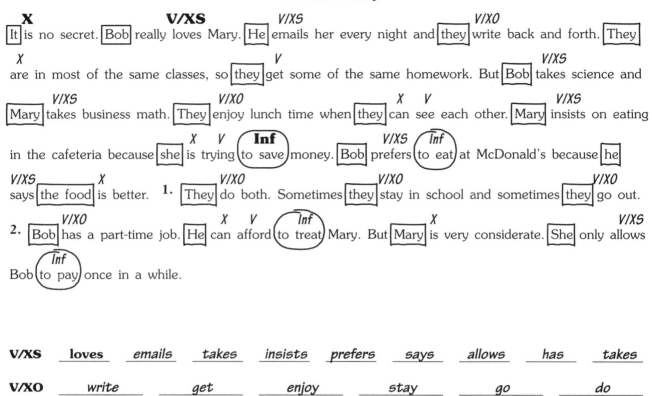

| V/XS | loves | emails | takes | insists | prefers | says | allows | has | takes |
| V/XO | write | | get | enjoy | | stay | go | | do |

➡ **Tricky, tricky, tricky!**

Change sentences 1 and 2 into yes/no questions. Where are the X-words and main verbs? Mark them.

    X   V
1. Do they do both? _____

    X   V
2. Does Bob have a part-time job? _____

Hidden X-Words in Main Verbs:
The Powerful X-Word *Did* #1

V/XD
Bob loved Mary. Where is the X-word?
The *d* on the main verb *love* means that the X-word *did* is hiding inside it.

Here is the proof:

Yes/No Question: Did Bob love Mary?

Negative Statement: Bob didn't love Mary.

Emphatic Statement: Bob did love Mary!

Find the hidden DID X-Words in the two sentences below and place a V/XD over them. Then change each to make a YES/NO QUESTION, a NEGATIVE STATEMENT, and an EMPHATIC STATEMENT, with an X over the X-word and a V over the main verb. All sentences talk about BEFORE time and about one or two subjects.

V/XD
The teacher lived in Virginia.

                   X   **V**
Yes/No Question: Did the teacher live in Virginia?

                           X   **V**
Negative Statement: No, the teacher didn't live in Virginia.

                         X   **V**
Emphatic Statement: The teacher did live in Virginia!

              V/XD
She and a neighbor worked at MSD.

                 X   *V*
Yes/No Question: *Did she and a neighbor work at MSD?*
_____

                        X   *V*
Negative Statement: *She and a neighbor didn't work at MSD.*
_____

                        X   *V*
Emphatic Statement: *She and a neighbor did work at MSD!*
_____

         V/XD
Both of them drove to school together each morning.

                 X   *V*
Yes/No Question: *Did both of them drive to school each morning?*
_____

                     X *V*
Negative Statement: *Both of them didn't drive to school each morning.*
_____

                     X *V*
Emphatic Statement: *Both of them did drive to school each morning!*
_____

Hidden X-Words in Main Verbs: The Powerful X-Word *Did* #2

Here is more practice with the hidden X-word DID. Find the hidden DID X-words in the sentences below and place a V/XD over them. Then change each to make a YES/NO QUESTION, a NEGATIVE STATEMENT, and an EMPHATIC STATEMENT, with an X over the X-word and a V over the main verb. **The main verbs look like X-words, but they mean *to own something (have)* or *to physically do some action (do)*. They are not X-words.**

Explain this concept to students by showing them that in ASL the main verbs are signed, but the X-words are not. All sentences talk about BEFORE time and about one or two subjects.

        V/XD   (*had* is the main verb here. It means "to own something.")
The boy had a lot of homework.
                  X   **V**
Yes/No Question: Did the boy have a lot of homework?
                     X   **V**
Negative Statement: The boy didn't have a lot of homework.
                     X   **V**
Emphatic Statement: The boy did have a lot of homework!

      V/XD   (*Did* is the main verb here. It means "to do something.")
He did his homework in the morning.
                  X   **V**
Yes/No Question: Did he do his homework in the morning?
                   X   **V**
Negative Statement: No, he didn't do his homework in the morning.
                   X   **V**
Emphatic Statement: Yes, he did do his homework in the morning!

        V/XD
The boy and girl had fun cleaning the house.
             X   *V*
Yes/No Question: *Did the boy and girl have fun cleaning the house?*
                  X   *V*
Negative Statement: *The boy and girl didn't have fun cleaning the house.*
                  X   *V*
Emphatic Statement: *The boy and girl did have fun cleaning the house!*

      V/XD
The girl had a lot of washing and ironing.
            X   *V*
Yes/No Question: *Did the girl have a lot of washing and ironing?*
               X   *V*
Negative Statement: *The girl didn't have a lot of washing and ironing.*
               X *V*
Emphatic Statement: *The girl did have a lot of washing and ironing!*

      V/XD
The boy did the cooking.
            X   *V*
Yes/No Question: *Did the boy do the cooking?*
                X *V*
Negative Statement: *The boy didn't do the cooking.*
               X *V*
Emphatic Statement: *The boy did do the cooking!*

Finding Hidden *Did*

Mark every X-word and X-V match as you have done before, but this time look for 10 hidden *did* X-words. Mark V/XD over the hidden *did* X-words. If you see the word *to* next to a *base-form verb*, circle the *to* and the *base-form verb* and label the circle INF, to mean *infinitive*, as shown below with *to smile*. Remember to box all your subjects and label all X-V matches. **List all V/XD in a group. The passage talks about BEFORE time and about completed actions, events, or feelings.**

Bob and Mary

V/XD   X   X

[Bob] met Mary when [they] were in junior high school. [They] were both on the swim team. At first

  V/XD   *V/XD* **Inf**   *V/XD*

[they] just looked at each other, but soon [they] started (to smile) at each other. [It] took Bob a few weeks

(Inf)   (Inf)   *V/XD*   X   (Inf)

(to have) the courage (to ask) Mary out. [They] lived near each other, so [it] wasn't hard for them (to take)

        (Inf)   *V/XD*

the bus to the mall and (to hang) out there for several hours on the weekends. But soon [Bob] needed

         X V   *V/XD*

money for college and [Mary] was getting a lot of homework, so [they] saw less and less of each other

              V/XD

on the weekends during high school. But, [they] saw each other in the hallways and at lunch. **1.** [They]

 V/XD   *V/XD*

also had one class together. **2.** [They] did their homework together too.

V/XD	met	looked	started	took	lived
	needed	saw	saw	had	did

➡ **Tricky, tricky, tricky!**

Change sentences 1 and 2 into yes/no questions. Where are the X-words and main verbs? Mark them.

   X   V
1. *Did they also have one class together?*

   X V
2. *Did they do their homework together too?*

ACTIVITY 34 Finding X-Words, X-Word and Main Verb Match-Ups, and Hidden X-Words #1

Put an X over all the alone X-words, XV over all the X-word main-verb match-ups, and either V/XS, V/XO, or V/XD over all the hidden X-words. The first two sentences are done for you. There are 5 alone X-words, 18 X-word main-verb match-ups, 3 V/XS, 4 V/XO, and 9 V/XD hidden X-words, counting repeats. Circle and label all infinitives INF. List all the X-words and main verbs in groups.

"The Midnight Ride"

V/XD
The midnight ride of Paul Revere happened April 18/April 19, 1775—a long time ago when the king

V/XD   **X**   *X V*
of England ruled this country. There were thousands of English soldiers in Boston. The king had sent

them there (to force)[INF] the people (to obey)[INF] his unjust laws. **V/XD** The soldiers guarded the streets of the town

X V and didn't allow anyone (to come)[INF] in or (to go)[INF] out without their permission. *X V* People would say, "The

V/XS   *V/XS*   *V/XS*
king makes us pay taxes but he gives us nothing in return. He sends soldiers among us (to take)[INF] away

X V (to fight)[INF]   *X*   *X V*
our liberty. We do not wish (to fight) against the king, but we are free men, and he must not send

soldiers (to oppress)[INF] us. We need (to be)[INF] *V/XO* ready (to defend)[INF] ourselves if the soldiers try (to harm)[INF] *V/XO* us."

X   *V/XD*
A group of men were not afraid of the king's soldiers. They camped in Charlestown, a village

X V   *X V*   *V/XD*
near Boston, and from its hills, they could watch what the king's soldiers were doing. The men decided

(to buy)[INF] gun powder and (to store)[INF] it in Concord, a city about 20 miles away, (to protect)[INF] themselves.

X   *X V*
Paul Revere was one of the men who was watching the English soldiers. One day, a friend of his

X V   *V/XD* *V/XD*
who was living in Boston secretly left and came (to see)[INF] him in Charlestown. He said, "I have something

(to tell)[INF] you. *X V* Some of the king's soldiers are going to Concord (to get)[INF] the gun powder. *X V* They are getting

ready (to start)[INF] tonight."

X V   *X V X V*
"Indeed!" said Paul Revere. "They'll get no gun powder if I can help it. I'll summon all the

farmers between Charlestown and Concord (to get)[INF] their guns and axes (to stand)[INF] up to the redcoats.

X V
You'll hang a lantern in the tower of the Old North Church in Boston if the soldiers are starting out

V/XO   *X V*
by land. If they cross the Charles River, you'll hang two lanterns."

➡️ **more on next page**

ACTIVITY 34   *(continued from page 142)*

                                                                        V/XD
And with the second light from the second lantern, Paul Revere knew which way the soldiers

  X   V   X   *Inf*
were heading. He was ready (to alert) the farmers.

Alone X-Words	were	are	were	was	was
X-V Matches	had sent	didn't allow	would say	do (not) wish	must (not) send
	could watch	were doing	was watching	was living	are going
	are getting	will get	can help	will summon	will hang
	are starting		will hang	were heading	
V/XS	makes		gives		sends
V/XO	need	try	have	cross	
V/XD	happened	ruled	guarded	camped	decided
	left	came	said	knew	

ACTIVITY 35 Finding X-Words, X-Word and Main Verb Match-Ups, and Hidden X-Words #2

Put an X over all the alone X-words, XV over all the X-word main-verb match-ups, and either V/XS, V/XO, or V/XD over all the hidden X-words. The first two sentences are done for you. There are 8 alone X-words, 15 X-word main-verb match-ups, 2 V/XS, 6 V/XO, and 27 V/XD hidden X-words, counting repeats. Circle and label all infinitives INF. List all the X-words and main verbs in groups.

"The Story of a Great Story"

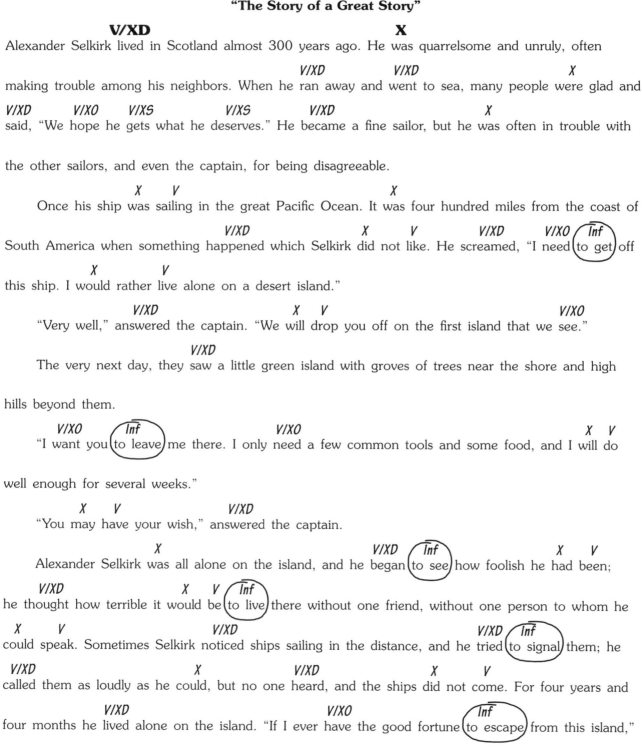

V/XD   **X**
Alexander Selkirk lived in Scotland almost 300 years ago. He was quarrelsome and unruly, often

                              V/XD   *V/XD*   *X*
making trouble among his neighbors. When he ran away and went to sea, many people were glad and

V/XD   *V/XO*   *V/XS*   *V/XS*   *V/XD*   *X*
said, "We hope he gets what he deserves." He became a fine sailor, but he was often in trouble with

the other sailors, and even the captain, for being disagreeable.

                  X   *V*   *X*
Once his ship was sailing in the great Pacific Ocean. It was four hundred miles from the coast of

                      V/XD   *X*   *V*   *V/XD*   *V/XO* Inf
South America when something happened which Selkirk did not like. He screamed, "I need (to get) off

        X   *V*
this ship. I would rather live alone on a desert island."

            V/XD   *X*   *V*   *V/XO*
"Very well," answered the captain. "We will drop you off on the first island that we see."

            V/XD
The very next day, they saw a little green island with groves of trees near the shore and high

hills beyond them.

    V/XO   Inf   *V/XO*   *X* *V*
"I want you (to leave) me there. I only need a few common tools and some food, and I will do

well enough for several weeks."

        X   *V*   *V/XD*
"You may have your wish," answered the captain.

           X   *V/XD* Inf   *X* *V*
Alexander Selkirk was all alone on the island, and he began (to see) how foolish he had been;

V/XD   *X* *V* Inf
he thought how terrible it would be (to live) there without one friend, without one person to whom he

X   *V*   *V/XD*   *V/XD* Inf
could speak. Sometimes Selkirk noticed ships sailing in the distance, and he tried (to signal) them; he

V/XD   *X*   *V/XD*   *X*   *V*
called them as loudly as he could, but no one heard, and the ships did not come. For four years and

          V/XD   *V/XO*   Inf
four months he lived alone on the island. "If I ever have the good fortune (to escape) from this island,"

➡ **more on next page**

V/XD   *X*   *V*   *X*   *V*   (Inf)

he said, "I will be kind and considerate to everyone. I will try (to make) friends instead of enemies."

              V/XD   *V/XD*   *V/XD*

Then to his great joy, a ship came nearer and anchored in the little harbor. He explained who he

X   *V/XD*   (Inf)   *V/XD*

was, and the captain willingly agreed (to take) him back to his own country. When he reached Scotland,

         X   (Inf)   *V/XD*

everybody was eager (to hear) about his adventures, and he soon found himself famous. A writer in

     V/XD   *X*   *V*   *V/XD*   *X*   *V*

England heard how Selkirk had lived alone on an island and decided it would make a wonderful story. He

V/XD

called his story, "The Adventures of Robinson Crusoe" and almost every child has read this famous story.

Alone X-Words	*was*	*were*	*was*	*was*	*was*
		could		*was*	*was*
X-V Matches	*was sailing*	*did (not) like*	*would (rather) live*	*will drop*	*will do*
	may have	*had been*	*would be*	*could speak*	*did (not) come*
	will be	*will try*	*had lived*	*would make*	*has read*
V/XS		*Gets*		*Deserves*	
V/XO	*hope*	*need*	*see*	*want*	*need*
		have			
V/XD	*lived*	*ran*	*went*	*said*	*became*
	happened	*screamed*	*answered*	*saw*	*answered*
	began	*thought*	*noticed*	*tried*	*called*
	heard	*lived*	*said*	*came*	*anchored*
	explained	*agreed*	*reached*	*found*	*heard*
		decided		*called*	

Edit the following sentences using the correction symbols on the right of each sentence to help you find the errors. *The sentences were written by students.*

1. Shira is looked for her dog.   **XV**
       X V
   Shira is looking for her dog. _____

2. All week Cubby was so upset in school. He fights with his friends.   **V/XD**
                V/XD
   All week Cubby was so upset in school. He fought with his friends. _____

   _____

3. Also I'm begun to thinking about her.   **XV INF**
       X   V   Inf
   Also I'm beginning to think about her. _____

4. Many people love it there. Plus, they has skiing too.   **V/XO**
                V/XO
   Many people love it there. Plus, they have skiing too. _____

5. He had a lot of hard work in Vietnam. He has a lot of jobs, and he survives it all. **V/XD V/XD**
               V/XD   *V/XD*
   He had a lot of hard work in Vietnam. He had a lot of jobs, and he survived it all. ___

   _____

6. He just like to takes some risks.   **V/XS INF**
         V/XS   *Inf*
   He just likes to take some risks. _____

7. My heart was beaten rapidly.   **XV**
          X   V
   My heart was beating rapidly. _____

8. Dr. Cuss did hitted a man's sleeve, but there no arm. But, did felt something. **XV X? S? XV**
       X V   *X*   *S X V*
   Dr. Cuss did hit a man's sleeve, but there was no arm. But, he did feel something. ___

   _____

Edit the following sentences using the correction symbols on the right of each sentence to help you find the errors.

Explain that the excerpt is part of a story. Have the students read through the excerpt before they begin correcting the mistakes.

Adapted from ***Charlotte's Web***
by E. B. White, pp. 5–7

1. Fern couldn't ate until her pig had some milk.   **XV**

          X   *V*
   Fern couldn't eat until her pig had some milk.

2. Mrs. Arable finds a baby's bottle and a rubber nipple.   **V/XD**

                 V/XD
   Mrs. Arable found a baby's bottle and a rubber nipple.

3. Fern taught the pig to sucking from the bottle.   **INF**

                 Inf
   Fern taught the pig to suck from the bottle.

4. The pig have a good appetite.   **V/XD**

         V/XD
   The pig had a good appetite.

5. The school bus was arriving.   **V/XD**

              V/XD
   The school bus arrived.

6. Fern is thinking about a name for her pig.   **Time**

        TIME
   Fern was thinking about a name for her pig.

7. She didn't noticed the children on the bus.   **XV**

         X   *V*
   She didn't notice the children on the bus.

8. "I will named my pig Wilbur," said Fern.   **XV**

      X   *V*
   "I will name my pig Wilbur," said Fern.

9. "Do you had a pig?" asked a child on the bus.   **XV**

      X   *V*
   "Do you have a pig?" asked a child on the bus.

10. "Yes, I did have a pig," said Fern.   **Time**

         TIME
    "Yes, I do have a pig," said Fern.

▶ **more on next page**

11. "Why did you picked Wilbur for a name?" asked the child.   **XV**

      X   V
   "Why did you pick Wilbur for a name?" asked the child.
___

12. "I liked the name Wilbur," said Fern.   **V/XO**

    V/XO
   "I like the name Wilbur," said Fern.
___

13. "It make the pig more human."   **V/XS**

     V/XS
   "It makes the pig more human.
___

14. "I takes care of it, and I feeds it everyday."   **V/XO V/XO**

   V/XO   *V/XO*
   "I take care of it, and I feed it everyday."
___

15. "Where the pig sleep?" asked the child.   **X?**

      X
   "Where does the pig sleep?" asked the child.
___

16. "The pig sleep in the barn," says Fern.   **V/XS V/XD**

     V/XS   *V/XD*
   "The pig sleeps in the barn," said Fern.
___

ACTIVITY 38 **Practice Editing III**

Edit the following sentences using the correction symbols on the right of each sentence to help you find the errors.

From **"Let's Trade"** in *Reading for Concepts, Book A*, p. 38

1. Long ago, people had to getting what they want by trading.   **INF V/XD**

          Inf   *V/XD*
   Long ago, people had to get what they wanted by trading.

2. Some people farm the land.   **V/XD**

          V/XD
   Some people farmed the land.

3. Other people make tools.   **V/XD**

          V/XD
   Other people made tools.

4. People trade tools for food.   **V/XD**

       V/XD
   People traded tools for food.

5. If people had too much meat, they could traded it for corn.   **XV**

                    X   V
   If people had too much meat, they could trade it for corn.

6. Many people want beautiful things.   **V/XD**

          V/XD
   Many people wanted beautiful things.

7. A farmer would trades milk for a piece of beautiful cloth.   **XV**

         X   V
   A farmer would trade milk for a piece of beautiful cloth.

8. Even today we traded with one another.   **V/XO**

          V/XO
   Even today we trade with one another.

9. When you buy candy, did you pay for it with bear fat?   **Time**

            TIME
   When you buy candy, do you pay for it with bear fat?

10. Of course not! You used money.   **V/XO**

          V/XO
    Of course not! You use money.

➡ **more on next page**

11. But you are still trade.   **XV**

              X   *V*

But you are still trading.
_____

12. You were still giving one thing for another.   **Time**

      TIME

You are still giving one thing for another.
_____

Practice Editing IV

Edit the following sentences using the correction symbols on the right of each sentence to help you find the errors.

Adapted from **"What Is It Worth?"** in *New Practice Readers: Book B*
by Donald G. Anderson, pp. 118–119

1. As you know, at one time, different countries use different measures. **V/XD**

   V/XD
   As you know, at one time, different countries used different measures.

2. But even inside the same country, measures was not always the same. **SX**

   S   X
   But even inside the same country, measures were not always the same.

3. When America was very young, each colony has its own money. **V/XD**

   V/XD
   When America was very young, each colony had its own money.

4. The coins did not had the same worth. **XV**

   X   V
   The coins did not have the same worth.

5. Other money comes from countries such as Spain, France and Portugal. **V/XD**

   V/XD
   Other money came from countries such as Spain, France and Portugal.

6. People become confused. **V/XD**

   V/XD
   People became confused.

7. They would bought things. **XV**

   X   V
   They would buy things.

8. But they can not be sure if they have their money's worth. **Time V/XD**

   TIME   V/XD
   But they could not be sure if they had their money's worth.

9. Then, one of our first presidents, Thomas Jefferson, thinks of a good plan. **V/XD**

   V/XD
   Then, one of our first presidents, Thomas Jefferson, thought of a good plan.

10. He was started the dollar system. **X**

    X
    He started the dollar system.

➡ **more on next page**

11. People learned count by tens.   **INF**

    Inf
    People learned to count by tens. _____

12. Ten cents make a dime. Ten dimes make a dollar.   **V/XD   V/XD**

        V/XD   *V/XD*
    Ten cents made a dime. Ten dimes made a dollar. _____

13. Today, we still used Jefferson's plan.   **V/XO**

          V/XO
    Today, we still use Jefferson's plan. _____

Editing for X-Words, Verbs, and Infinitives

Explain that the excerpt is part of a story about a weird schoolteacher who takes her class on odd types of trips. Have the students read through the excerpt before they begin correcting the mistakes.

Adapted from ***The Magic School Bus at the Waterworks***
by Joanna Cole and Bruce Degen, pp. 7–16

1. Our class really have bad luck.	**V/XS**
2. We gotten Ms. Frizzle, the strangest teacher in school.	**V/XD**
3. Ms. Frizzle make us grow green mold on old pieces of bread.	**V/XS**
4. Other classes went on trips to the zoo.	**V/XO**
5. We are go to the WATERWORKS!!	**XV**
6. Ms. Frizzle forces us to spend a whole month in the library.	**V/XD**
7. We were collected ten interesting facts about water.	~~**X**~~
8. The old school bus is waiting for us.	**Time**
9. It looks a lot different.	**V/XD**
10. All the students wearing scuba diving clothes.	**X?**
11. Ms. Frizzle didn't seeming to noticing.	**XV INF**
12. She just drives on.	**V/XD**
13. Then, Ms. Frizzle does the weirdest thing ever.	**V/XD**
14. She tells everyone to getting out of the bus.	**V/XD INF**
15. The kids didn't wants to going.	**XV INF**
16. Frizzie says she would giving more homework.	**V/XD XV**
17. Mountains was down there!!	**SX**

Edit the following sentences, using the corrections symbol or symbols to the right of each sentence to help you find the errors.

Adapted from ***The Magic School Bus at the Waterworks***
by Joanna Cole and Bruce Degen, pp. 7–16

1. Our class really *has* have bad luck.   **V/XS**

2. We *got* gotten Ms. Frizzle, the strangest teacher in school.   **V/XD**

3. Ms. Frizzle *makes* make us grow green mold on old pieces of bread.   **V/XS**

4. Other classes went *go* on trips to the zoo.   **V/XO**

5. We are *going* go to the WATERWORKS!!   **XV**

6. Ms. Frizzle *forced* forces us to spend a whole month in the library.   **V/XD**

7. We ~~were~~ collected ten interesting facts about water.   ~~**X**~~

8. The old school bus *was* is waiting for us.   **Time**

9. It *looked* looks a lot different.   **V/XD**

10. All the students *were* ∧ wearing scuba diving clothes.   **X?**

11. Ms. Frizzle didn't *seem* seeming to *notice* noticing.   **XV INF**

12. She just *drove* drives on.   **V/XD**

13. Then, Ms. Frizzle *did* does the weirdest thing ever.   **V/XD**

14. She *told* tells everyone to *get* getting out of the bus.   **V/XD INF**

15. The kids didn't *want* wants to *go* going.   **XV INF**

16. Frizzie *said* says she would *give* giving more homework.   **V/XD XV**

17. Mountains *were* was down there!!   **SX**

Section 3

- **Sentence Patterns**
- **Editing Practice**

Key teaching points:

Trunks are basic sentences to which other trunks or sentence parts can be added.

How they are added determines punctuation.

ACTIVITY 40 Review of Changing Statements into Yes/No Questions

Change each of the following statements into YES/NO questions. Label the statements and questions as shown.
Remember: If you see an X-word, move it in front of the subject. If you do not see an X-word, it is hidden. Pull the hidden X-word (either *does*, *do*, or *did*) out of its main verb and move it in front of the subject too.

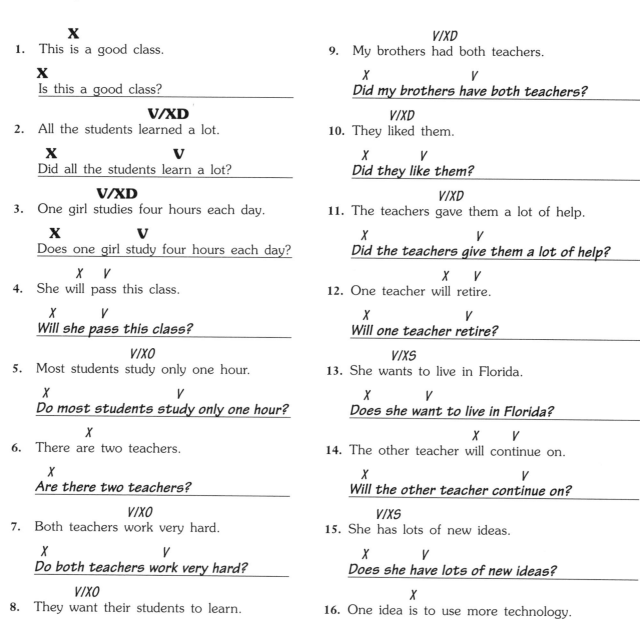

      X
1. This is a good class.

      X
Is this a good class?

          V/XD
2. All the students learned a lot.

      X   **V**
Did all the students learn a lot?

          V/XD
3. One girl studies four hours each day.

      X   **V**
Does one girl study four hours each day?

      X *V*
4. She will pass this class.

    X   *V*
Will she pass this class?

        V/XO
5. Most students study only one hour.

  X   *V*
Do most students study only one hour?

        X
6. There are two teachers.

    X
Are there two teachers?

        V/XO
7. Both teachers work very hard.

  X   *V*
Do both teachers work very hard?

        V/XO
8. They want their students to learn.

  X   *V*
Do they want their students to learn?

      V/XD
9. My brothers had both teachers.

    X   *V*
Did my brothers have both teachers?

      V/XD
10. They liked them.

   X   *V*
Did they like them?

       V/XD
11. The teachers gave them a lot of help.

   X   *V*
Did the teachers give them a lot of help?

        X *V*
12. One teacher will retire.

   X   *V*
Will one teacher retire?

      V/XS
13. She wants to live in Florida.

   X   *V*
Does she want to live in Florida?

          X *V*
14. The other teacher will continue on.

   X   *V*
Will the other teacher continue on?

      V/XS
15. She has lots of new ideas.

   X   *V*
Does she have lots of new ideas?

          X
16. One idea is to use more technology.

  X
Is one idea to use more technology?

ACTIVITY 41　**What Is a Trunk?**

A trunk is a basic English sentence—a sentence without any "extras"—like one that tells when or why. It is a subject and a predicate with only one main verb. It can easily turn into a yes/no question. Make trunks by matching the subjects (on the left) with the predicates (on the right) that make sense. Start each trunk with a capital letter and end with a period. Use the lines below to write your trunks.

TRUNK

SUBJECT	PREDICATE
The Maryland School for the Deaf	freezes at 32 degrees Fahrenheit
Washington, D.C.	are the Yankees and the Mets
Serious students	is impossible to read in the dark
There	can be fun
Water	is the capital of the United States
It	are a billion people living in China
Learning to cook	has two campuses
The two New York baseball teams	are in middle school
Sixth, seventh, and eighth graders	always come to class on time

TRUNK

1. The Maryland School for the Deaf has two campuses.

2. Washington, D.C., is the capital of the United States.

3. Serious students always come to class on time.

4. There are a billion people living in China.

5. Water freezes at 32 degrees Fahrenheit.

6. It is impossible to read in the dark.

7. Learning to cook can be fun.

8. The two New York baseball teams are the Yankees and the Mets.

9. Sixth, seventh, and eighth graders are in middle school.

ACTIVITY 42 Changing Trunks into Yes/No Questions

In your mind, change trunks 1–9 in activity 41 into yes/no questions. Did it work? Now write 5 of your own trunks below and change each to a yes/no question. *Answers will vary.*

1. _____

_____

2. _____

_____

3. _____

_____

4. _____

_____

5. _____

_____

➡ Did each trunk turn into a yes/no question?

ACTIVITY 43 Joining Trunks: T, + T with *and*

Join the following trunks with the joiner word *and*. Make sure each trunk can turn into a yes/no question. You'll need a comma before the joiner word. Label each sentence T, + T as shown. Write Ts over the verbs or X-words in the sentences.

1. Peter and Sue wanted to buy a car.
    They wanted to buy one quickly.

         T   **,** **+**   **T**
    Peter and Sue wanted to buy a car, and they wanted to buy one quickly.

2. They read the ads in newspapers.
    They looked in showrooms.

      T   *, +*   *T*
    They read the ads in newspapers, and they looked in showrooms.

3. Peter asked his friends at work.
    Sue posted a sign in their apartment building.

       T   *, +*   *T*
    Peter asked his friends at work, and Sue posted a sign in their apartment building.

4. Peter received no responses at work.
    No one responded to Sue's sign.

       T   *, +*   *T*
    Peter received no response at work, and no one responded to Sue's sign.

5. They saw a car with a "For Sale" sign in its window.
    They asked the owner how much the car cost.

      T   *, +*   *T*
    They saw a car with a "For Sale" sign in its window, and they asked the owner how

    much the car cost.

6. The car was pretty new.
    It was the right price. Sold!

      T   *, +*   *T*
    The car was pretty new, and it was the right price. Sold!

➡️ In a T, + T pattern, the joiner word *and* can be replaced with a semi-colon as seen below.

Peter and Sue wanted to buy a car, and they wanted to buy one quickly.

Peter and Sue wanted to buy a car; they wanted to buy one quickly.

ACTIVITY 44 **Joining Trunks: T, + T with *but***

But shows contrasting ideas between two trunks. Join a trunk from the left with a trunk from the right that makes sense, using the joiner word *but*. Make sure each trunk can turn into a yes/no question. You'll need a comma before the joiner word. Write 7 good sentences in the blanks below. Label each sentence T, + T as shown.

T	**T**
I studied hard	people call me Susan
Computers are remarkable	she was able to find her keys quickly
The driver wasn't hurt	it felt more like summer
The room was a mess	the homework was still due
My real name is Sue	the car was destroyed
It was winter	I failed anyway
The teacher was absent	they can't think for people

        T   , +   T

1. I studied hard, but I failed anyway.

          T   , +   T

2. Computers are remarkable, but they can't think for people.

          T   , +   T

3. The driver wasn't hurt, but the car was destroyed.

          T   , +   T

4. The room was a mess, but she was able to find her keys quickly.

          T   , +   T

5. My real name is Sue, but people call me Susan.

        T   , + T

6. It was winter, but it felt more like summer.

          T   , +   T

7. The teacher was absent, but the homework was still due.

ACTIVITY 45   **Joining Trunks: T, + T with *so***

So shows the result or effect of a first trunk. Join a first trunk from the left with a result or effect trunk from the right that makes sense, using the joiner word *so*. Make sure each trunk can turn into a yes/no question. You'll need a comma before the joiner word. Write 7 good sentences in the blanks below. Label each sentence T, + T as shown.

T	**T**
The teacher caught the students cheating	she stayed up all night reading it
The airplane tickets were too expensive	they decided to stay indoors
The books were overdue	they decided to drive
Peter and Sue love warm weather	she called their parents
Olivia was gaining too much weight	we returned them to the library
The snow fell at the rate of one inch per hour	she threw out the ice cream
The book was incredibly interesting	they bought a home in Florida

        T   **, +**   **T**

1. The teacher caught the students cheating, so she called their parents.

        T   *, +*   *T*

2. *The airplane tickets were too expensive, so they decided to drive.*

     T   *, +*   *T*

3. *The books were overdue, so we returned them to the library.*

      T   *, +*   *T*

4. *Peter and Sue love warm weather, so they bought a home in Florida.*

    T   *, +*   *T*

5. *Olivia was gaining too much weight, so she threw out the ice cream.*

     T   *, +* *T*

6. *The snow fell at the rate of one inch per hour, so they stayed indoors.*

    T   *, +* *T*

7. *The book was incredibly interesting, so they stayed up all night reading it.*

ACTIVITY 46 **Joining Trunks: T, + T with *or***

Or trunks talk about an additional choice from a first trunk. Join a first trunk from the left with a different choice or result trunk from the right that makes sense, using the joiner word *or*. Make sure each trunk can turn into a yes/no question. You'll need a comma before the joiner word. Write 7 good sentences in the blanks below. Label each sentence T, + T as shown.

T	**T**
We'll go to the theater	it will receive an F
They'll fly to Las Vegas	you'll get a headache later
The essay needs to be rewritten	they'll go by train
She'll work in the city as a dog walker	he'll wait until the spring
He'll play soccer in the fall	she'll work at the beach as a babysitter
He'll either go to the movies	he'll go to the bowling alley
You should eat something now	we'll go bowling

         T   **, + T**

1. We'll go to the theater, or we'll go bowling.

       T   *, +*   *T*

2. They'll fly to Las Vegas, or they'll go by train.

        T   *, +*   *T*

3. The essay needs to be rewritten, or it will receive an F.

      T   *, +*   *T*

4. She'll work in the city as a dog walker, or she'll work at the beach as a babysitter.

      T   *, +*   *T*

5. He'll play soccer in the fall, or he'll wait until spring.

      T   *, +*   *T*

6. He'll either go to the movies, or he'll go to the bowling alley.

       T   *, +*   *T*

7. You should eat something now, or you'll get a headache later.

ACTIVITY 47 **Practice with Joiners**

Join each pair of trunks with a comma and the joiner that makes most sense. Choose *AND, BUT, SO,* or *OR.* Label each T, + T.

After this activity, it will be helpful to ask students to create their own T,+T sentences using each of the joiners. Have them label all sentences as seen below.

1. I prepared the dinner.
   Peter cleaned up after it.

        T   **, +**   **T**
   I prepared the dinner, and Peter cleaned up after it.

2. We invited them to come.
   They had other things to do.

         T   *, +*   *T*
   We invited them to come, but they had other things to do.

3. My husband was sick.
   We decided not to go to the party.

         T   *, +*   *T*
   My husband was sick, so we decided not to go to the party.

4. You'll need to cover the candy.
   The ants won't crawl all over it.

      T   *, +*   *T*
   You'll need to cover the candy, so the ants won't crawl all over it.

5. We were hungry.
   We bought some food.

      T   *, +*   *T*
   We were hungry, so we bought some food.

6. The dog needs to go out.
   It will do something on the rug.

      T   *, +*   *T*
   The dog needs to go out, or it will do something on the rug.

7. Living in a dorm is fun.
   It's a great way to make friends.

       T *, +* *T*
   Living in a dorm is fun, and it's a great way to make friends.

8. Students need to read 100 pages a week.
   Their vocabulary will not improve.

       T   *, +*   *T*
   Students need to read 100 pages a week, or their vocabulary will not improve.

ACTIVITY 48   **One Trunk with Two Predicates: T =**

Here are some T, +T patterns from activities 43–46 where the subjects of each trunk are the same.

In this new pattern, call the students' attention to the verb or X-word that follows the joiner word. If these words are nouns or adjectives, the pattern will not be T=. It will most likely be T, as in She ate a hamburger and French fries for lunch *or* The book was interesting, informative, and very helpful to me.

T, + T   *They* read the ads in newspapers, and *they* looked in showrooms.

T, + T   *The car* was pretty new, and *it* was the right price.

T, + T   *I* studied hard, but *I* failed anyway.

T, + T   *It* was winter, but *it* felt more like summer.

T, + T   *The essay* needs to be rewritten, or *it* will receive an F.

If the subjects of two trunks are the same, you can drop the second subject and the comma. Then you have a T = pattern! T = patterns start with a verb or X-word after *and*, *but*, *so*, and *or*.

T =   They read the ads in the newspapers and looked in showrooms.

T =   The car was pretty new and was the right price.

T =   I studied hard but failed anyway.

T =   It was winter but felt more like summer.

T =   The essay needs to be rewritten or will receive an F.

Change the following T, + T patterns into T = patterns:

T, + T   The girl took the pencil, and she put it in a drawer.

T =   The girl took the pencil and put it in a drawer.

T, + T   Michael was a good friend, but he was sometimes dishonest.

T =   *Michael was a good friend but was sometimes dishonest.*

T, + T   Jerry turned off the lights, but he couldn't fall asleep for a while.

T =   *Jerry turned off the lights but couldn't fall asleep for a while.*

T, + T   She wasn't feeling well, so she decided to leave.

T =   *She wasn't feeling well so decided to leave.*

ACTIVITY 49 One Trunk with Three (or more) Predicates Joined by *and*

Trunks with three or more predicates joined by *and* need commas to separate all predicates:

The young mother fed the baby, washed the dishes, and went to bed.
He gets up *every* morning, brushes his teeth, washes his face, eats breakfast, and goes to work.
I come home, watch some television, eat a snack, and do my homework.

Combine the groups of sentences below into *one sentence each* using the pattern T =.

1. The two women borrowed money.   They rented an office.   They started their own business.

   The two women borrowed money, rented an office, and started their own business.

2. The two friends shopped for clothes.
   They ate lunch out.
   They took the subway home.

   The two friends shopped for clothes, ate lunch out, and took the subway home.

3. The students got the notes for the final exam.
   They set up study groups.
   They passed the course.

   The students got the notes for the final exam, set up study groups, and passed the course.

4. The teacher entered the room.   She opened her bag.   She passed out the test.

   The teacher entered the room, opened her bag, and passed out the test.

5. She had a headache.
   She felt ill.
   She fainted.

   She had a headache, felt ill, and fainted.

6. He was late for class.
   He missed his presentation.
   He realized he would fail the assignment.

   He was late for class, missed his presentation, and realized he would fail the assignment.

Practice with T, + T and T =

Can you identify the sentence patterns below? Use T for a single trunk, T, +T for two trunks combined with a joiner word, and T= for one trunk with two or more predicates.

    T   It was the first snow of the season.

    T =   It started early in the morning and continued through the night.

   T, + T   It was supposed to stop at 3 a.m., but it continued on until the morning.

    T =   Sarah woke up and wondered if her school would be closed.

    T   There hadn't been a snow day for a long, long time.

    T   The last one was seven years before.

    T =   She was in kindergarten and remembered the day.

    T =   She and her mom baked cookies in the morning, took a nap in the afternoon, and did some coloring in the evening.

   T, + T She was older now, so she wanted to spend the day with her friends.

    T =   She wanted to videophone them but realized that the telephone lines were down.

    T   That meant no email as well.

    T =   She turned on the television and read the captions about school closings.

    T   It was her lucky day!

    T   All schools in the county were closed!

    T =   She got washed, got dressed, and thought about walking to her friend's house.

   T, + T She tried to open the front door, but it would not budge.

    T   The snow outside was up to the door knob!

    T =   She closed the door and went upstairs to tell her mom.

    T   They decided to bake cookies.

    T   It was the perfect snow-day activity!

Sentence Combining with T, + T and T =

Combine the groups of sentences below into *one sentence each* using the patterns T, + T or T =. Watch out for capitals, periods, and commas.

"My Dog Twister"

1. I have a black Labrador retriever.
   Her name is Twister.

   I have a black Labrador retriever, and her name is Twister.

2. She was trained to assist blind people.
   She failed the final test.

   She was trained to assist blind people, but she failed the final test.

   She was trained to assist blind people but failed the final test.

3. She is not very friendly with other dogs.
   She loves people.

   She is not friendly with other dogs, but she loves people.

   She is not friendly with other dogs but loves people.

4. She has jet black fur.
   She has white around her paws.
   She has grey around her mouth.

   She has jet black fur, has white around her paws, and has grey around her mouth.

5. She knows commands such as sit, stay, down, and come.
   She likes doing them.

   She knows commands such as sit, stay, down, and come, and she likes doing them.

   She knows commands such as sit, stay, down, and come, and likes doing them.

6. She is never more than two inches away from me.
   I have to be careful not to step on her.

   She is never more than two inches away from me, so I have to be careful not to step on her.

ACTIVITY 52   **Linkers and Trunks (LT)**

A linker connects the meaning of the sentence it begins with the meaning of the sentence before it. Let's see how some authors use linkers.

Explain the meaning of this passage to the students, making sure they understand the context for the use of the linkers. Additional linkers are listed in activity 53 and in Appendix D.

"The Hotel Owner's Mistake"

Some men were sitting by the door of a hotel in Baltimore. As they looked all the way down the street, they saw a farmer on horseback riding toward the hotel. He was riding very slowly, and both he and his horse were covered with mud. *Finally*, the farmer arrived at the hotel.

"Do you have a room here for me?" he asked the hotel owner.

Now the owner prided himself upon keeping a first-class hotel, and he feared that his guests would not like the rough-looking farmer. So, he answered, "No, sir. Every room is full. *However*, the only place I could put you would be in the barn."

"Well, *first*," answered the stranger, "I will see if there are empty rooms at the Planters' Tavern around the corner," and he rode away.

Later on, a well-dressed gentleman came into the hotel and said, "I wish to see Mr. Thomas Jefferson."

"Mr. Jefferson?" asked the owner, "the Vice President of the United States?"

"Yes," said the gentleman. "I met him as he rode into town, and he said that he intended to stop at this hotel."

"I turned Mr. Jefferson away because he was covered in mud. What an idiot I was! *Now*, I must run over to Planters' Tavern and bring him back."

So, he went to the other hotel, where he found the vice president sitting with some friends in the lobby. "Mr. Jefferson," he said, "I have come to ask your pardon. I thought you were some old farmer. Come back to my hotel, and I will give you the best room in the house."

"No," said Mr. Jefferson. "A farmer is as good as any other man. *Therefore*, if there is no room for a farmer, there can be no room for me."

ACTIVITY 53 Other Linkers and What They Mean

Note that linkers begin with a capital letter and are followed by a comma.

Linkers that mean AND:

               L   **T**

She likes to dance, sew, and skate. *In addition*, she enjoys working in the garden.

Linkers that mean BUT:

           L   **T**

He is allergic to chocolate. *However*, he continues to eat it.
                           Still,

Linkers that mean SO:

               L   **T**

They are missing three assignments. *As a result*, they may not go to the dance.
                         Therefore,

Linkers that mean DIFFERENT WAY:

                           L   **T**

The project required a lot of time, money, and energy. *On the other hand*, it was an excellent

learning experience.

Linkers that EXPLAIN:

               L   **T**

Fat-free foods are not free of calories. *In other words*, you can gain weight eating them.

Linkers that ADD ADDITIONAL DETAIL:

               L   **T**

She did very well in school this term. *In fact*, she got all As.
                     Actually,

ACTIVITY 54 **Practice with Linkers**

Which linker would make *the most* sense in the pairs of sentences below? Rewrite them with the linker. Use Appendix D to help you. Watch your periods, capitals, and commas. Label the linker *L* and the trunk *T*.

1. She struggled with the assignment. She got it!

                                      L   **T**
    She struggled with the assignment. Finally, she got it!

2. He passed the test. He got the highest grade.

                          L   *T*
    He passed the test. In fact, he got the highest grade.

3. She likes to read, cook, and swim. She likes to watch old-time movies.

                                         L   *T*
    She likes to read, cook, and swim. In addition, she likes to watch old-time movies.

4. They like to camp out. They don't like to shower outdoors.

                         L   *T*
    They like to camp out. However, they don't like to shower outdoors.

5. He never read the assigned books. He failed the class.

                                 L   *T*
    He never read the assigned books. Therefore, he failed the class.

6. They decided not to go to the mall. They went to the gym.

                               L   *T*
    They decided not to go to the mall. Instead, they went to the gym.

7. They didn't enjoy staying in the house all day. They got a lot of chores done.

                                          L   *T*
    They didn't enjoy staying in the house all day. However, they got a lot of chores done.

8. The spaghetti sauce was delicious. It was the best they had ever eaten.

                                 L   *T*
    The spaghetti sauce was delicious. In fact, it was the best they had ever eaten.

9. She was told that she was late to work too many times and that the job would be given to someone else. She was fired.

    She was told that she was late to work too many times and that the job would be given
                          L   *T*
    to someone else. As a result, she was fired.

ACTIVITY 55 Practice Editing for Sentence Patterns I

Errors in sentence patterns below are marked with correction symbols in the right margin. Correct the sentences just for the sentence patterns based on the correction symbols.

1. We started to trust each other, expressed our secret personalities.　　　　**T=**

    We started to trust each other *and* expressed our secret personalities.

2. Interpreters did not show up. However, mainstream classes did not help me to improve.　　**T LT**

    Interpreters did not show up. *Therefore*, mainstream classes did not help me to improve.

3. An interpreter explained why she was absent, I still did not understand.　　**T, +T**

    An interpreter explained why she was absent, but I still did not understand.

4. He had to know what he was supposed to do during the war. He went to boot camp to train for it.　　**T, +T**

    He had to know what he was supposed to do during the war, so he went to boot

    camp to train for it.

5. He finished training in San Diego, California. He went and got on an air force plane to go to Vietnam.　　**T LT=**

    He finished training in San Diego, California. Then, he went and got on an air force

    plane to go to Vietnam.

6. We decided to ask him questions, we interviewed him.　　**T, +T**

    We decided to ask him questions, so we interviewed him.

7. Gino wagged his tail, and brought his toys to Tarlie, she smiled and played with him.　　**T= T=**

    Gino wagged his tail and brought his toys to Tarlie. She smiled and played with him.

8. Gino and Tarlie spent the rest of their lives together and they were full of happiness, Tarlie thanked God for inventing animals.　　**T, +T T**

    Gino and Tarlie spent the rest of their lives together, and they were full of

    happiness. Tarlie thanked God for inventing animals.

9. Teenagers want to act mature, but can act childish.　　**T, +T**

    Teenagers want to act mature, but they can act childish.

ACTIVITY 56 **Practice Editing for Sentence Patterns II**

Errors in sentence patterns are marked with correction symbols in the right margin. Correct the sentences just for the sentence patterns based on the correction symbols.

1. It was their parents' 40th wedding anniversary so the son and daughter planned a surprise party.   **T, +T**

   It was their parents' 40th wedding anniversary, so the son and daughter planned a surprise

   party.

2. The son and daughter were both in their twenties, and lived in the city. Their parents lived in a small town miles away.   **T= LT**

   The son and daughter were both in their twenties and lived in the city. *However,* their

   parents lived in a small town miles away.

3. They wanted to have the party in their parents' town, they had to drive out to the small town several times to speak with restaurant owners.   **T, +T**

   They wanted to have the party in their parents' town, so they had to drive out to the small

   town several times to speak with restaurant owners.

4. The son preferred a luncheon. Therefore, the daughter wanted a dinner.   **T LT**

   The son preferred a luncheon. On the other hand, the daughter wanted a dinner.

5. They argued back and forth. In addition, they decided that a luncheon would save them money.   **T LT**

   They argued back and forth. Finally, they decided that a luncheon would save them money.

6. The son and daughter wanted to write invitations by hand, there wasn't enough time.   **T, +T**

   The son and daughter wanted to write invitations by hand, but there wasn't enough time.

7. They talked about calling the guests on the phone to invite them. In fact, they decided to use a Web site that allows guests to reply online to party invitations.   **T LT**

   They talked about calling the guests on the phone to invite them. Instead, they decided

   to use a Web site that allows guests to reply online to party invitations.

➡ **more on next page**

8. Only 50 people responded to the online invitation. Therefore, 75 people came to the party!   **T   LT**

    Only 50 people responded to the online invitation. However, 75 people came to the party!

9. The parents screamed with delight, and cried and felt overwhelmed on the day of the party.   **T= = =**

    The parents screamed with delight, cried, and felt overwhelmed on the day of the party.

10. They were not dressed appropriately, it was proof that they were surprised!   **T, +T**

    They were not dressed appropriately, but it was proof that they were surprised!

ACTIVITY 57 Front and End Shifters (FT and TE)

There are words or groups of words that can come before or after a trunk to add more information about the trunk. These words or groups of words can be shifted from the front of the trunk (FT) to the end of the trunk (TE) or from the end of the trunk (TE) to the front of the trunk (FT) without changing meaning. Shifters most often tell us WHEN, WHERE, or WHY about a trunk.

"Which Was the King?"

F   **T**
On a beautiful day in May, King Henry the Fourth of France was hunting in a forest with a group of men.
                         T   **E**
King Henry the Fourth of France was hunting in a forest with a group of men on a beautiful day in May.

F   **T**
Because he wanted to enjoy the longer way back to town by himself, he told his men to ride home by the shorter main road.
     T   **E**
He told his men to ride home by the shorter main road because he wanted to enjoy the longer way

back to town by himself.

F   **T**
As he came out of the forest, he saw a little boy waiting patiently by the roadside.
   T   **E**
He saw a little boy waiting patiently by the roadside as he came out of the forest.

The little boy wanted to meet the king.

CAREFUL!! NOTHING TO SHIFT HERE.

   T   **E**
He was waiting patiently because he heard the king was hunting in the forest.
F   **T**
Because he heard the king was hunting in the forest, he was waiting patiently.

F   **T**
"If that is what you wish, you can ride with me to town," [said the king].
   T   **E**
"You can ride with me to town if that is what you wish," [said the king].

T (question)   **E**
"How will I know who the king is if there are a lot of men surrounding him?" [asked the boy]
F   **T (question)**
If there are a lot of men surrounding him, how will I know who the king is?" [asked the boy]

F   **T**
"Except for the king, all the other men will take off their hats," [said the king].
     T   **E**
"All the other men will take off their hats except for the king," [said the king].

⮕ **more on next page**

F   **T**
When the king and boy arrived at the main road, all the men seemed amused.
          T   **E**
All the men seemed amused when the king and boy arrived at the main road.

F   **T**
As they usually do, the men greeted the king by taking off their hats.
          T   **E**
The men greeted the king by taking off their hats as they usually do.

                              T   **E**
[The boy said,] "The king must be either you or I because we both have our hats on."
                    F   **T**
[The boy said,] "Because we both have our hats on, the king must be either you or I."

➡ Which shifters need a comma: FT or TE? *FT*

Can shifters change into yes/no questions? YES or NO? *NO*

ACTIVITY 58 **Shifting Shifters**

Only shifters can shift. Shift the beginning of each sentence below to the end of the sentence and re-write it. If you can't shift anything, leave the space blank. Label your trunks and shifters.

Adapted from: ***Harvey Slumfenburger's Christmas Present***
by John Burningham

1. At last, Santa and the reindeer arrived home.
                   T   *E*
    Santa and the reindeer arrived home at last.

2. Because they had been delivering presents, the reindeer were tired.
                T   *E*
    The reindeer were tired because they had been delivering presents.

3. All the children got presents.

    _____

4. After they ate, the reindeer went to bed.
             T   *E*
    The reindeer went to bed after they ate.

5. One of the reindeer was not feeling well.

    _____

6. In the morning, it still was not feeling well.
           T   *E*
    It still was not feeling well in the morning.

7. Santa realized that one present for Harvey Slumfenburger was not delivered.

    _____

8. Without all the reindeer, how would Santa deliver the present?
          T   *E*
    How would Santa deliver the present without all the reindeer?

9. While eating breakfast, Santa thought of a plan.
          T   *E*
    Santa thought of a plan while eating breakfast.

10. If he could get a little help from his neighbors, he would deliver the present without the reindeer.
         T   *E*
    He would deliver the present without the reindeer if he could get a little help from his neighbors.

➡ Which shifters need a comma: FT or TE? _FT_

Can shifters change into yes/no questions? YES or NO? _NO_

ACTIVITY 59 **Shifting Shifters**

Only shifters can shift. Shift the end of each sentence below to the front of the sentence and re-write it. Remember to add a comma after the front shifter. If you can't shift anything, leave the space blank. Label your trunks and shifters.

"Cinderella"

1. Cinderella stayed home and did all the housework while her stepsisters went to parties and balls.

       F   *T*
   While her stepsisters went to parties and balls, Cinderella stayed home and did all the

   housework.

2. Her name was Cinderella because she spent so much time cleaning the ashes and cinders.

       F   *T*
   Because she spent so much time cleaning the ashes and cinders, her name was Cinderella.

3. Now it happened that the king was to give a ball.

4. The stepsisters were thrilled when they received an invitation.

       F   *T*
   When they received an invitation, the stepsisters were thrilled.

5. They had sent for the best dressmaker by the end of the day.

       F   *T*
   By the end of the day, they had sent for the best dressmaker.

6. Cinderella helped her stepsisters dress for the ball even though she was upset about not receiving an invitation.

       F   *T*
   Even though she was upset about not receiving an invitation, Cinderella helped her stepsisters

   dress for the ball.

7. Cinderella watched from the kitchen window as the stepsisters drove away in their fine carriage.

       F   *T*
   As the stepsisters drove away in their fine carriage, Cinderella watched from the kitchen window.

8. She sat down by the fire and began to cry when the carriage was out of sight.

       F   *T*
   When the carriage was out of sight, she sat down by the fire and began to cry.

➡ **more on next page**

9. She heard a voice from out of nowhere.

   F   *T*
   From out of nowhere, she heard a voice. _____

10. "You must listen carefully if you want to go to the ball."

    F   *T*
    "If you want to go to the ball, you must listen carefully." _____

11. "You'll need to bring me the largest pumpkin you can find from outside in the garden."

    F   *T*
    "From outside in the garden, you'll need to bring me the largest pumpkin you can find." _____

➡ Which shifters need a comma: FT or TE? __*FT*__

Can shifters change into yes/no questions? YES or NO? __*NO*__

ACTIVITY 60 A Word about Fragments

Turn each of the following into yes/no questions. If you can, write TRUNK. If you can't, write FRAGMENT.

1. It isn't easy to learn American Sign Language.   **TRUNK**
   yes/no question: Isn't it easy to learn American Sign Language?

2. Because it's a different kind of language.   **FRAGMENT**
   yes/no question: Is because it a different kind of language?

3. When people try to learn it.   *FRAGMENT*
   yes/no question: *Do when people try to learn it?*

4. They can express themselves well.   *TRUNK*
   yes/no question: *Can they express themselves well?*

5. But have a hard time understanding it.   *FRAGMENT*
   yes/no question: *Do but have a hard time understanding it?*

6. That's different from learning other languages.   *TRUNK*
   yes/no question: *Is that different from learning other languages?*

7. Because understanding language is easier than expressing it.   *FRAGMENT*
   yes/no question: *Is because understanding language easier than expressing it?*

➡ Fragments will never turn into yes/no questions because they are not trunks. They might be *shifters*!

Now change sentences 1 and 2 above into a TE pattern here:

   T   E
It isn't easy to learn American Sign Language because it is a different kind of language.

Change sentences 3, 4, and 5 into a FT= pattern here:

   F   T   =
When people try to learn it, they can express themselves well but have a hard time understanding it.

Change sentences 6 and 7 into a TE pattern here:

   T   E
That's different from learning other languages because understanding language is easier than

expressing it.

ACTIVITY 61 Another Word about Fragments

Try to turn each of the following into yes/no questions. If you can, write TRUNK. If you can't, write FRAGMENT.

1. When I was a little girl.   **FRAGMENT**
   yes/no question: *Was when I a little girl?*

2. I went to the beach everyday in the summer.   **TRUNK**
   yes/no question: Did I go to the beach everyday in the summer?

3. If it was a sunny day.   *FRAGMENT*
   yes/no question: **Was if it a sunny day?**

4. At about noon time.   *FRAGMENT*
   yes/no question: *NO X-WORD OR VERB*

5. I ate meat, potatoes, and a vegetable.   *TRUNK*
   yes/no question: *Did I eat meat, potatoes, and a vegetable?*

6. Because my mother didn't want to cook a big meal.   *FRAGMENT*
   yes/no question: *Didn't because my mother want to cook a big meal?*

7. When she came home from the beach.   *FRAGMENT*
   yes/no question: *Did when come home from the beach?*

8. We didn't realize that this was a healthy way to eat.   *TRUNK*
   yes/no question: *Didn't we realize that this was a healthy way to eat?*

9. Because it was in the 1950s.   *FRAGMENT*
   yes/no question: *Was because it in the 1950s?*

10. When many people didn't know about healthy lifestyles.   *FRAGMENT*
    yes/no question: *Didn't when many people know about healthy lifestyles?*

Now change numbers 1 and 2 above into a FT pattern here:
  F   *T*
When I was a little girl, I went to the beach every day in the summer.

Now change numbers 3, 4, 5, 6, and 7 into a FFTEE pattern here:
  F   *F*   *T*   *E*
If it was sunny, at about noon time, I ate meat, potatoes, and a vegetable because my mother didn't
              E
want to cook a big meal when she came home from the beach.

Now change numbers 8, 9, and 10 into a TEE pattern here:
  T   *E*   *E*
We didn't realize that this was a healthy way to eat because it was the 1950s when many people

didn't know about healthy lifestyles.

ACTIVITY 62 **Inserts (TI)**

Inserts add interest to a sentence by adding detail in the middle or at the end of the sentence. You can remove an insert and the sentence will be complete and correct. Inserts do not shift. They always have punctuation on both sides.

From *Homecoming*
by Cynthia Voigt, p. 14

    T   **I**

1. They had hamburgers and French fries and, *after Dicey thought it over*, milkshakes.

    T   **I**

2. They could have one more meal before they ran out of money, *or maybe two more*.

    T   **I**

3. The little ones horsed around in the back, *teasing, wrestling, tickling, quarreling, and laughing.*

Adapted from *The Ant Bully*
by John Nickle, p. 1

   T   **I**

4. Sid, *the neighborhood bully*, was especially mean to Lucas.

   T   **I**

5. Lucas, *however*, was not mean to Sid.

   T   **I**

6. The Civil War *(1861–1865)* killed more Americans than any other war in history.

   T   **I**

7. There were several famous battles of the war: *Antietam, Bull Run, Gettysburg, and Vicksburg.*

   T   **I**

8. Abraham Lincoln, *president during the Civil War*, was respected throughout the world.

   T   **I**

9. Many people praised his kindly spirit—*even his enemies.*

➡ What punctuation can start or end inserts?

Commas, parentheses, colons, periods, and dashes.

ACTIVITY 63 **Inserting Inserts**

Rewrite each sentence with the insert in the right place and with punctuation on both sides of the insert.

1. T: John Fitzgerald Kennedy was shot to death on November 22, 1963.
   I: the youngest man ever elected president

   John Fitzgerald Kennedy, the youngest man ever elected president, was shot to death on November 22, 1963.

2. T: Kennedy won the presidency after several debates with his opponent.
   I: Vice President Richard M. Nixon.

   Kennedy won the presidency after several debates with his opponent, Vice President Richard M. Nixon.

3. T: Kennedy was the first president of the Roman Catholic faith.
   I: (1917–1963)

   Kennedy (1917–1963) was the first President of the Roman Catholic faith.

4. T: His parents moved the family to better neighborhoods.
   I: each time moving into bigger and better homes

   His parents moved the family to better neighborhoods, each time moving into bigger and better homes.

5. T: They lived in a variety of cities.
   I: Brookline, Riverdale, and Bronxville

   They lived in a variety of cities: Brookline, Riverdale, and Bronxville.

6. T: He entered Harvard in 1936.
   I: majoring in government and international relations

   He entered Harvard in 1936, majoring in government and international relations.

7. T: Jack spent 1939 traveling in Europe.
   I: as his family called him

   Jack, as his family called him, spent 1939 traveling in Europe.

8. T: *Why England Slept* became a best-selling book.
   I: his last writing assignment at Harvard

   Why England Slept, his last writing assignment at Harvard, became a best-selling book.

Underline the sentence pattern that best describes each sentence below.

From *Drip! Drop! How Water Gets to Your Tap*
by Barbara Seuling

1. Water comes in three forms: a liquid, a gas, and a solid.   FT   TE   <u>TI</u>

2. Water is salty, as in the oceans, or frozen in glaciers.   FT   TE   <u>TI</u>

3. It doesn't matter how much water evaporates because it always comes back to earth as rain, snow, sleet, or hail.   FT   <u>TE</u>   TI

4. Large objects are filtered out of water— fish, boots, plastic bags, leaves.   FT   TE   <u>TI</u>

5. Minerals, such as sulfur, are taken out of water.   FT   TE   <u>TI</u>

6. It can be a problem if water flows too slowly or too fast.   FT   <u>TE</u>   TI

"The Paddle-Wheel Boat"

7. More than a hundred years ago, two boys were fishing in a small river.   <u>FT</u>   TE   TI

8. They sat in a heavy flat-bottomed boat, each holding a fishing rod.   FT   TE   <u>TI</u>

9. When they wanted to move the boat from one place to another, they had to push against a long pole whose lower end reached the bottom of the river.   <u>FT</u>   TE   TI

10. The boys needed a lot of time to get anywhere because the boat crept over the water no faster than a snail.   FT   <u>TE</u>   TI

11. If they wanted to move faster, they had to invent a way.   <u>FT</u>   TE   TI

12. After a great deal of trying, they did succeed in making two paddle wheels.   <u>FT</u>   TE   TI

13. They fastened each of these wheels to the end of an iron rod, first passing the rod through the boat from side to side.   FT   TE   <u>TI</u>

14. They bent the rod in the middle, making a crank for turning.   FT   TE   <u>TI</u>

15. When the work was finished, the old fishing boat had a paddle wheel on each side which dipped just a few inches into the water.   <u>FT</u>   TE   TI

16. One of the boys, Robert Fulton, kept on planning and thinking.   FT   TE   <u>TI</u>

17. We know him as the inventor of the steamboat because he went on to make a paddle boat that could be run by steam.   FT   <u>TE</u>   TI

ACTIVITY 65 Identifying All Sentence Patterns

Underline the sentence pattern that best describes each sentence below.

Adapted from: **Ant Cities**
by Arthur Dorros, pp. 9–22

1. Underneath an ant hill, there may be miles of tunnels and hundreds of rooms.

   T   T,+T   T=   LT   <u>FT</u>   TE   TI

2. It is dark inside the hill, but the ants stay cozy.

   T   <u>T,+T</u>   T=   LT   FT   TE   TI

3. Worker ants do many different kinds of work in the rooms of the hill.

   T   T,+T   T=   LT   FT   <u>TE</u>   TI

4. It is like a city, a busy city of ants.

   T   T,+T   T=   LT   FT   TE   <u>TI</u>

5. In one room of the nest, a queen ant lays eggs.

   T   T,+T   T=   LT   <u>FT</u>   TE   TI

6. Worker ants carry the ants to other rooms and take care of them.

   T   T,+T   <u>T=</u>   LT   FT   TE   TI

7. All of the other ants in the ant city grow from the eggs.

   <u>T</u>   T,+T   T=   LT   FT   TE   TI

8. At first, the tiny eggs grow into larvae.

   T   T,+T   T=   LT   <u>FT</u>   TE   TI

9. The worker ants feed the larvae and lick them clean.

   T   T,+T   <u>T=</u>   LT   FT   TE   TI

10. Harvester ants will bite if you disturb their nest.

    T   T,+T   T=   LT   FT   <u>TE</u>   TI

11. When one ant finds food, the others follow.

    T   T,+T   T=   LT   <u>FT</u>   TE   TI

ACTIVITY 66 Practice Editing for Sentence Patterns III

Errors in sentence patterns below are marked with symbols in the right margin. Correct the sentences based on the symbols and use the symbols to label the sentences.

1. My dad Randy works for the Canadian Forest Department.   **TI**

        T   *I*

    My dad, Randy, works for the Canadian Forest Department.

2. Buck is my favorite dog. he works for my dad. he pulls the sleds.   **T T T**

        T   *T*   *T*   **(3 sentences)**

    Buck is my favorite dog. He works for my dad. He pulls the sleds.

3. Buck doesn't like to be boss but he is a great leader.   **T, +T**

       T   *, +*   *T*

    Buck doesn't like to be boss, but he is a great leader.

4. When my dad came back. I was so excited, because I had missed Buck.   **FTE**

         F   *T*   *E*   **(one**

    When my dad came back, I was so excited because I had missed Buck.   **sentence)**

5. I played with him all day, and didn't see my mom call me for dinner.   **T=**

       T   *=*

    I played with him all day and didn't see my mom call me for dinner.

6. My favorite building of all is the MSD gym called Benson Gym. Which has a swimming   **TI**
   pool, basketball court, and bowling alley.

                      T   *I*

    My favorite building of all is the MSD gym called Benson Gym, which has a

    swimming pool, basketball court, and bowling alley.

7. When I was on my way to the field. I heard someone yelling loudly to me.   **FT**

            F   *T*

    When I was on my way to the field, I heard someone yelling loudly to me.

8. Charlie a boy I know is very mischievous, he makes spitballs in class puts thumb tacks   **TI**
   under seats puts cherry bombs in the toilets which make horrible sounds.   **T= =I**

      T   *I*   *T*   *=*   **(two**

    Charlie, a boy I know, is very mischievous. He makes spitballs in class, puts   **sentences)**

                     =   *I*

    thumbtacks under seats, and puts cherry bombs in the toilets, which make

    horrible sounds.

➡ **more on next page**

9. One day, Charlie was in class he was making spitballs and spit on his teacher.

          L   T   T   =

    One day, Charlie was in class. He was making spitballs and spit on his teacher.

    LT T=
    (two
    sentences)

10. The next day the principal went to Charlie's house he saw Charlie and his parents making spitballs on the kitchen table.

              L   T   , +   T

    The next day, the principal went to Charlie's house, and he saw Charlie and his
                           /

    parents making spitballs on the kitchen table.

    LT, +TI
    (one
    sentence)

ACTIVITY 67 Practice Editing for Sentence Patterns IV

Errors in sentence patterns below are marked with symbols in the right margin. Correct the sentences based on the symbols and use the symbols to label the sentences.

1. We visited Rose Hill Manor, we went into a log cabin.   **T=**

        T   **=**

    We visited Rose Hill Manor and went into a log cabin.

2. In 2050 each MSD student will have two laptops. One will be for school, the other one   **FT**
    will be left at home for homework.   **T, +T**
        F   **T**   **T**   **, +**   **(two**
    In 2050, each MSD student will have two laptops. One will be for school, and   **sentences)**
        T

    the other one will be left at home for homework.

3. The dog was so thirsty. It went to the toilet for water.   **T, +T**
        T   *, +*   *T*
    The dog was so thirsty, so it went to the toilet for water.

4. For a few months. She took care of the dog they played a lot and they looked like a cute   **FT**
    couple—a dog and an old person.   **T= I**
        F   *T*   *T*   *=*   **(two**
    For a few months, she took care of the dog. They played a lot and looked like a   **sentences)**
        I

    cute couple—a dog and an old person.

5. Because she refused to eat. She started to lose a lot of weight and it made her more   **FT, +T**
    depressed.   **(one**
        F   *T*   *, +*   *T*   **sentence)**
    Because she refused to eat, she started to lose a lot of weight, and it made

    her more depressed.

6. He was hoping his father would show up. While he was playing basketball.   **TE**
      T   *E*
    He was hoping his father would show up while he was playing basketball.

7. When he arrived home. There was his dad lying down watching TV.   **FTI**
        F   *T*   *I*
    When he arrived home, there was his dad, lying down watching TV.

➡ more on next page

Section 3 • Editing Practice

8. My mother did not work outside the home. When I was growing up. There always was   **T**
    the smell of rice and beans slowly cooking in the kitchen.   **FTI**
                T   *F*   **(two**
    My mother did not work outside the home. When I was growing up, there always   **sentences)**
       T   *I*
    was the smell of rice and beans, slowly cooking in the kitchen.

9. She never sat with us, because she preferred to stand and serve us.   **TE**
                  T   *E*
    She never sat with us because she preferred to stand and serve us.

10. By the time she was ready to sit down. I had left the kitchen.   **FT**
              F   *T*
    By the time she was ready to sit down, I had left the kitchen.

Practice Editing for Sentence Patterns V

Errors in sentence patterns below are marked with symbols in the right margin. Correct the sentences based on the symbols and use the symbols to label the sentences.

Adapted from: ***Killing Mr. Griffin***
by Lois Duncan, pp. 8–11

1. For the last year of her life Susan had dreamed about David every night.   **FT**
         F   **T**
    For the last year of her life, Susan had dreamed about David every night.

2. In some of the dreams he smiled at her, however, in other dreams he didn't notice her.   **FT**
                F   T   L   F   T   **L FT**
    In some of the dreams, he smiled at her. However, in other dreams, he didn't   **(two sentences)**

    notice her.

3. Susan took off her glasses, and wiped the dust from them.   **T=**
            T   =
    Susan took off her glasses and wiped the dust from them.

4. David had moved away from her, when she put them on again.   **TE**
          T   E
    David had moved away from her when she put them on again.

5. The only handsome boys were the McConnells and most of the time she hated all three   **T, +FT**
    of them.
                      T   , +   F   T
    The only handsome boys were the McConnells, and most of the time, she hated

    all three of them.

6. She waited in the classroom doorway looking around the room.   **TI**
          T   I
    She waited in the classroom doorway, looking around the room.

7. She smiled at two girls but they were talking to each other, and didn't seem to notice her.   **T, +T=**
      T   , +   T   =
    She smiled at two girls but they were talking to each other and didn't seem to

    notice her.

➡ **more on next page**

8. She was a straight-A student. As a result, students never asked her about homework.   **T LT**

   T   L   T

She was a straight-A student. However, students never asked her about

homework.

9. The mid-term exam had been a disaster for everyone, or the final was going to be even   **T, +T**
harder.

       T   , + T

The mid-term exam had been a disaster for everyone, and the final was going

to be even harder.

10. They thought that Mr. Griffin their teacher was too hard a teacher.   **TI**

   T   I

They thought that Mr. Griffin, their teacher, was too hard a teacher.

Editing for Sentence Patterns

Edit the following sentences using the correction symbol or symbols to the right of each sentence to help you find the errors.

Adapted from: ***Killing Mr. Griffin***
by Lois Duncan, pp. 11–16

Susan opened her pocketbook, and took out a pen. **T=**

_____

A few minutes later Mr. Griffin stepped through the doorway pulling the door shut **FTI**
behind him.

_____

_____

The day had begun and Susan did not have a positive feeling. **T,+T**

_____

Other teachers might not appear at all, and Mr. Griffin was always there. **T,+T**

_____

Mr. Griffin responsible as always was dressed in a blue suit. **TI**

_____

Susan took out her homework, and passed it forward luckily, she would not have to read **T= LT**
it aloud in class. **(two sentences)**

_____

_____

David said, "I did the assignment, it blew out of my notebook." **T,+T**

_____

Mr. Griffin annoyed by this comment explained that he has never accepted late papers. **TI**

_____

_____

➡ **more on next page**

His hand went into his jacket pocket then it brought out a small plastic bottle.   **T   LT
(two sentences)**

_____

Without looking at it he snapped it open.   **FT**

_____

Edit the following sentences using the correction symbol or symbols to the right of each sentence to help you find the errors.

Adapted from: **Killing Mr. Griffin**
by Lois Duncan, pp. 11–16

Susan opened her pocketbook, and took out a pen.   **T=**

Susan opened her pocketbook and took out a pen.

A few minutes later Mr. Griffin stepped through the doorway pulling the door shut   **FTI**
behind him.

A few minutes later, Mr. Griffin stepped through the doorway, pulling the door

shut behind him.

The day had begun and Susan did not have a positive feeling.   **T,+T**

The day had begun, and Susan did not have a positive feeling.

Other teachers might not appear at all, and Mr. Griffin was always there.   **T,+T**

Other teachers might not appear at all, but Mr. Griffin was always there.

Mr. Griffin responsible as always was dressed in a blue suit.   **TI**

Mr. Griffin, responsible as always, was dressed in a blue suit.

Susan took out her homework, and passed it forward luckily, she would not have to read   **T= LT**
it aloud in class   **(two sentences)**

Susan took out her homework and passed it forward. Luckily, she would not

have to read it aloud in class.

David said, "I did the assignment, it blew out of my notebook."   **T,+T**

David said, "I did the assignment, but it blew out of my notebook."

Mr. Griffin annoyed by this comment explained that he has never accepted late papers.   **TI**

Mr. Griffin, annoyed by this comment, explained that he has never accepted

late papers.

➧ **more on next page**

His hand went into his jacket pocket then it brought out a small plastic bottle.

T   LT
(two sentences)

His hand went into his jacket pocket. Then, it brought out a small plastic bottle.

Without looking at it he snapped it open.

FT

Without looking at it, he snapped it open.

Section 4

- **Boxes and Main Words**

- **Countable and Uncountable Boxes**

- ***THE* Boxes**

- **Referents**

- **Editing Practice**

Key teaching points:

Main words (nouns) live in boxes.

They can show one or many and can be replaced with referents.

ACTIVITY 69 Boxes and Main Words

Boxes are places where nouns live with other words that work for them. They are also places where words like *it, they, he, she, them* can substitute for nouns. Boxes can be found before the verb—in subject position (do you remember how to find the subject of a sentence?), or after the verb. Every box must have at least one noun (or its substitute) and that noun (or its substitute) is the *main word* of the box. It tells us what the box is really about. An asterisk (*) is above the main words in the boxes below.

Adapted from ***The Magic School Bus Inside the Human Body***
by Joanna Cole and Bruce Degen, pp. 6–26

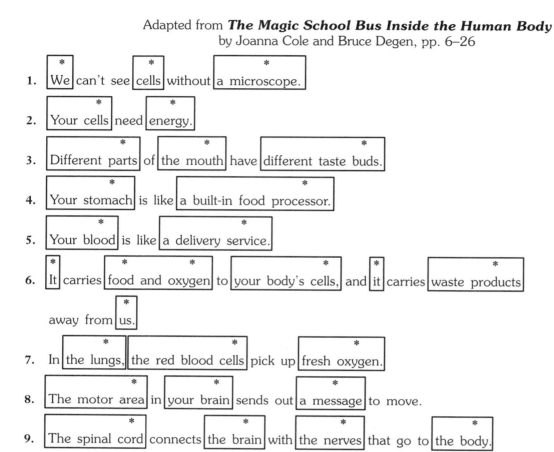

ACTIVITY 70 Practice with Boxes

Place an asterisk (*) over the main words in the boxes below.

Adapted from "Good Earth" in *New Practice Readers*
by Anderson, Stone, and Burton, p. 136

1. The earth* is covered with soil.*

2. Most soil* is made of ground-up bits* of rocks.*

3. Rocks* mix with dead leaves,* parts* of dead plants, and dead animals,* too.

4. All these things,* mixing together for a long, long, time,* make soil.*

Now . . . find the boxes in the following sentences and place an asterisk above the main words in them.

Adapted from *From Plants to Blue Jeans*
by L'Hommedieu, pp. 4–11

1. Blue jeans* were invented by Levi Strauss.*

2. These tough pants* have been worn by all sorts* of people.*

3. Blue jeans* begin on a cotton farm.*

4. Special machines* plant cotton seeds* in many rows.*

5. Small white flowers* form on the little cotton plants.*

6. The flowers* change color* and die.

7. They* leave tiny pods.*

8. The pods* are called cotton bolls.*

More Practice with Boxes

Find the boxes in the following sentences and place an asterisk (*) above the main word or words in them.

"The Year Is 1902"
From: www.goofball.com/jokes/facts/2003016101

The year is 1902, about one hundred years ago.

The average life expectancy in the U.S. was 47.

Only 14 percent of the homes in the U.S. had a bathtub.

Only 8 percent of the homes had a telephone.

A three-minute call from Denver to New York City cost 11 dollars.

There were only 8,000 cars in the U.S. and only 144 miles of paved roads.

The maximum speed limit in most cities was 10 mph.

Alabama, Mississippi, Iowa, and Tennessee were each more heavily populated than California.

The tallest structure in the world was the Eiffel Tower.

The average wage in the U.S. was 22 cents an hour.

The average U.S. worker made between $200 and $400 per year.

A competent accountant could expect to earn $2,000 per year. Sugar cost 4 cents a pound.

Most women only washed their hair once a month and used borax or egg yolks for shampoo.

The five leading causes of death in the U.S. were: pneumonia and influenza, tuberculosis, diarrhea, heart disease, and stroke.

The American flag had 45 stars. Arizona, Oklahoma, New Mexico, Hawaii, and Alaska hadn't been admitted to the Union yet.

The population of Las Vegas, Nevada, was 30.

Crossword puzzles, canned beer, and iced tea hadn't been invented.

ACTIVITY 72 Focusing on Nouns

Study the nouns on the left and the nouns on the right, then answer the questions at the bottom of the page.

suitcase/bag/trunk
a
another
each

luggage

suitcases/bags/trunks
2, 3, 4 . . .
many

coin/bill/check/quarter
a
another
each

money

coins/bills/checks/quarters
2, 3, 4 . . .
many

sofa/lamp/chair/table
a
another
each

furniture

sofas/lamps/chairs/tables
2, 3, 4 . . .
many

bat/racket/base/glove
a
another
each

equipment

bats/rackets/bases/gloves
2, 3, 4 . . .
many

➡ Can you show one or many of the nouns on the left? YES NO

Can you show one or many of the nouns on the right? YES NO

ACTIVITY 73 Countable and Uncountable Boxes

Boxes that show one and many are called *countable boxes*. Some ways to show one or many are to use words such as *a, an, another, each, many* and to use *numbers*. You can also add an *s*. Boxes that do not show one or many are called *uncountable boxes*. See Appendix F for nouns/boxes that can be both countable and uncountable as well as some other uncountable nouns/boxes. If you want to know if a noun is countable or uncountable, check a dictionary. In most learner's dictionaries of American English, uncountable nouns will be labeled like this: spaghetti, n. [U].

Study the boxes on the left to see how the main words inside them show one or many. Study the boxes on the right to see how the main words do not show one or many. Read across.

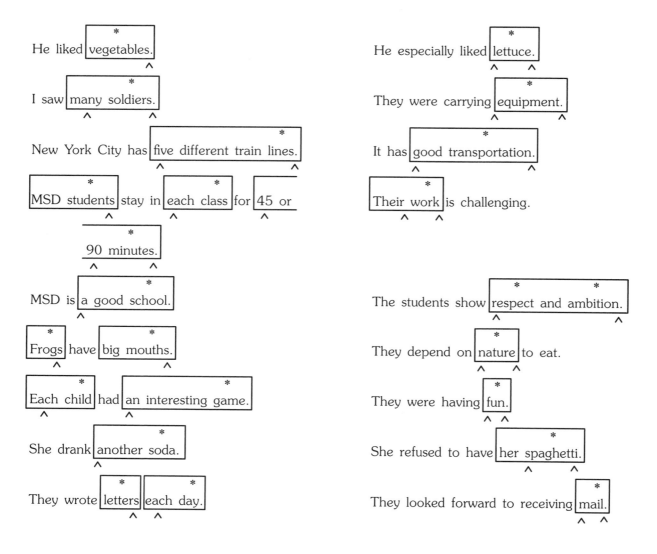

ACTIVITY 74 Practice with Countable and Uncountable Boxes

In the boxes below, place an asterisk over the main words and ^ to the left or right of the main words to show one or many if the main words are countable. If the main words are uncountable, place a *u* inside the box. Use activities 72 and 73 and Appendix F to help you.

1. He really needed ┃***u** help.┃

2. Della wanted to buy ┃a special gift.┃ *** ^

3. ┃His friends┃ live far away. *** ^

4. He had ┃great experiences┃ with ┃animals┃ as ┃a little kid.┃ *** ^ · *** ^ · *** ^

5. I prefer to eat healthfully and not take ┃medicine.┃ **u*

6. She gave ┃incorrect information┃ to ┃her friends.┃ **u* · *** ^

7. For her birthday, she got ┃a chocolate Labrador retriever.┃ *** ^

8. She writes in ┃two diaries┃each night.┃ *** ^ · *** ^ ^

9. Some houses need ┃fresh air.┃ **u*

10. They looked like ┃a cute couple.┃ *** ^

11. Gino would never leave her for ┃another girl.┃ *** ^

12. Joshua ran to get ┃dog medicine.┃ **u*

ACTIVITY 75 Practice Correcting Countable and Uncountable Errors

In the boxes below, use ^ to show countable errors and then correct them. Write a small u above uncountable errors and correct them as well. Use activities 72–73 and Appendix F to help you.

1. He came to the car and asked Julia if she really needed | a help. | (u)
   ^

   He came to the car and asked Julia if she really needed help.

2. She really wanted to buy | one special gifts | for Jim for Christmas.
   ^   ^

   She really wanted to buy one special gift for Jim for Christmas.

   She really wanted to buy special gifts for Jim for Christmas.

3. Her internship experience gave her | a wonderful opportunities. |
   ^   ^

   Her internship experience gave her a wonderful opportunity.

4. The little girl had | many piece | of | chalks. | (u)
   ^   ^   ^

   The little girl had many pieces of chalk.

5. They will allow Joshua to get | another dogs. |
   ^   ^

   They will allow Joshua to get another dog.

6. NYC has | good transportations. | (u)
   ^

   NYC has good transportation.

7. I saw a small bowl. It was made with | woods. | (u)
   ^

   I saw a small bowl. It was made with wood.

8. There aren't | many tree | near the beach.
   ^   ^

   There aren't many trees near the beach.

9. | Their homeworks | is always done well. (u)
   ^

   Their homework is always done well.

Writers use THE to show readers special things or things readers already know about. Readers might know about them because:

1. There is only one in the world.

    The sun . . . the moon . . . the Gulf of Mexico . . . the Bahamas . . .
    the Atlantic . . . the United States of America . . . the Titanic . . .
    the *Frederick Post*

2. They are made special by what follows them.

    The player who finishes first will win.   (not just any player)
    Please give me *the cup that is broken*.   (not just any cup)

3. They refer back to something already mentioned.

    Mr. Frappa, who owned *a grocery store* on Maple Avenue, kept
    a large black book with the names of people who owed him money.
    When I walked in *the store*, I could see *the book*.
    (Adapted from De Young 1999, p.7)

4. There is only one in the environment you are in or can assume there's one in the environment you are reading
    about.

    Let's go to *the library*.   (Students are at school.)
    Isn't *the park* beautiful!   (People are in a park.)
    When I walked in, I could see it on *the counter*.   (A person was in a place
                                                  with one counter.)

5. Writers/speakers assume you already know what they are talking about outside the environment.

    Wasn't *the dress* perfect for her?   (Friends had already seen a dress.)
    The President's plan is good.   (People learned about the plan before.)
    What did you think of *the movie*?   (Friends saw a movie.)
    Let's go to *the movies*.   (People know what movies are.)

ACTIVITY 77 Recognizing Reasons for *THE* Boxes

Why does the author C. Coco De Young use *the* the way she does in the following passages from *A Letter to Mrs. Roosevelt* (pp. 6–7)? The numbers above the words *the* below refer to the reasons described in activity 76. Do you agree?

Papa owned a shoe repair shop on Bedford Street. I often walked to work with him when there was
                                                              1
no school. Every morning at six o'clock he crossed over the First Street Bridge, stopped to greet Mr.
                    2   **3**   **2**   **4**
Bobb, who operated the train tower on the bridge, then walked the long trek past the steel mill. Papa
                                                                                    2
stopped whistling and tipped his hat in respect as he passed St. John's Church. At the corner near
 1   **3**
the Swank Building, he started to whistle again, and continued until he reached the shop. As Papa
          4   **2**
unlocked the door, he would pause to breathe in the balmy scents of leather and shoe polish. Then
          4   **4**
he'd turn on the lights, walk behind the counter, and put on his apron.

          5   **3**   **2**
       In the late afternoon, Papa closed the shop and walked past the bank on Main Street. There was
                    3
a time when he would stop in the bank every Friday, just before closing. That was when he carried a
                                                                                    3
small sack of money, proof of a busy week. He would smile as he proudly handed the sack over to
 2   **4**   **3**
the teller behind the counter. Sometimes Mr. Lockhard, the bank president, would smile back and shake
                                        3   **2**
Papa's hand. Not anymore. Now Papa walked by the bank jingling the small change in his pocket,

sometimes carrying a basket of fresh fruit and vegetables.

                                        2   **3**
       Today I heard him tell Mama that Mr. Lockhard stood in the window of the bank yesterday.

Papa tipped his hat, but Mr. Lockhard didn't seem to notice as he stared out at Main Street. He
                                                            3
stopped shaking Papa's hand a long time ago, when Papa stopped carrying the money sack. Now
 3
Papa used the pocket change to pay our food bill.

Practice with *THE* Boxes #1

Draw a box around the *the* boxes below and write a number over the *the* word to show the reason for its use. Use activity 76 to help. *Read the excerpt to the students before they begin the activity.*

Adapted from **"Freedom"** in ***Wayside School Is Falling Down***
by Louis Sachar, pp. 36–37

Myron crumbled a cracker on [2 | the windowsill] next to his desk, then looked away. He knew Oddly came

only when nobody was looking.

A little while later a bird landed on [3 | the windowsill] and ate [3 | the crumbs.] Myron watched him out of

[2 | the corner] of his eye.

He was a black bird with a pink breast. Myron had named him "Oddly."

"Is that your dumb bird again?" asked Kathy.

"No," said Myron. "Oddly is not *my* bird. I don't own him. He doesn't live in a cage. Oddly is free!"

"You're a birdbrain," said Kathy.

Myron watched Oddly fly away. He wished he could fly away across [1 | the sky] with Oddly.

Oddly probably thinks I live in a cage, he realized. Whenever he sees me, I'm sitting in this same

desk. He probably thinks this desk is my cage!

So Myron got out of his chair and sat on [4 | the floor.]

"Myron, what are you doing out of your seat?" asked Mrs. Jewls.

"I want to sit on [4 | the floor.]" said Myron.

"Get back to your seat," ordered Mrs. Jewls.

I *do* live in a cage, he thought. And I have to stay in [3 | the cage] until [4 | the bell] rings!

Draw a box around the *the* boxes below and write a number over the *the* word to show the reason for its use. Use activity 76 to help. *Read the excerpt to the students first.*

"Two Great Painters"

There was once a painter whose name was Zeuxis, and he could paint pictures so life-like that they were

mistaken for **[2]** the real things which they represented. At one time, he painted **[2]** the picture of some fruit

which was so real that birds flew down and pecked at it. This made him very proud of his skill.

"I am **[1]** the only man in **[1]** the world who can paint a picture so true to life," he said.

There was another famous artist whose name was Parrhasius. When he heard of **[2]** the boast which

Zeuxis had made, he said to himself, "I will see what I can do."

So he painted a beautiful picture which seemed to be covered with a curtain. Then he invited

Zeuxis to come and see it.

Zeuxis looked at it closely. "Pull **[3]** the curtain aside and show us **[3]** the picture," he said.

Parrhasius laughed and answered, "**[3]** The curtain is **[3]** the picture."

"Well," said Zeuxis, "you have beaten me this time, and I shall boast no more. I deceived only

[3] the birds, but you have deceived me, a painter."

Some time after this, Zeuxis painted another wonderful picture. It was that of a boy carrying a

basket of ripe red cherries. When he hung this painting outside his door, some birds flew down and

tried to carry **[3]** the cherries away.

"Ah! This picture is a failure," he said. "If **[3]** the boy had been as well painted as **[3]** the cherries **[3]** the birds

would have been afraid to come near him."

ACTIVITY 80 **Practice with *THE* Boxes #3**

Draw a box around the *the* boxes below and write a number over the *the* word to show the reason for its use. Use activity 76 to help. *Read the excerpt to the students before they begin the activity.*

From **"Splendor"** in *Reading Fluency, Level C*
by Lois Lowry, p. 29

To Becky's surprise, her mother smiled. "You have your baby-sitting money in **⁵**[the bank,] Beck," she

said. "And it's your very first real dance. If you want to spend that much on a special dress—well, it's

up to you."

"Mom," said Angela, "nobody dances with seventh graders anyway. **⁵**[The seventh-grade boys]

won't dance. They all stand around in **⁵**[the corners] with each other. And **⁵**[the eighth-grade boys] only

dance with **⁵**[the eighth-grade girls.] So what's **²**[the point] of spending all your money on a dress if no

one's going to dance with you? I *told* Becky she could wear my blue dress to **³**[the dance.] The one I

wore last year."

"I don't want to wear a hand-me-down dress, not to **³**[the Christmas dance,]" Becky exploded.

"*You* didn't have to wear someone else's dress when you were in seventh grade!"

"Becky," Angela pointed out in her logical, patronizing way, "I didn't have an older sister. So who

could hand a dress down?"

"It's not my fault I was born second."

"Shhh," said their mother. "Calm down. You buy **³**[the dress,] honey, if it's what you want. It's

important to have a very special dress now and then."

ACTIVITY 81 Referents

Referents are words that replace or refer to boxes. This way, you do not have to keep repeating the boxes themselves. Words like *he/him*, *she/her*, *they/them* and *it* are referents. They are also called *pronouns*. In the passage below, *Ref* is written above the referents. Draw arrows from these referents to the boxes they replace or refer to. *(Ref* over It in line 7 below refers to the entire phrase* to make his daughters doctors.)

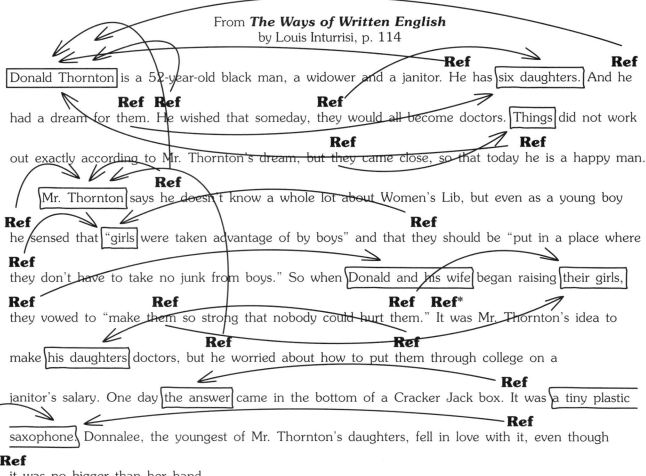

From **The Ways of Written English**
by Louis Inturrisi, p. 114

Donald Thornton is a 52-year-old black man, a widower and a janitor. He has six daughters. And he had a dream for them. He wished that someday, they would all become doctors. Things did not work out exactly according to Mr. Thornton's dream, but they came close, so that today he is a happy man.

Mr. Thornton says he doesn't know a whole lot about Women's Lib, but even as a young boy he sensed that "girls" were taken advantage of by boys" and that they should be "put in a place where they don't have to take no junk from boys." So when Donald and his wife began raising their girls, they vowed to "make them so strong that nobody could hurt them." It was Mr. Thornton's idea to make his daughters doctors, but he worried about how to put them through college on a janitor's salary. One day the answer came in the bottom of a Cracker Jack box. It was a tiny plastic saxophone. Donnalee, the youngest of Mr. Thornton's daughters, fell in love with it, even though it was no bigger than her hand.

That Christmas Donnalee was given a real saxophone. Then Jeannette, the second child, had to have a guitar. Then came Betty who wasn't musical, so she got a tambourine. Yvonne was next. She played the alto sax. Then Linda took up the drums. Rita, the last girl, learned the piano.

Soon all six girls began to play together as a group. They called themselves "The Thornton Sisters."

The group soon managed to get itself into show business. As a result of their success, the Thorntons were able to save enough money to finance their children's education.

➡ **more on next page**

So far there are three "Drs. Thornton." All three have promised their father to use their maiden

Ref

name professionally to show respect for him. The other three daughters are now in medical school

pursuing their studies.

Understanding Different Forms of Referents

Referents that refer to the same box can be spelled differently. List all the boxes on the left from in the story about the Thornton Sisters (activity 81) and then all their referents on the right, in the correct column.

Referents

Boxes	Before The Verb	After The Verb
Donald Thornton (Mr. Thornton)	he	
six daughters	they	them
Things	they	
girls	they	
Donald and his wife	they	
their girls		them
his daughters		them
the answer	It	
a tiny plastic saxophone	it	it
Betty	she	
Yvonne	she	
all six girls	They	
their father		him

➡ Which referents come before the verb? _he_ , _they_ , _it_ , _she_

Which referents come after the verb? _them_ , _it_ , _him_

ACTIVITY 83 Choosing the Correct Referent

In the passage below, choose the correct referent in parentheses so that it matches its box and write *Ref* above the correct referent. Draw a box around its box and an arrow from the referent to its box.

Adapted from **"The Gossiper"** in ***Chicken Soup for the Teenage Soul***
by Cannfield, Hansen, and Kirberger, pp. 41–42

A woman repeated a bit of gossip about a neighbor. Within a few days the whole community knew the

story. The neighbor was deeply hurt. Later, the woman responsible for spreading the gossip learned

Ref   *Ref*
that (it/she) was not true. (She/He) was very sorry and went to a wise old sage to find out what

Ref
(she/he) could do to stop the gossip.

       Ref   *Ref*
      "Go to the marketplace," (he/him) said, "and purchase a chicken, and have (it/him) killed. Then

                Ref
on your way home, pluck its feathers and drop (it/them) one by one along the road." Although

         Ref
surprised by this advice, the woman did what (he/it) said.

      The next day the wise man said, "Now, go and collect all those feathers you dropped

        Ref
yesterday and bring (it/them) back to me."

The woman followed the same road, but to her dismay the wind had blown all the feathers away.

        Ref
After searching for hours, (they/she) returned with only three in her hand. "You see," said the sage,

     Ref   *Ref*
"it's easy to drop (it/them), but it's impossible to get (it/them) back. So it is with gossip. It doesn't

             Ref
take much to spread gossip, but once you do, you can never take (it/them) back."

ACTIVITY 84 **More Practice with Referents**

Write *Ref* above the incorrectly matched referent in the sentences below. Draw a box around its box and put an asterisk over the main word in the box. Draw an arrow from the referent to its box. Then, correct the referent.

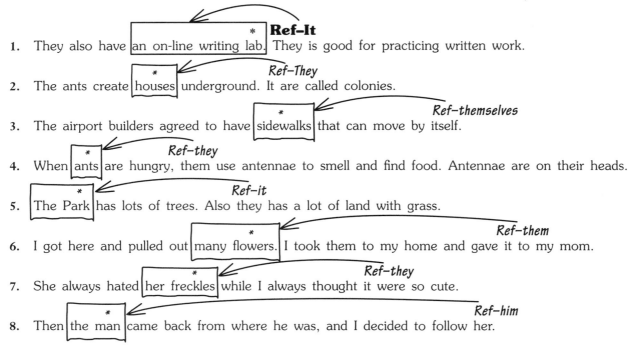

1. They also have an on-line writing lab. They is good for practicing written work. **Ref–It**

2. The ants create houses underground. It are called colonies. *Ref–They*

3. The airport builders agreed to have sidewalks that can move by itself. *Ref–themselves*

4. When ants are hungry, them use antennae to smell and find food. Antennae are on their heads. *Ref–they*

5. The Park has lots of trees. Also they has a lot of land with grass. *Ref–it*

6. I got here and pulled out many flowers. I took them to my home and gave it to my mom. *Ref–them*

7. She always hated her freckles while I always thought it were so cute. *Ref–they*

8. Then the man came back from where he was, and I decided to follow her. *Ref–him*

In the sentences below, boxes are repeated. Write *Ref?* above the repeated box and correct it with an appropriate referent. The first one is done for you.

Ref?–it
9. I grabbed the flag and waved the flag.

Ref?–It
10. The dog was so thirsty. The dog showed its thirsty face.

Ref?–He   *Ref?–her*
11. Tarlie realized that Gino, the dog, was very loyal to her. Gino always slept with Tarlie.

12. Jerry thinks that he might need to spend more time with the hamster to appreciate what his sister

Ref?–it
sees in the hamster.

Ref?–it
13. Classes will be canceled tomorrow because tomorrow is a holiday.

Ref?–them
14. Leave the books outside my office. Someone will come to pick the books up later.

ACTIVITY 85 Practice Editing Inside Boxes and for Referents I

Edit the following sentences using the correction symbol or symbols inside each sentence to help you find the errors. The first one is done for you.

Adapted from **"Secrets from the Desert"** in *Reading Fluency, Level C*
by Camille L. Z. Blachowicz, p. 22

1. It all started with a goat. At least, that's the way the story goes.

  1 the
2. The story comes from a shepherd boy in Middle East.

       boy
3. This boys lived in Jordan. One day, in 1947, he and his goats were out in the desert,
       ^
  1 *the*
  near Dead Sea.

                                                      stone   **3** *the*
4. One of the goats ran off. The boy saw it go into a cave. He threw a stones into a cave to scare
                                                          ^
  the goat out.

           Ref *he*
5. When the stone landed, the boy heard something break.

               3 *the*
6. The boy ran off and brought a friend back to cave.

      Ref *they*   **3** *the*
7. Together he climbed into dark, dry cave.

          3 *the*
8. There they saw what a stone had hit.

                              jars
9. Lying on the floor were some old pottery jar.
                                        ^
     jars   **Ref** *they*   *years*
10. These jar weren't just old—it were ancient. They were 2,000 year old.
       ^   ^
                          papers   *boys*
11. Rolled up in the jars were some old paper as old as the jars. The boy did not know it then,
                                ^   ^
    papers   **Ref** *They* **2** *the*   **3** *the*
    but the paper were of great importance. It were first part of Dead Sea Scrolls.
          ^
  Researchers   *scientists*
12. Researcher and scientist call the Dead Sea Scrolls one of the greatest finds ever.
        ^   ^

ACTIVITY 86 Practice Editing Inside Boxes and for Referents II

Edit the following sentences using the correction symbol or symbols inside each sentence to help you find the errors.

Adapted from **"Women at War"** in *Reading Fluency, Level D*
by Camille L. Z. Blachowicz, p. 9

1. Between 1961 and 1973, more than 7,000 military women served in Vietnam.

2. At that time, women were not trained for fighting. Most were *nurses* nurse.

3. Many served in *hospitals* hospital that were located near the action.

4. Army nurses had to deal with their patients' pain and **u**–*suffering* sufferings.

5. Some *soldiers* soldier, as a result of their wounds, would be crippled for **u**–*life* lifes.

6. Often **2** *the* last face that a dying *soldier* soldiers saw was **2** *the* face of a *nurse* nurses.

7. Connie Curtley was a nurse in Vietnam. Her many *memories* memory of the *war* wars are painful.

8. **Ref** *She* They describes the smell of the dirty uniforms that **Ref** *she* they cut off the wounded men.

9. At times, Curtley treated so many wounded *men* man that her own *clothes* cloth were soaked in **u**–*blood* bloods.

10. Curtley said her uniform was so full of dried blood, **Ref**–*it* they was hard.

11. *Years* Year after a **3** *the* war, nurses still have trouble shaking these memories.

Edit the following sentences using the correction symbol or symbols inside each sentence to help you find the errors.

Adapted from **"Race Through the Sand"** in ***Reading Fluency, Level C***
by Camille L. Z. Blachowicz, p. 23

1
1. So you like to run? Then maybe Marathon of the Sands is the race for you.

2. Of course, you'll have to fly to Morocco. Once there, you'll have to run 140 mile in seven day.

ʌ　　　　　　ʌ

u
3. And you'll have to do it in 120° heats.

Ref
4. Organizers boast that the Marathon is "the world's toughest footrace." They has six stages, each

1
taking place in hot Sahara Desert.

Ref
5. Runners just don't run. Runners run in the sand. They just don't carry a water bottle.

6. They carry on their backs all the good that they will need over the course of the seven-day race.

ʌ

7. This means cloth, sleeping bag, compass, and flare are packed in their backpacks.

ʌ　　　　　　ʌ　　　　ʌ　　　ʌ

8. And, oh, yes, each runners also carries a snakebite kits.

ʌ　　　　　　　　　　ʌ

u
9. Each year, about 500 peoples sign up to run this races.

ʌ

10. Because of the harsh conditions, it would seem that many runner would perish.

ʌ

Ref
11. While most people don't die, it do pay a price.

u
12. Some collapse with heat exhaustions.

EDITING QUIZ IV **Answers**

Edit the following sentences using the correction symbol or symbols inside each sentence to help you find the errors.

Adapted from **"Race Through the Sand"** in *Reading Fluency, Level C*
by Camille L.Z. Blachowicz, p. 23

1. So you like to run? Then maybe *the* Marathon of the Sands is the race for you.

2. Of course, you'll have to fly to Morocco. Once there, you'll have to run 140 miles ∧ in seven days. ∧

3. And you'll have to do it in 120° **u**–*heat* heats.

4. Organizers boast that the Marathon is "the world's toughest footrace." They has six stages, each **Ref**-*It*

    taking place in hot *the* Sahara Desert.

5. Runners just don't run. Runners run in the sand. **Ref**-*They* They just don't carry a water bottle.

6. They carry on their backs ∧ all the goods ∧ that they will need over the course of the seven-day race.

7. This means clothes, ∧ sleeping bags, ∧ compasses, ∧ and flares ∧ are packed in their backpacks.

8. And, oh, yes, each *runner* runners ∧ also carries a snakebite *kit* kits. ∧

9. Each year, about 500 **u**–*people* peoples sign up to run this *race* races. ∧

10. Because of the harsh conditions, it would seem that many runners ∧ would perish.

11. While most people don't die, it **Ref**-*they* do pay a price.

12. Some collapse with heat **u**–*exhaustion* exhaustions.

Appendices

X-Words: Before and Now

Before	At some time before . . . maybe continuing into now	Now
did		does
		do
had	has	
	have	
would		will/would
could		can/could
should		shall/should
might		may/might
		must
was		is
were		are
		am

Appendix B
X-Words: 1 or 2 or Many

1	2 or Many
is	are
was	were
has	have
does	do

will/would	will/would
can/could	can/could
shall/should	shall/should
may/might/must	may/might/must
had	had
did	did

Appendix C
Some Main Verb Forms

<table>
<tr><th colspan="3">**With X-Words That Show**</th><th colspan="3">**With X-Words That Hide**</th></tr>
<tr><td colspan="6">(Time and how many are in the X-words)</td></tr>
<tr><th>BASE</th><th>*ING*</th><th>*D-T-N*</th><th>V/XS</th><th>V/XO</th><th>V/XD</th></tr>
<tr><td>do, does, did will, would can, could shall, should may, might, must</td><td>is, am, are, was, were</td><td>has, have, had</td><td>(hidden *does*)</td><td>(hidden *do*)</td><td>(hidden *did*)</td></tr>
<tr><td>abandon</td><td>abandoning</td><td>abandoned</td><td>abandons</td><td>abandon</td><td>abandoned</td></tr>
<tr><td>accept</td><td>accepting</td><td>accepted</td><td>accepts</td><td>accept</td><td>accepted</td></tr>
<tr><td>allow</td><td>allowing</td><td>allowed</td><td>allows</td><td>allow</td><td>allowed</td></tr>
<tr><td>ask</td><td>asking</td><td>asked</td><td>asks</td><td>ask</td><td>asked</td></tr>
<tr><td>bark</td><td>barking</td><td>barked</td><td>barks</td><td>bark</td><td>barked</td></tr>
<tr><td>be</td><td>being</td><td>been</td><td>—</td><td>—</td><td>—</td></tr>
<tr><td>bother</td><td>bothering</td><td>bothered</td><td>bothers</td><td>bother</td><td>bothered</td></tr>
<tr><td>call</td><td>calling</td><td>called</td><td>calls</td><td>call</td><td>called</td></tr>
<tr><td>change</td><td>changing</td><td>changed</td><td>changes</td><td>change</td><td>changed</td></tr>
<tr><td>choose</td><td>choosing</td><td>chosen</td><td>chooses</td><td>choose</td><td>chose</td></tr>
<tr><td>come</td><td>coming</td><td>come</td><td>comes</td><td>come</td><td>came</td></tr>
<tr><td>consider</td><td>considering</td><td>considered</td><td>considers</td><td>consider</td><td>considered</td></tr>
<tr><td>convince</td><td>convincing</td><td>convinced</td><td>convinces</td><td>convince</td><td>convinced</td></tr>
<tr><td>deserve</td><td>deserving</td><td>deserved</td><td>deserves</td><td>deserve</td><td>deserved</td></tr>
<tr><td>destroy</td><td>destroying</td><td>destroyed</td><td>destroys</td><td>destroy</td><td>destroyed</td></tr>
<tr><td>die</td><td>dying</td><td>died</td><td>dies</td><td>die</td><td>died</td></tr>
<tr><td>distract</td><td>distracting</td><td>distracted</td><td>distracts</td><td>distract</td><td>distracted</td></tr>
<tr><td>do</td><td>doing</td><td>done</td><td>does</td><td>do</td><td>did</td></tr>
<tr><td>doubt</td><td>doubting</td><td>doubted</td><td>doubts</td><td>doubt</td><td>doubted</td></tr>
<tr><td>drive</td><td>driving</td><td>driven</td><td>drives</td><td>drive</td><td>drove</td></tr>
<tr><td>expect</td><td>expecting</td><td>expected</td><td>expects</td><td>expect</td><td>expected</td></tr>
<tr><td>feel</td><td>feeling</td><td>felt</td><td>feels</td><td>feel</td><td>felt</td></tr>
<tr><td>fight</td><td>fighting</td><td>fought</td><td>fights</td><td>fight</td><td>fought</td></tr>
<tr><td>find</td><td>finding</td><td>found</td><td>finds</td><td>find</td><td>found</td></tr>
</table>

With X-Words That Show			With X-Words That Hide		
			(Time and how many are in the X-words)		
BASE	*ING*	*D-T-N*	**V/XS**	**V/XO**	**V/XD**
do, does, did will, would can, could shall, should may, might, must	is, am, are, was, were	has, have, had	(hidden *does*)	(hidden *do*)	(hidden *did*)
fix	fixing	fixed	fixes	fix	fixed
get	getting	gotten	gets	get	got
give	giving	given	gives	give	gave
go	going	gone	goes	go	went
grieve	grieving	grieved	grieves	grieve	grieved
guide	guiding	guided	guides	guide	guided
have	having	had	has	have	had
hate	hating	hated	hates	hate	hated
hear	hearing	heard	hears	hear	heard
invent	inventing	invented	invents	invent	invented
interrupt	interrupting	interrupted	interrupts	interrupt	interrupted
kill	killing	killed	kills	kill	killed
know	knowing	known	knows	know	knew
leave	leaving	left	leaves	leave	left
let	letting	let	lets	let	let
live	living	lived	lives	live	lived
look	looking	looked	looks	look	looked
lose	losing	lost	loses	lose	lost
make	making	made	makes	make	made
marry	marrying	married	marries	marry	married
meet	meeting	met	meets	meet	met
mention	mentioning	mentioned	mentions	mention	mentioned
motivate	motivating	motivated	motivates	motivate	motivated
obey	obeying	obeyed	obeys	obey	obeyed
pay	paying	paid	pays	pay	paid
polish	polishing	polished	polishes	polish	polished
put (on)	putting (on)	put (on)	puts (on)	put (on)	put (on)
raise	raising	raised	raises	raise	raised

With X-Words That Show			With X-Words That Hide		
		(Time and how many are in the X-words)			
BASE	ING	D-T-N	V/XS	V/XO	V/XD
do, does, did will, would can, could shall, should may, might, must	is, am, are, was, were	has, have, had	(hidden *does*)	(hidden *do*)	(hidden *did*)
reach	reaching	reached	reaches	reach	reached
read	reading	read	reads	read	read
relieve	relieving	relieved	relieves	relieve	relieved
ride	riding	ridden	rides	ride	rode
rise	rising	risen	rises	rise	rose
say	saying	said	says	say	said
see	seeing	seen	sees	see	saw
seem	seeming	seemed	seems	seem	seemed
send	sending	sent	sends	send	sent
stand	standing	stood	stands	stand	stood
stop	stopping	stopped	stops	stop	stopped
take	taking	taken	takes	take	took
think	thinking	thought	thinks	think	thought
try	trying	tried	tries	try	tried
understand	understanding	understood	understands	understand	understood
walk	walking	walked	walks	walk	walked
want	wanting	wanted	wants	want	wanted

Linkers

"Sequence in Time" Linkers

Finally,
The next day,
First, Second, etc.
Then
Later (on),
Meanwhile,
At the same time,
Now,

"And" Linkers

In addition,
Also,

"But" Linkers

However,
Still,
Instead,

"So" Linkers

As a result,
Therefore,

"Different Way" Linkers

On the other hand,

"Explanation" Linkers

In other words,
For example,
For instance,

"Detail" Linkers

In fact,
Actually,

Appendix E
Common Shifter Words and Phrases

Time Shifters

Before school, I called my mother.

After school, I called my mother.

During school, I called my mother.

When school started, I called my mother.

At 12 PM, I called my mother.

Last night, I called my mother.

Everyday, I call my mother.

A few days ago, I called my mother.

In a couple of days, I will call my mother.

Next week, I will call my mother.

While I was eating, I called my mother.

Reason Shifters

Since he was sick, he left school.

Because he was sick, he left school.

Contrast Shifters

Although he was sick, he came to school.

Even though he was sick, he came to school.

Though he was sick, he came to school.

Condition Shifters

If it rains, we won't have a picnic.

Even if it rains, we will have a picnic.

Unless it rains, we will have a picnic.

Where Shifters

Underneath an ant hill, there can be miles of tunnels.

About three feet from us, the bear stood straight up on its back legs.

Appendix F
Countable and Uncountable Nouns/Boxes

Some nouns can be both countable and uncountable depending on the meaning intended.

Countable	Uncountable
(Here the meaning is about specific times or things.)	(Here the meaning is "in general.")
*	*
We had a good time.	Good students use time well.
*	*
The young wife bought a cooked chicken for dinner.	I eat only chicken.
*	*
May I take a chocolate?	Chocolate is made with milk.
*	*
The rich man has three homes.	The college student left home.
*	*
The old man had a long and healthy life.	Live life to the fullest everyday!

Some Other Uncountable Nouns

spaghetti, pollution, tennis,

ice, gold, dirt, anger, happiness,

salt, courage, snow, electricity,

violence, patience, sunshine,

garbage, homework, clothing,

peace, work, vocabulary, news

Appendix G
X -Word Grammar Correction Symbols

X?   missing X-word

X?
I getting a light blue scooter on Friday.
^

X̸   too many X-words

X
All the windows are ~~is~~ very strong.

      unnecessary X-word

X
I ~~were~~ enjoyed this trip a lot.

WX   wrong X-word

WX
Why does she sick?

TIME   wrong time reference

Time
How do you tell your Mom that soldiers

had stopped you . . .?

S X   wrong match-up of subject and X-word

S   **X**
Many dogs does obey him. He's a leader.

X V   wrong match-up of X-word and main verb

X   **V**
And she saw Shira was rocked outside. And

X   **V**
she was watched and waiting for Jessy.

V/X   wrong form of a hidden X-word

(hidden *does*)

He does work for my dad. He just

V/XS
pull the sled like other dogs.

(hidden *do*)

V/XO
I felt much better right now.

(hidden *did*)

Jerry brought the hamster home

V/XD
and shows it to his parents.

INF   wrong form of infinitive

Inf
I'm beginning to thinking of a better gift.

T, + T   missing joiner and/or comma

T **,+**   **T**
It rained. The picnic ended.

This appendix is adapted from Kurz and Glock 2000.

T=	second subject can be dropped	**T** Choco began to jump around Bertha and **=** ~~Choco~~ cheered her up.
T=	a joiner needs to be added and/or a comma can be dropped	**T** We trusted each other / **and** **=** expressed our secret personalities.
L T	add a/choose a better linker	**L In fact,** He just loves plain pizza. ~~Anyway,~~ he will stop snow boarding and zoom to make a call for pizza.
F T	front shifter needs attachment	**F** **T** When I was on my way. I saw someone yelling at me.
T E	end shifter needs attachment	**T** **E** She started to lose a lot of weight. Because she refused to eat.
T I	insert needs proper punctuation	**T I** My dad, Randy works for the government.
	something wrong in a: countable box	She wanted a special gifts. ^
	uncountable box	^U They have a good transportation.
	the box	**5** James went to park with his dog.
Ref	wrong match-up of referent	I got there and pulled many flowers and **Ref** took it home.
Ref?	referent needed	I grabbed the flag and **Ref?** waved the flag.

Appendix H
Model Essays

Crossed Cultures
by Luke

In the story "Mrs. Dutta Writes a Letter" by Chitra Divakaruni, Mrs. Dutta, an Indian woman, moves from Calcutta, India, to San Francisco, California. She moves to America to live with her son, Sagar, and his family after a long illness. After several months in her new country and home, Mrs. Dutta decides to move back to Calcutta due to the cultural conflict that existed between her and her daughter-in-law, Shyamoli. I strongly agree with the decision that Mrs. Dutta made to go back to her country.

Mrs. Dutta wanted to spend time with her family because she desperately missed her son Sagar and was thrilled when she actually moved in with him. She thought things would go well when she moved in, but she didn't expect that things were going to happen so differently. For example, Mrs. Dutta, at an early age, learned to get up every morning at 5 a.m. to make tea for her husband and family, but during her stay in California, it seems that Sagar doesn't respect this tradition. One day, she mistakenly dropped the alarm clock when she just wanted to make tea for everyone. Sagar tells her "Mother, please don't get up so early in the morning. All that noise in the bathroom, it wakes us up, and Molli has such a long day at work." Mrs. Dutta did not feel appreciated and felt upset after Sagar's statement. Her cultural beliefs and traditions are getting in the way

of her ability to get along with and be a part of her family.

Mrs. Dutta was very surprised after she saw her grandchildren react to their

parents and to Mrs. Dutta herself. For instance, Mrs. Dutta was in the bathroom

and Shyamoli told her daughter, Mrinalini, to use the bathroom downstairs

and Mrinalini's reaction was "it's not fair, why can't she go downstairs." After

Mrs. Dutta heard what her grandchild said, she felt badly about the way her

grandchildren talk to their parents. She feels it's too Americanized, and that they

don't have respect for their elders. Mrs. Dutta was also surprised that Shyamoli,

as a mother, did not discipline her children for being so disrespectful.

Mrs. Dutta is forcing herself to be happy, but she's living a lie. She gets

a letter from her best friend from Calcutta asking her how everything is in

California with her son, Sagar. Mrs. Dutta wants to write back but doesn't want

to be very negative about her experience because she doesn't want people in her

country to know that she is ashamed of how Shyamoli and Sagar are acting;

she doesn't want others to know the truth about what happened and how she

is feeling. She is unable to express what is really happening in America even to

her best friend, and that, I think, is bad. She is going against herself by trying to

make things sound better than they are. If she were to go back home, she could

again be herself. She wouldn't have to try to blend in while going against all of

her own beliefs. In America, she is acting opposite of who she really is.

If Sagar and Shyamoli had known that Mrs. Dutta was unhappy, I think they still wouldn't change their behavior. Shyamoli, as a daughter-in-law, is too embarrassed to hang her clothes outside, as preferred by Mrs. Dutta, because she doesn't want her neighbors to look down at her and think that they are deprived and can't afford to buy a dryer. It seems that Mrs. Dutta can't possibly do anything there to help or be valued enough as a grandmother and a mother to her family because they will not allow her to be herself. She always wanted to come and spend time with her family and always pictured that everything would be perfect. The picture that hung in her bedroom in Calcutta allowed her to fantasize about her family and what it would be like when she came to America, but everything was completely different the moment she arrived. Maybe it would be good for Sagar and Shyamoli to visit Mrs. Dutta in India for them to see and understand their culture.

Abel's Misfortune
by Molly

In the first chapter of *In This Sign* by Joanne Greenberg, the main character of the novel, Abel, is heading for a life of debt. Once after work, on the way home, a car in a showroom of cars caught his attention. Standing for a while, he admired the beautiful cars. The car salesman in the showroom invited Abel to come in and started to advertise with a lot of talk how good the car is. So the salesman, Dengel, convinced Abel to buy the car. Abel did not realize that he only put down a small payment for the car and ignored requests for monthly payments which came by mail. I think that Abel and Dengel were both to blame for Abel's life of debt.

Abel is guilty. When Dengel was speaking to him about the car, Abel pretended to understand. "He didn't need to hear the words to feel the honor, so he smiled and nodded to show how glad he was because of it." Dengel continued to convince Abel to buy the car and Abel "nodded yes, and yes again." I understand Abel's behaviors; he wants to feel respected as he said, ". . . he called me 'sir.'" He didn't want Dengel to find out that he's Deaf because his attitude to him would change. Then Dengel gave some papers to Abel, and the Deaf man signed a contract without reading it. This is why he didn't know about owing monthly payments.

Mr. Dengel is like a hunter whom Abel falls prey to. "Sometimes the man came out and took someone by the arm and smiled to him to come and sit behind the wheel and notice this thing or that, try the horn, try the lights.

Once, Abel was that person." The car salesman was buttering Abel up to convince him to buy the car. Moreover, Dengel talked with a cigar in his mouth that didn't allow Abel to read his lips. I wonder how Dengel couldn't notice something was wrong with Abel while he was talking on and on. The nodding without saying any word a long time should have seemed suspicious. I think Dengel is just self-interested. He, as any businessman, needs money. His main interest was to sell cars, so he didn't care if the customer understood.

I think this trouble would not happen to Abel today because the present time is more civilized. Now Deaf people's lives are different than before when Deaf people always were ashamed of being Deaf and not feeling equal to hearing people. In the future, Abel should let Dengel know beforehand that he is Deaf and ask him to write what he is going to say or ask him politely to take out the cigar from his mouth and try to move his lips clearly. It's hard to guess about Dengel's behavior. In my life, I have never experienced an occasion with an unscrupulous salesperson. I think that a Dengel today would act properly if he is aware that a customer is Deaf. At first, he would ask Abel if he can read lips. If he cannot do that, then, the salesman certainly will write.

Conflict Between Immigrant Parents and Their Children
by Olga

In "An American Dream" by Rosemarie Santini and "The Struggle to Be an All-American Girl" by Elizabeth Wong, we see a conflict of values between younger and older generations. In both stories, the children of immigrant parents prefer American culture and tradition and do not follow their family's tradition. I will offer some reasons for their feelings.

"Where are the children?" asks Grandmother Ida Rinaldi. Grandmother Ida cooked a special dinner to feed her family. She expects them to be together because this is her cultural tradition. However, her grandchildren, John and Paul DeGiovanni, were not at home even though they knew that their family was waiting for them for dinner. John and Paul were busy at the DeGiovanni beach club, swimming and getting ready for a party. They preferred to hang out with their friends and not to be home with their family. "We . . . respected our parents and our family" said Ida's husband Mr. Rinaldi. In addition, he said, "we worked hard." His grandchildren will go to college without having to work; they have everything that they need. They were not the same as he was as a hard-working teenager.

Other conflict between immigrant parents and their children appeared in "The Struggle to be an All-American Girl" by Elizabeth Wong. Elizabeth's mother forced her children to learn and to respect Chinese traditions even though they did not want to. "In Chinese school the children learned mainly language, reading, and writing. The lessons always began with an exercise in politeness." The students in

Chinese school had to learn to be polite and always respect elderly people. They learned Chinese languages by heart. Elizabeth's mother wanted her children to learn to speak Chinese because in Chinatown there were many Chinese people who speak Chinese. She wanted Elizabeth to be able to speak with these people, celebrate Chinese holidays, and eat Chinese food. But Elizabeth did not like the Chinese language because of the loud voice people used with it. Moreover, Elizabeth said, "Nancy Drew, my favorite book heroine, never spoke Chinese."

In my opinion, John and Paul will not resolve the problem with their grandparents. They are not children anymore who need fixing to follow old traditions. They already chose and will hold on to more American ways of life. These ways are comfortable for them, and they do not want to be responsible or help their parents and grandparents. I think it is boring for them to stay home with their family. They prefer to have fun and hang out. Elizabeth and her brother were unhappy with their Chinese school, and it was so hard for them to learn Chinese traditions. Their souls and traditions are now American, and they will not follow Chinese traditions. Elizabeth spoke English in Chinatown even though she knew Chinese. It means forcing her to speak Chinese will be hopeless, and she will not obey what her mother wants. The children of immigrant families in America will choose their own preferred style and culture without their parents' approval. American schools and other teens will influence these children, and it will be hard to teach or explain deeply to them about their own culture and traditions. Their parents have to accept this because they made their children live in America.

Appendix I
Model Essays Grammatically Analyzed

Crossed Cultures
by Luke

Grammatical Focus:

Subjects
X-Words
X-V Matches
Hidden X-Words
Infinitives

In the story "Mrs. Dutta *[V/XS]* Writes a Letter" by Chitra Divakaruni, Mrs. Dutta, an Indian woman, *[V/XS]* moves from Calcutta, India to San Francisco, California. She moves *[V/XS]* to America to live *[Inf]* with her son, Sagar, and his family after a long illness. After several months in her new country and home, Mrs. Dutta *[V/XS]* decides to move *[Inf]* back to Calcutta due to the cultural conflict *[V/XD]* that existed between her and her daughter-in-law, Shyamoli. I *[V/XO]* strongly agree with the decision that Mrs. Dutta *[V/XD]* made to go *[Inf]* back to her country.

Mrs. Dutta *[V/XD]* wanted to spend *[Inf]* time with her family because she desperately missed *[V/XD]* her son, Sagar, and was thrilled when she *[X]* actually moved *[V/XD]* in with him. She *[V/XD]* thought things would *[X]* go *[V]* well when she moved *[V/XD]* in, but she *[X]* didn't *[V]* expect that things were *[X]* going *[V]* to happen *[Inf]* so differently. For example, Mrs. Dutta, at an early age, learned *[V/XD]* to get up *[Inf]* early morning at 5 am to make *[Inf]* tea for her husband and family, but during her stay in California, it *[V/XS]* seems that Sagar *[X]* doesn't *[V]* respect this tradition. One day, she mistakenly dropped the alarm clock when she just wanted to make tea for everyone. Sagar tells her, "Mother, please don't get up so early in the morning. All the noise in the bathroom, it wakes us up, and Molli has such a long day at work." Mrs. Dutta did not feel appreciated and felt upset after Sagar's statement. Her cultural beliefs and traditions are getting in the way of her ability to get along with and be a part of her family.

Mrs. Dutta was very surprised after she saw her grandchildren react to their parents and to Mrs. Dutta herself. For instance, Mrs. Dutta was in the bathroom and Shyamoli told her daughter, Mrinalini, to use the bathroom downstairs, and Mrinalini's reaction was "it's not fair, why can't she go downstairs?" After Mrs. Dutta heard what her grandchild said, she felt badly about the way her grandchildren talk to their parents. She feels their behavior is too Americanized, and that they don't have respect for their elders. Mrs. Dutta was also surprised that Shyamoli, as a mother, did not discipline her children for being so disrespectful.

Mrs. Dutta is forcing herself to be happy, but she's living a lie. She gets a letter from her best friend from Calcutta asking her how everything is in California with her son. Mrs. Dutta wants to write back but doesn't want to be very negative about her experience because she doesn't want people in her country to know that she is ashamed of how Shyamoli and Sagar are acting; she doesn't want others to know the truth about what happened and how she is feeling. She is unable to express what is really happening in America even to her best friend and [that,] [I] think, is bad. [She] is going against herself by trying (to make) [things] sound better than [they] are. If [she] went back home, [she] could again be herself. [She] wouldn't [have¹ to try] (to blend in) while going against all of her own beliefs. In America, [she] is acting opposite of who [she] really is.

If [Sagar and Shyamoli] had known that [Mrs. Dutta] was unhappy, [I] think [they] still wouldn't change their behavior. [Shyamoli, as a daughter-in-law,] is too embarrassed (to hang) her clothes outside, as preferred by Mrs. Dutta, because [she] doesn't want her neighbors (to look down) at her and (think) that [they] are deprived and can't afford (to buy) a dryer. [It] seems that [Mrs. Dutta] can't possibly do anything there (to help) or (be) valued enough as a grandmother and a mother to her family because [they] will not allow her (to be) herself. [She] always wanted (to come) and (spend) time with her family and always pictured that everything would be perfect. [The picture] that hung in her bedroom in Calcutta allowed her (to fantasize) about her family and what [it] would be like when [she] came to America, but [everything] was completely different the moment [she] arrived. Maybe [it] would be good for Sagar and Shyamoli (to visit) Mrs. Dutta in India for them (to see) and (understand) their culture.

---

1. *Have to* is a semimodal similar in meaning to *must*.

Abel's Misfortune
by Molly

Grammatical Focus:

Subjects
X-Words
X-V Matches
Hidden X-Words
Infinitives
Sentence Structure

1
In the first chapter of *In This Sign* by Joanne Greenberg, the main   **1 FTI**
                          X   *V*   **2**
character, Abel, is heading for a life of debt. Once after work, on the   **2 FFT**
                                                  V/XD
way home, a car in a showroom of cars caught his attention.

3   *V/XD*   **4**
Standing for a while, he admired the beautiful cars. The car salesman   **3 FT**
                        V/XD   *Inf*   *V/XD*   *Inf*
in the showroom invited Abel (to come in) and started (to advertise)   **4 T=**

                                        X **5**
with a lot of talk how good the car was. So, the salesman, Dengel,   **5 LTI**
   V/XD   *Inf*   **6** *X*   *V*   *V/XD*
convinced Abel (to buy) the car. Abel did not realize that he only put   **6 T=I**
                                                  V/XD
down a small payment for the car and ignored requests for monthly

                              7 *V/XO*   *X*
payments, which came by mail. I think that Abel and Dengel were   **7 T**
        Inf
both (to blame) for Abel's life of debt.

   8 *X*   **9**   *X*   *V*
Abel is guilty. When Dengel was speaking to him about the car,   **8 T**
     V/XD   *Inf*   **10** *X*   *V*   *Inf*
Abel pretended (to understand) "He didn't need (to hear) the words   **9 FT**
   Inf   *V/XD*   *V/XD*   *Inf*
(to feel) the honor, so he smiled and nodded (to show) how glad he   **10 T,+T=**
   X   **11**   *V/XD*   *Inf*   *Inf*
was because of it." Dengel continued (to convince) Abel (to buy) the   **11 T,+T**
           V/XD   **12**   *V/XO*
car, and Abel "nodded yes, and yes again." I understand Abel's   **12 T;T**
           V/XS *Inf*   *V/XD*   *V/XD*
behaviors; he wants (to feel) respected as he said, ". . .he called me

13   *X*   *V*   *Inf*   *X*

'sir.'" [He] didn't want Dengel (to find out) that [he]'s Deaf because   **13 TE**

           X   *V*   **14**   *V/XD*

[his attitude] to him would change. Then, [Dengel] gave some papers to   **14 L,T,+T**

            V/XD   **15**   *X*

Abel, and [the Deaf man] signed a contract without reading it. [This] is   **15 T**

    X   *V*

why [he] didn't know about owing monthly payments.

   16   *X*   *V/XS*   **17**

   [Mr. Dengel] is like a hunter whom [Abel] falls prey to. "Sometimes   **16 T**

     V/XD   *V/XD*   *V/XD*

[the man] came out and took someone by the arm and smiled to him   **17 LT= =**

Inf   *Inf*   *Inf*   *Inf*

(to come) and (sit) behind the wheel and (notice) this thing or that, (try)

        Inf   **18**   *X*   **19**

the horn, (try) the lights. Once, [Abel] was that person." [The car   **18 LT**

     X   *V*   *Inf*   *Inf*

salesman] was buttering Abel up (to convince) him (to buy) the car.   **19 T**

20   *V/XD*   *X*   *V*

Moreover, [Dengel] talked with a cigar in his mouth [that] didn't allow   **20 LT**

    Inf   **21** *V/XO*   *X*   *V*

Abel (to read) his lips. [I] wonder how [Dengel] couldn't notice [something]   **21 TE**

X   *X*   *V*   **22**

was wrong with Abel while [he] was talking on and on. [The nodding   **22 T**

                    X   *Aux²*   *V*

without saying any word a long time] should have seemed suspicious.

23 *V/XO*   *X*   **24**   *V/XS*

[I] think [Dengel] is just self-interested. [He, as any businessman,] needs   **23 T**

       25   *X*   *Inf*   *X*   *V*

money. [His main interest] was (to sell) cars, so [he] didn't care if   **24 TI**

          V/XD

[the customer] understood.   **25 T,+T**

26 *V/XO*   *X*   *V*

   [I] think [this trouble] would not happen to Abel today because   **26 TE**

            X   **27**   *X*

[the present time] is more civilized. Now, [Deaf people's lives] are   **27 LT**

                            X

different than before when [Deaf people] always were ashamed of

                      28

being Deaf and not feeling equal to hearing people. In the future,   **28 LT= =**

---

2. Middle verbs in three-word verb phrases are called auxiliaries.

Abel should let Dengel know beforehand that he is Deaf and ask him to write what he is going³ to say or ask him politely to take out the cigar from his mouth and try to move his lips clearly. It's hard **29 T**

to guess about Dengel's behavior. In my life, I have never experienced **30 FT** an occasion with an unscrupulous salesperson. I think Dengel today **31 TE** would act properly if he is aware that a customer is Deaf. At first, he **32 LT** would ask Abel if he can read lips. If he cannot do that, then, **33 FLT** the salesman certainly will write.

---

3. *Is going to* is a semimodal similar in meaning to *will*.

Conflict Between Immigrant Parents and Their Children
by Olga

Grammatical Focus:

Putting it all together!
Subjects
X-Words
X-V Matches
Hidden X-Words
Infinitives
Sentence Structure
Boxes and Referents

1 In "The American Dream" by Rosemarie Santini and "The Struggle to   **1 FT**

be an All-American Girl" by Elizabeth Wong, we see a conflict of

values between younger and older generations. **2** In both stories, the   **2 FT=**

children of immigrant parents *prefer* American culture and tradition and

do not follow their family's tradition. **3** I will offer some reasons for their   **3 T**

feelings.   **4 T(Q)**

4 "Where are the children?" asks Grandmother Ida Rinaldi. **5** Grand-   **5 T**

mother Ida cooked a special dinner to feed her family members. **6** She   **6 TE**

expects them to be together because this is her cultural tradition.

7 However, her grandchildren, John and Paul DeGiovanni, were not at   **7 LTIE**

home even though they knew that their family was waiting for them

for dinner. **8** John and Paul were busy at the DeGiovanni beach club,   **8 TI**

swimming and getting ready for a party. **9** They preferred to hang out   **9 T**

with their friends and not to be home with their family. **10** "We . . .   **10 TI**

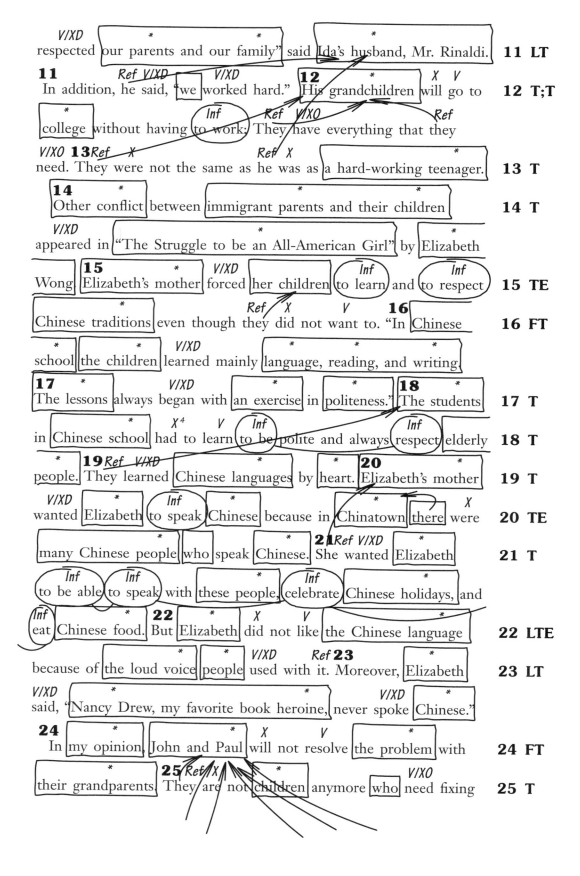

V/XD
respected our parents and our family" said Ida's husband, Mr. Rinaldi.　**11 LT**

11　*Ref V/XD*　*V/XD*　**12**
In addition, he said, "we worked hard." His grandchildren will go to　**12 T;T**

Inf　*Ref V/XD*　*Ref*
college without having to work. They have everything that they

V/XO **13**Ref　X　*Ref X*
need. They were not the same as he was as a hard-working teenager.　**13 T**

14
Other conflict between immigrant parents and their children　**14 T**

V/XD
appeared in "The Struggle to be an All-American Girl" by Elizabeth

15　*V/XD*　*Inf*　*Inf*
Wong Elizabeth's mother forced her children to learn and to respect　**15 TE**

Ref X　V　**16**
Chinese traditions even though they did not want to. "In Chinese　**16 FT**

V/XD
school the children learned mainly language, reading, and writing.

17　*V/XD*　**18**
The lessons always began with an exercise in politeness." The students　**17 T**

*X*⁴　V　*Inf*　*Inf*
in Chinese school had to learn to be polite and always respect elderly　**18 T**

19 *Ref V/XD*　**20**
people. They learned Chinese languages by heart. Elizabeth's mother　**19 T**

V/XD　*Inf*　X
wanted Elizabeth to speak Chinese because in Chinatown there were　**20 TE**

21Ref V/XD
many Chinese people who speak Chinese. She wanted Elizabeth　**21 T**

Inf　*Inf*　*Inf*
to be able to speak with these people, celebrate Chinese holidays, and

Inf　**22**　X　V
eat Chinese food. But Elizabeth did not like the Chinese language　**22 LTE**

V/XD　*Ref* **23**
because of the loud voice people used with it. Moreover, Elizabeth　**23 LT**

V/XD　*V/XD*
said, "Nancy Drew, my favorite book heroine, never spoke Chinese."

24　X　V
In my opinion, John and Paul will not resolve the problem with　**24 FT**

25Ref X　*V/XO*
their grandparents. They are not children anymore who need fixing　**25 T**

4. *Had to* in line 18 is a semimodal similar in meaning to *must*.

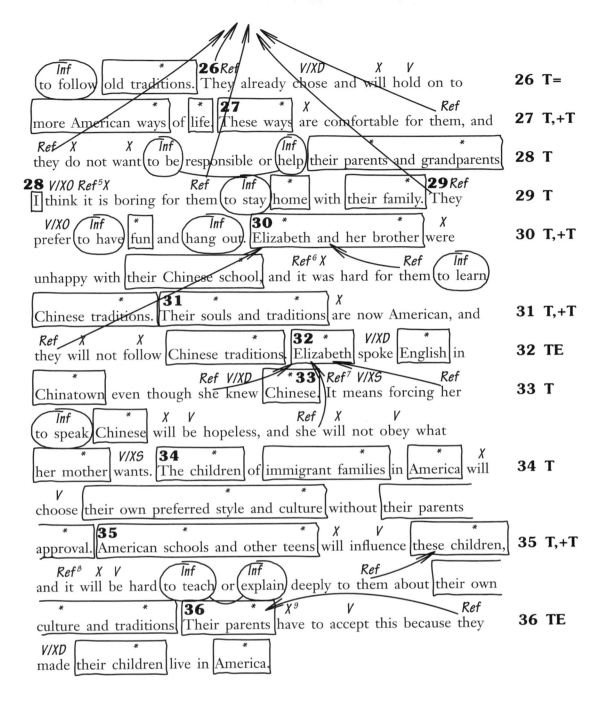

26 to follow old traditions. They already chose and will hold on to   **26 T=**

27 more American ways of life. These ways are comfortable for them, and   **27 T,+T**

28 they do not want to be responsible or help their parents and grandparents   **28 T**

29 I think it is boring for them to stay home with their family. They   **29 T**

30 prefer to have fun and hang out. Elizabeth and her brother were   **30 T,+T**

unhappy with their Chinese school, and it was hard for them to learn

31 Chinese traditions. Their souls and traditions are now American, and   **31 T,+T**

32 they will not follow Chinese traditions. Elizabeth spoke English in   **32 TE**

33 Chinatown even though she knew Chinese. It means forcing her   **33 T**

to speak Chinese will be hopeless, and she will not obey what

34 her mother wants. The children of immigrant families in America will   **34 T**

choose their own preferred style and culture without their parents

35 approval. American schools and other teens will influence these children,   **35 T,+T**

and it will be hard to teach or explain deeply to them about their own

36 culture and traditions. Their parents have to accept this because they   **36 TE**

made their children live in America.

5. *It* in line 28 refers to the entire phrase *to stay home with their family.*

6. *It* between lines 30–31 refers to the entire phrase *to learn Chinese traditions.*

7. *It* in line 33 refers back to the idea that *Elizabeth spoke English in Chinatown even though she knew Chinese.*

8. *It* between lines 35–36 refers to the entire phrase *to teach or explain deeply to them about their own culture and traditions.*

9. *Have to* is a semimodal similar in meaning to *must.*

References

Anderson, Donald G. 1997. *New Practice Readers, Book B.* 3rd ed. New York: Phoenix Learning Resources.

Anderson, Donald G., Clarence Stone, and Ardis Edwards Burton. 1997. *New Practice Readers, Book A.* 3rd ed. New York: Phoenix Learning Resources.

Baldwin, James. 2004. "The King and the Bees." In *Fifty Famous People* by James Baldwin. Retrieved on June 25, 2010 from www.gutenberg.org/etext/6168.

———. 2004. "The Landlord's Mistake." In *Fifty Famous People* by James Baldwin. Retrieved on June 25, 2010 from www.gutenberg.org/etext/6168.

———. 2004. "The Midnight Ride." In *Fifty Famous People* by James Baldwin. Retrieved on June 25, 2010 from www.gutenberg.org/etext/6168.

———. 2004. "The Paddle-Wheel Boat." In *Fifty Famous People* by James Baldwin. Retrieved on June 25, 2010 from www.gutenberg.org/etext/6168.

———. 2004. "Saving the Birds." In *Fifty Famous People* by James Baldwin. Retrieved on June 25, 2010 from www.gutenberg.org/etext/6168.

———. 2004. "The Story of a Great Story." In *Fifty Famous People* by James Baldwin. Retrieved on June 25, 2010 from www.gutenberg.org/etext/6168.

———. 2004. "Two Great Painters." In *Fifty Famous People* by James Baldwin. Retrieved on June 25, 2010 from www.gutenberg.org/etext/6168.

———. 2004. "Which Was the King?" In *Fifty Famous People* by James Baldwin. Retrieved on June 25, 2010 from www.gutenberg.org/etext/6168.

Baum, L. Frank. 2003. "The Glass Dog." In *American Fairy Tales* by L. Frank Baum. Retrieved on June 25, 2010 from http://www.gutenberg.org/files/4357/4357-h/4357-h.htm.

Blachowicz, Camille L. Z., ed. 2004. *Reading Fluency, Level C.* New York: Glencoe.

Blachowicz, Camille L. Z., ed. 2004. *Reading Fluency, Level D.* New York: Glencoe.

Burningham, John. 1993. *Harvey Slumfenburger's Christmas Present.* Cambridge, MA: Candlewick Press.

Canfield, Jack, Mark Victor Hanson, and Kimberly Kirberger, eds. 1997. *Chicken Soup for the Teenage Soul.* Deerfield Beach, FL: Health Communications.

Cole, Joanna, and Bruce Degen. 1986. *The Magic School Bus at the Waterworks.* New York: Scholastic.

———. 1989. *The Magic School Bus Inside the Human Body.* New York: Scholastic.

Curtis, Jamie Lee. 1993. *When I Was Little*. New York: HarperCollins.

de Maupassant, Guy. 1907. "The Necklace." In *The Short-Story: Specimens Illustrating Its Development*, ed. Brander Matthews. New York: American Book Company. Retrieved on July 15, 2007, from www.bartleby.com/195/20.html.

De Young, C. Coco. 1999. *A Letter to Mrs. Roosevelt*. New York: Random House.

Dorros, Arthur. 1987. *Ant Cities*. New York: HarperCollins.

Duncan, Lois. 1990. *Killing Mr. Griffin*. New York: Random House.

Inturrisi, Louis. 1980. *The Ways of Written English*. New York: Language Innovations, Inc.

Jiang, Ji Li. 1997. *Red Scarf Girl: A Memoir of the Cultural Revolution*. New York: HarperCollins.

Kunz, Linda, and Laurie Gluck. 2000. "X-Word Grammar Intermediate." The English Language Center, LaGuardia Community College, The City University of New York.

L'Hommedieu, John. 1997. *From Plant to Blue Jeans*. New York: Children's Press.

Lowry, Lois. 2004. "Splendor." In *Reading Fluency*, ed. Camille L. Z. Blachowicz, 29. New York: Glencoe.

Nickle, John. 1999. *The Ant Bully*. New York: Scholastic.

Paterson, Katherine. 1979. "Angels and Other Strangers." In *A Christmas Treasury*, 57–74. New York: Scholastic.

Reading for Concepts, Book A. 3rd ed. 1999. New York: Phoenix Learning Resources.

Robnoxious. 2003. "The Year Is 1902." Retrieved on January 10, 2003, from www.goofball.com/jokes/facts/2003016101.

Rylant, Cynthia. 1982. *When I Was Young in the Mountains*. New York: Puffin Unicorn.

———. 1998. *The Bird House*. New York: Scholastic.

Sachar, Louis. 1989. *Wayside School Is Falling Down*. New York: Avon Books.

Seuling, Barbara. 2000. *Drip! Drop! How Water Gets to Your Tap*. New York: Holiday House.

Voigt, Cynthia. 1981. *Homecoming*. New York: Fawcett Juniper.

White, E. B. 1952. *Charlotte's Web*. New York: Harper & Row.

Index

A

academic writing, 91

Allen, Robert, 55

"Alone in the Crowd" (Wixtrom), 83

"An American Dream" (Santini), 20

American Sign Language (ASL): characteristics of narrative in, 5; conferencing with teachers and, 93; translating essays into, 86–87

analysis of grammar in second drafts, 43–50

Angelillo, Janet, *Writing About Reading*, 20

"Another Evening at the Club" (Riatt), 82

answering guides, 15

Anzaldúa, Gloria, "Lifeline," 15

arrows, double-headed, marking text with, 19

ASL. See American Sign Language

assessment: evaluation rubrics and, 77–79; exit exam for English department, 86, 91, 93–94; of first drafts across term, 82–84; NCTE best practices for, 93–94; of own work, 83, 84, 85; reframing, 79–81; of third and fourth drafts across term, 84–85

aural ability and writing ability, 3, 8–11

B

Bean, John C., *Engaging Ideas*, 13, 19

blogs, 21–22

boxes, 73–74

brackets, marking text with, 18, 19

Broad, Bob, *What We Really Value*, 78

Brueggemann, Brenda Jo, 13–14

C

Carver, Raymond, "Cathedral," 35

"Cathedral" (Carver), 35

Chorost, Michael, 7

chunks, thinking in, 22–24

circling unfamiliar words when marking text, 18–19

City University of New York (CUNY)/ACT writing test, 6, 10, 91, 94

Clay, Marie, 19

collocations, 42–50, 84

commas and front shifters, 69

comments on first drafts, examples of, 36–40

comprehension questions, 15

concluding statements, 40

conferences with students: benefit of, 33–34; on one essay over time, 79–81; writing, talk, and, 92–93

content and craft in teaching of writing, 34, 40

context and emotion, 31

contrastive analysis, 9

corpus linguistics, 42–43

correction symbols (X-Word Grammar), 59, 60, 62, 76

craft and content in teaching of writing, 34, 40

CUNY/ACT writing test, 6, 10, 91, 94

D

Deaf and hard of hearing students: access to information for exam topics and, 94; classroom equipment for, 16; as Generation 1.5 students, 10; learning contexts for, 95; print as supplemental mother tongue for, 7–8; student models for, 91; writing process and, 89, 90–91

definitions of unfamiliar words, finding, 15, 19

de Maupassant, Guy, "The Necklace," 16–18, 19, 84

DeSena, Laura Hennessey, 20

developmental writing, look of, 12

Didion, Joan, 25

discussion-board software, 21–22

discussion notes: filling in, 22–23; formulating, 20–21

Divakaruni, Chitra, "Mrs. Dutta Writes a Letter," 82

documentation, teaching, 22

document cameras, 16

Dolch word-picture cards, 7

Dynamic Criteria Map, 78

E

educational-standards movement, 88–89

emotion and context, 31

end shifters, 69–70

Engaging Ideas (Bean), 13, 19

English as a Second Language (ESL) instruction, 9

Esquivel, Laura, *Like Water for Chocolate*, 13, 20

essays: exposure to, 25; final drafts of, 52, 86–87; "Immaturity," 31–34; models for, 25, 26, 91; number of drafts of, 85–86; peer-written, 26; prewriting activities, 24; "A Red Tablecloth," 4–5; required number of, 89; second drafts of, 41, 43–50; "Stranger in the Nest," 26–31, 34. *See also* first drafts of essays; third drafts of essays

evaluation rubrics, 77–79

exit exam for English department, 86, 91, 93–94

F

final drafts of essays: presentation of, 86–87; as treasured, 52

first drafts of essays: about stereotyping, 35–40; becoming responsive readers of, 33–34; progress in across term, 82–84; sample conclusions to, 2–3

Fjeldstad, Mary, *The Thoughtful Reader*, 15–16

focused reading notes, 19

forwarding, 20

fragments, dealing with, 70–71

front shifters, 69–70

G

Generation 1.5 students, 9–10

Glickfeld, Carole, "What My Mother Knows," 35

Gluck, Laurie, 55

grammar: analysis of in second drafts, 43–50; approaches to instruction in, 53–54; definitions of, 53; editing and, 91–92; errors in, focusing on, 51–53; lexical approach and, 50; overlaying onto writing assignments, 10, 76; proficiency in, 84–85. *See also* X-Word Grammar

Grammar and the Teaching of Writing (Noguchi), 53–54

grammar translation, 9

Greenberg, Joanne: "And Sarah Laughed," 8; *In This Sign*, 23, 31, 85

guides, 15

H

hard of hearing students. *See* Deaf and hard of hearing students

Harris, Joseph, *Rewriting: How to do Things with Texts*, 20

hidden X-words, 61–64

Hill, Jimmie, "Revising Priorities," 49–50

how many, showing, 58

Huot, Brian, *(Re)Articulating Writing Assessment for Teaching and Learning*, 79

I

"Immaturity" essay, 31–34

infinitive verb form, teaching, 63

inserts, 71–72

"In the City of the Deaf" (Sternberg), 26

In This Sign (Greenberg), 23, 31, 85

J

joiners, 65–66

K

Kunz, Linda Ann, 54–55, 60, 69

L

language, interlinked nature of, 54, 75–76

language wars, 8–9, 10–11

leaning on print, 7–8

Lewis, Michael, *Teaching Collocation*, 41–42, 50, 54

lexical approach, 50. *See also* collocations

"Lifeline" (Anzaldúa), 15

Like Water for Chocolate (Esquivel), 13, 20

linkers and trunks, 68–69

Livingston, Sue, *Rethinking the Education of Deaf Students*, 94–95

M

marking text, 15–19

models for writing essays, 25, 26, 91. *See also* touchstone texts

"Mrs. Dutta Writes a Letter" (Divakaruni), 82

N

narrative in written compared to spoken discourse, 5

National Council of Teachers of English (NCTE), "Beliefs about the Teaching of Writing," 88–94

native English speakers, mental lexicons of, 41–42

"The Necklace" (de Maupassant), 16–18, 19, 84

Newbury House Dictionary of American English, 15

Nia, Isoke Titilayo, 25–26

Noguchi, Rie R., *Grammar and the Teaching of Writing*, 53–54

notetaking, 21

nouns, errors related to, 52–53, 73–74

O

one trunk with two or more predicates sentence pattern, 66–67

online discussions, 21–22

oral ability and writing ability, 3, 6, 8–11

oral/aural language development, obsession with, 8–9, 10–11

outlines, writing from, 23–24

P

peer-written essays, 26

phrasal assistance: English lexicon and, 49–50; types of, 47–48

presentations of final drafts, 86–87

print as supplemental mother tongue for Deaf students, 7–8

progress: evaluation rubrics and, 77–79; in first drafts across term, 82–84; number of drafts written and, 41, 81, 85–86; on one essay over time, 79–81; in third and fourth drafts across term, 84–85; trail of work and, 93

Q

question marks, marking text with, 18, 19

R

reading proficiency and writing ability, 5–8, 92. *See also* writing-into-reading activities

(Re)Articulating Writing Assessment for Teaching and Learning (Huot), 79

"A Red Tablecloth" essay, 4–5

referents, 74–75

reframing assessment, 79–80

responsive readers, becoming, 34–40

Rethinking Rubrics in Writing Assessment (Wilson), 78, 79–80

Rethinking the Education of Deaf Students (Livingston), 94–95

"Revising Priorities" (Hill), 49–50

Rewriting: How to do Things with Texts (Harris), 20

Riatt, Alifa, "Another Evening at the Club," 82

rubrics for evaluation, 77–79

run-on sentences, 67

S

Santini, Rosemarie, "An American Dream," 20

"And Sarah Laughed" (Greenberg), 8

second drafts of essays: collocation and grammar in, 43–50; prewriting activities, 41

sector analysis, 55

semicolons, use of, 66

sentence patterns: errors in, 52; inserts, 71–72; linkers and trunks, 68–69; one trunk with two or more predicates, 66–67; shifter positions, 69–70; in third essays, 67–68; trunk plus trunk, 65–66; trunks, 64–65

social networking tools, 21–22

spoken discourse compared to written discourse, 4–5

stereotyping: assignments on theme of, 13; first draft of essay about, 35–40; second draft of essay about, 43–50; third draft of essay about, 48–49, 50

Sternberg, Martin, "In the City of the Deaf," 26

"Stranger in the Nest" essay: annotations for, 28–31; description of, 26; rewrites of, 34; text of, 27–28

"The Struggle to Be an All-American Girl" (Wong), 20

subjects, discovering, 57

"summarizer" role for online discussions, 22

T

Talese, Gay, 25

talk and writing, 92–93

"talking back" to text, 20

Tannen, Deborah, 4

teacher's guide, 56

Teaching Collocation (Lewis), 41–42, 50, 54

text: marking, 15–19; "talking back" to, 20

texts: conventions of finished and edited, 91–92; touchstone, 25–33; for writing assignments, 12–14, 20

the, errors with, 74

themes, grouping readings by, 20

thinking: about reading, 20–22; in chunks, 22–24; writing as tool for, 90–91

third drafts of essays: boxes and, 73–74; example of, 48–49; hidden X-words and, 62–64; power of X-words and, 59; progress in across term, 84–85; referents and, 75; sentence patterns and, 67–69, 70–71, 72; tasks completed by time of, 51; verb match-ups and, 60–61; working with lexicon and, 50

The Thoughtful Reader (Fjeldstad), 15–16

time, showing, 58

timed writing tasks, 94

touchstone texts: criteria for, 25–26; examples of, 26–33; file of, 33

translating essays into ASL, 86–87

trunk plus trunk sentence pattern, 65–66

trunk sentence pattern, 64–65

Twenty Questions game, 57

U

underlining when marking text, 18, 19

V

verbs: errors in, 52; teaching, 60–61, 63–64

W

Ward, Marc, 84

wavy lines, marking text with, 18–19

"What My Mother Knows" (Glickfeld), 35

What We Really Value (Broad), 78

whiteboards, 21

Wilson, Maja, *Rethinking Rubrics in Writing Assessment*, 78, 79–80

Wixtrom, Christine, "Alone in the Crowd," 83

Wong, Elizabeth, "The Struggle to Be an All-American Girl," 20

word patterns, recurring, 42–43

writing: becoming responsive readers of, 34–40; NCTE best practices and, 88–94; as process, 89; purposes for, 91; talk and, 92–93; thinking about reading and, 20–22; as tool for thinking, 90–91. *See also* writing-into-reading activities

writing ability: oral ability, aural ability, and, 3, 8–11; reading proficiency and, 5–8, 92

Writing About Reading (Angelillo), 20

writing assignments, texts for, 12–14, 20

writing-into-reading activities: focused reading notes, 19; guides or comprehension questions, 15; marking text, 15–19; notetaking, 21

written discourse compared to spoken discourse, 4–5

X

X-Word Grammar: benefits of, 10, 55, 75–76; boxes, 73–74; components of, 56; correction symbols, 59, 60, 62, 76; hidden X-words, 61–64; how many, showing, 58; main verb match-ups and, 60; as part of writing course, 55–56; progress with, 84; referents, 74–75; shifter positions, 69–70; subjects, discovering, 57; time, showing, 58; yes/no questions, 57, 64–65, 69–70. *See also* sentence patterns

Y

yes/no questions, making, 57, 64–65, 69–70